FROM CONCEPTION TO ADULTHOOD—EXPLORE THE HIDDEN BOND BETWEEN PARENT AND CHILD

Every day modern medicine is confirming what holistic healers and parapsychologists have long believed: that the mind has a nearly limitless ability to connect psychically with loved ones, to heal, and to intuit the most intimate feelings of others. In this remarkable work, Carl Jones demonstrates the importance of psychic parenting—and shows you how you can develop your mind power with your children. Here are startling true-life examples of psychic communication between parent and child, including:

- Crisis telepathy—cases in which ESP saved the lives of the children involved.
- Uncanny dreams that accurately described a scene occurring to a son or daughter hundreds of miles away—and dreams that have predicted the future.
- Apparitions of a deceased mother or father at the moment of their death.
- The everyday ESP that probably all parents and children share.

FROM PARENT TO CHILD: The Psychic Link

CARL JONES

A Warner Communications Company

Warner Books, Inc., 666 Fifth Avenue, New York, NY 10103
A Warner Communications Company

Printed in the United States of America
First Printing: April 1989
10 9 8 7 6 5 4 3 2 1

Designed by Giorgetta Bell McRee

Library of Congress Cataloging-in-Publication Data

Jones, Carl.
From parent to child.

1. Extrasensory perception. 2. Parent and child—Miscellanea. I. Title.
BF1321.J66 1989 133.8 88-26118
ISBN 0-446-38761-4 (pbk.) (U.S.A.)
0-446-38762-2 (Canada)

To Jan, Carl, Paul and Jonathan

ACKNOWLEDGMENTS

My thanks to James G. Matlock, librarian and archivist of the American Society for Psychical Research, for his help with the research and for reading the manuscript and making many valuable suggestions.

Thanks to Sally Ann Drucker, a parapsychologist who has done extensive research on children and ESP, for reading through the manuscript, catching several errors, and making suggestions.

Thanks to Athena Drewes, a child psychologist, for her extensive bibliography on children and ESP.

Thanks to Berthold E. Schwarz, M.D., a pioneer in the field of parent-child ESP, for his suggestions and encouragment.

I am very grateful for the help of the many childbirth professionals who have assisted me in researching the parapsychology of pregnancy and the psychic world of the unborn child and of babies, especially Pat Jones, certified nurse midwife of Houston, Texas, who offered many valuable anecdotes.

Special thanks to the innumerable parents who shared their ESP experiences with me.

Above all, thanks to my wife Jan, who read through the manuscript many times, typed it, and made many suggestions.

CONTENTS

FROM PARENT TO CHILD: The Psychic Link

1

The ESP Connection

Every day, men learn they are going to become fathers. Yet it is always a dramatic event when a man first discovers the news that will change his life forever. For Berthold Eric Schwarz, psychiatrist, it was even more than that. It was magical—something out of a fairy tale.

Except that it didn't happen in a Gothic castle on a windswept moor, but in his oak-paneled office in Montclair, New Jersey. The doctor was listening patiently to a middle-aged woman on the couch talk about herself. She was intensely angry. She was experiencing what psychiatrists call "transference." Her unresolved feelings, perhaps stemming from something in her childhood, were transferred to emotions about her doctor. She was jealous of Dr. Schwarz's wife, Ardis, even though she had never met her.

Many patients have strong feelings about their psychiatrists and their spouses now and then. But few have ever expressed them quite like this patient did.

She was angrily glaring at Dr. Schwarz. Her face reddened with jealousy. She was telling him how she envied his wife. Then in a burst of fury, she lashed out with: "And your wife is pregnant!"

The psychiatrist struggled to maintain his professional composure. "If she is, it's news to me," he said. The remark had been totally unrelated to anything they had been discussing.

The woman on the couch had no way of knowing whether or not Ardis was pregnant. Yet she was consumed with jealousy about Ardis's pregnancy, a pregnancy of which the physician knew nothing. It must be a fantasy, he thought. Of course it was. It had to be, he told himself. Until later in the day when he talked with his wife.

She had been waiting for the right time to break the news, to tell him that their life would soon be changed. Ardis was pregnant.

But how did the patient know? Was the patient's sudden outburst a flash of psychic knowledge? Had she unconsciously used the power of ESP to get her psychiatrist's attention? If she had, it certainly worked.

That wasn't the first time ESP had revealed vital information to Berthold Schwarz about his family. The earliest major psychic event in his life occurred in 1945 when he was on leave from the Navy during World War II. While returning home, he became suddenly gripped with the horrible and increasing certainty that his younger brother Eric, who had been fighting in General Patton's Third Army in Germany, had been killed in action. He couldn't shake off the grim thought. As he approached his home, he recognized a few cars belonging to his family and friends parked in the street. As he walked through the door, it was no surprise to learn that his premonition was all too true. A telegram had come bearing the tragic news of Eric's death in a small town in Germany.

Weeks before the telegram arrived, his mother had already been prepared for the news. On the day that Eric died in combat, she was alone in her Montclair, New Jersey, home. Suddenly for no apparent reason, she sank to her knees and began to cry. She noted the time. Later when her husband came home, she told him what she felt—what she knew to be true. And she waited. She waited for weeks.

Then the telegram came and told her what she already knew. The time of her son's death coincided precisely with the time she had fallen on her knees in anguish.

Mrs. Schwarz never made a big deal about her psychic experiences, though she had many in the course of her life. She didn't read tea leaves or consult fortune-tellers. She didn't dabble in the "occult." She simply accepted extrasensory perception as a normal part of her life, especially when it came to her children.

But Berthold Schwarz had been jolted by the psychic experiences he and his mother had had in relation to his brother's death. They opened the door to what was to become a lifelong interest in parent-child ESP. He wondered how common such things were. How did they work? Were such occurrences just the tip of an iceberg? Was ESP a part of all parent-child relationships? Were parents and offspring linked in some hidden realm beyond the senses, allowing thoughts to pass between them even when they were separated by thousands of miles? Could ESP encompass less spectacular events and perhaps even be a part of everyday life?

When Dr. Schwarz became a father, as his angry patient had predicted, he turned his attention to answering these questions. He began to pay attention to possible extrasensory experiences with his own children. This soon led him to an awareness that shaped the course of his life, and that could very well revolutionize our concept of the parent-child relationship.

One of the first ESP episodes between parent and child that he recorded occurred one evening while he was reading a text. His daughter Lisa, who was not quite two years old, was in the room with him. His mind drifted. He thought of telephoning a friend and asking him if he would like to go out to a restaurant. He couldn't make up his mind whether to call his friend and satisfy his gastronomic urge or continue reading.

Suddenly Lisa looked up and said, "Telephone."

Neither she nor her father were near a telephone. Was his two-year-old daughter reading his mind? Had she somehow picked up on his unexpressed desire? Could this be possible? Could a little girl attune to her father's thoughts? Perhaps it was a coincidence, thought Dr. Schwarz. An incredibly well-timed coincidence.

Or was it telepathy?

Telepathy is the transference of thoughts or feelings from one mind to another without the use of the physical senses. The word comes from the Greek roots "tel" meaning "far off" or "distant," and "pathy" meaning "experience" or "feeling": the feeling or experience of knowledge at a distance. Telepathy is just as likely to occur with persons who are separated by half the world as with those who are in the same room. And the information is transmitted from mind to mind instantaneously—unlike anything we know of in the physical universe.

Telepathy is one of many forms of *psi* (short for psychic phenomena).

In the 1930s, J. B. Rhine, the father of experimental parapsychology (the science that investigates psi) began, under the guidance of Professor William McDougall, scientifically controlled studies of telepathy at Duke University in Durham, North Carolina. Methods of testing were developed. A pack of cards called "Zener" cards were designed to test for thought transference. The pack consists of twenty-five cards, each having one of five geometric symbols: a star, square, waves, circle, and cross. In testing for telepathy, one person attempts to "send" the image on the card to another, the "receiver."

Clairvoyance, or extrasensory cognition not obtained from another animate mind, was also investigated. To test for clairvoyance, the investigator would not look at the card until after the subject had made a "guess."

The percentage of correct hits in some experiments was so great that nothing but psi could explain the results.

For example, an assistant director of the Parapsychology Laboratory at Duke University, J. B. Pratt, carried out a series of experiments with Hubert Pearce, a student in the Divinity School, which have since become immortalized in parapsychological literature as the Pearce-Pratt experiments. In a research room on the top floor of a building in the main Duke campus, Dr. Pratt laid out ESP cards in the middle of the table with their symbols facing down. Meanwhile, Pearce remained in a cubicle in the stacks at the back of the library, a hundred yards away. While in his cubicle he attempted to identify the cards that were laid down on the table by Pratt. The results were later compared. The experiment was repeated with several hundred trials. The number of hits was so astounding that the possibility of chance was one in a million times a million times a million times a million.[1]

Another experiment was conducted by the British mathematician S. G. Soal in the 1930s. He was well known for his skepticism regarding ESP at the time. However, he was objective in his experiment involving 160 people at 128,356 trials. When the results were examined for telepathy, the odds of chance were one in several billion billion. Apparently this was enough to convince Soal of the reality of ESP. He later became president of the Society for Psychical Research.[2]

However, thanks largely to prejudice against the inexplicable, it wasn't until forty years later that the American Association for the Advancement of Science recognized parapsychology as a legitimate subject for scientific research.

If it perplexes the rational mind to conceive of ESP operating outside the framework of space—that is, that thoughts could be transfered equally effectively across the room or around the world—it staggers the imagination to think that psi might also transcend time. Could a subject identify a future order of cards in the Zener pack? The very question seemed preposterous. Tests were performed at Duke. Again the results were significant enough to establish psi. *Precognition*—psychic knowledge of future events—was demonstrated. To most people this form of psi is most familiar in the context of precognitive dreams.

Though some still don't like to believe it, hundreds of

documented reports testify that ESP occurs in the controlled setting of the laboratory. Innumerable reports of spontaneous psi collected the world over testify that it happens in the home.

Dr. Schwarz began writing down possible telepathic episodes that occurred among himself, his wife, Ardis, and their two children, Lisa and Eric. Just how often did telepathy occur between parent and child? Over the next few years Dr. Schwarz amassed what is probably the most detailed and exhaustive collection of parent-child ESP episodes ever recorded in one family.

Five hundred and five episodes were published in his book, *Parent-Child Telepathy: A Study of the Telepathy of Everyday Life.* But this was only a fraction of the accounts he recorded with scrupulous care and self-effacing honesty. He didn't stop writing down ESP experiences in his family until he had 1,521 of them.

Most of the episodes he recorded consisted of minor details passed from mind to mind, such as the time his daughter Lisa said "telephone" while he was wondering whether to continue reading or telephone his friend for a night out. Like photos in a family album, they are of little interest to anyone outside the immediate family. A few of the episodes are memorable psychic events, such as one account that describes how Dr. Schwarz awakened in the middle of the night from a nightmare at the same instant his daughter woke from an almost identical dream. But all are remarkable. All highlight the same phenomenon: psychic communication between parent and offspring.

After several years of keeping painstaking records, Dr. Schwarz gave up recording the episodes. "Why bother writing them down?" he says. "They happen all the time. And what's more, they probably happen to all parents, or at least to most. We'd all probably notice such experience if only we paid attention to them."

Dr. Schwarz had the answer he was looking for. He had begun with the tip of the iceberg—the startling events occurring around the time of his brother's death. That was his peak experience, the episode he couldn't forget because it centered on such grim news. Then, like Freud, he went deeper. He discovered that ESP, like Freud's unconscious, encompassed far more territory than most people imagine. ESP was a part of everyday life, at least as far as Dr. Schwarz and his family were concerned.

Do all parents have an ESP connection with their offspring, a link that transcends both space and time? Are parents and children united in a world beyond the senses? Can all parents take a quantum leap across the generation gap with the hidden power of mind? Is empathy really another form of extrasensory communication between parent and child? Is ESP behind parents' intuitions?

Dr. Schwarz suggests that we will find the answers to these questions by looking within ourselves. "If you spend time surveying your own experiences with your child," he says, "really looking closely and being open-minded about it, you might have the surprise of your life. You might discover that the parent-child relationship widens to incomprehensible boundaries."

Obviously the sheer volume of psychic communications in Dr. Schwarz's family is unusual. The attention he gave to even the most minor ESP occurrences may partly explain how he was able to record so many episodes. Extrasensory experiences seem to occur more frequently to those who are looking for them. Just thinking of ESP may be a way of fine-tuning the mind to the "frequency" of extrasensory perception. Personal extrasensory talent in his household no doubt also contributed to the high volume of ESP episodes he recorded.

However, the events Dr. Schwarz records are by no means unique. The overwhelming majority of parents have experienced ESP in one of its countless variations: inexplicably sensing your unborn child is a boy or a girl; thinking about your daughter the instant before she phones; sensing there is something wrong and later discovering that your son is ill. There are few parents who can claim never to have had a possible ESP experience with their child.

Extrasensory communication can occur between any two people regardless of their relationship. As innumerable experimental tests have shown, ESP takes place in the controlled setting of the laboratory between persons who don't even know one another.

However, spontaneous telepathy—mind to mind communication that occurs between two persons without the intent of either to send or receive a message—is most common between those who are close: husband and wife, lovers, good friends, parent and child.

Spontaneous telepathy occurs most frequently within the immediate family, and it is more common between parent and child than in any other relationship. Parapsychologist Ian Stevenson conducted a survey to find who among family members experienced the highest percentage of telepathic experiences. As can be expected, his survey showed that the majority took place between mother and child.

Carl Jung called the mother-child relationship an archetypal situation par excellence for the occurrence of ESP. Mother and offspring have a closer biological and emotional relationship than others. They are frequently in one another's thoughts. This is particularly so in times of crisis when spontaneous ESP is most likely to occur.

Many parapsychologists agree that the early mother-child relationship may be the prototype of all other relationships involving telepathy. In fact, telepathy often occurs between two people when one of them is *acting in place of a parent.*

For instance, ESP is particularly common between therapist and patient. The episode with the patient who psychically perceived that Dr. Schwarz's wife, Ardis, was pregnant is a striking example. But that was not an isolated case.

Viennese psychiatrist Wilhelm Stekel first reported the occurrence of telepathy during psychotherapy in 1921. Sigmund Freud later reported telepathic episodes that he said followed the same laws of the unconscious as other material. Dr. Jule Eisenbud, a psychiatrist with a private practice in Denver, Colorado, and a well known parapsychologist, states: "Soon after I began my psychoanalytic and psychiatric practice, it became apparent to me, as it had to others, that patients in their dreams and associations occasionally mirrored my experiences; moreover, they mirrored affects and conflicts I would rather have repressed."[3] He began to pay attention to and use the material in therapy and found that it added a significant dimension to the psychotherapeutic process.

Dr. Schwarz believes that the psychotherapist-patient relationship is fertile soil for psi because it in many ways mirrors the parent-child relationship. In the course of psychotherapy, feelings are elicited for the therapist that might otherwise be directed to a mother or a father. He finds telepathic communication particularly common between doctor and patient when either of them leaves on vacation. "Like the young dependent child," he writes, "the patient is upset and must utilize auxiliary methods of communication."[4]

Another psychiatrist, Dr. Joost A. M. Meerloo, former associate professor of psychiatry at the New York School of Psychiatry, suggests that telepathy between therapist and patient is most likely to come to the fore when the patient has regressed to that phase of his or her past in which he or she lived in the normal symbiotic dependence with the mother.[5]

Mother and child seem to share a special psychic bond.

Elaine Shrager, Ph.D., of New York University, believed that young children would score highest on an ESP test if their own mother rather than another mother tried to send them a message. To prove her point, she used M&M candies and 38 children aged three and a half to five and a half. One hundred M&M's—twenty each of the five colors—were placed in a brown paper bag. A mother shook the bag before each trial and then selected one M&M blindly. She then looked at the candy and tried to mentally communicate its color to a child in another room. Children whose own mothers tried to send the message scored highest.

Many open-minded health professionals have taken note of the frequency of ESP experiences in the parent-child relationship. "There seems to be a connection between parents and children that defies all known laws of science," remarks San Diego psychiatrist Martin Greenberg, a pioneer in the field of parent-infant bonding and author of *The Birth of a Father.* "When someone comes into my office and tells me he has had a psychic experience—telepathic communication with his child, a vision of his mother at the moment of her death—I don't understand it. But I take it seriously. Such things as psychic dreams and mind-to-mind communication between parents and children, so common under conditions of great stress, seem to suggest that the love bond transcends all barriers. It is awesome."

Awesome, yet it happens every day in thousands of homes the world over.

"Scores of parents tell me about their telepathic experiences," says Dr. Schwarz. "They tell me, the psychiatrist, in private, hoping I'll explain it to them. But I can't explain it. I can only say it's part of life. It happens all the time."

We call ESP "paranormal" because no sensory channel has yet been discovered which mediates the information. However, ESP may be a natural and normal part of the parent-child relationship. Perhaps all parents and offspring share a lifelong ESP connection, a link that knows no geographical barriers. And if so, perhaps the paranormal is not so paranormal after all.

For millenia psi has startled, fascinated, perplexed, and inspired people from every walk of life in all corners of the globe. It is acknowledged in every society. It is part of every major religion. It is the backbone of the occult. And it has come under the scrutiny of the laboratory where scientists have sought the answers to the same questions people have been asking for centuries: What is the purpose of psychic phenomena? Why telepathy? Why clairvoyance? Why do dreams reveal information unknown to the dreamer? How does ESP work? The answers to these questions have been sought in everything from the new physics to extraterrestrial communication. However, some suggest that we will perhaps come to the answers to all these questions, and indeed to the very root of psi, if we turn to a source far closer to our homes.

To our children.

Psi may be an integral part of the love bond we share with our children, a bond that unites parents and offspring in the deepest levels of the psyche and affects the very roots of our being. And according to some parapsychologists, psi may be a part of the parent-offspring bond in all mammalian species.

An experiment with rabbits supposedly conducted in the Soviet Union bears out this theory.[6] Scientists implanted electrodes in a female rabbit's brain and while she was kept on shore in a laboratory, her babies were taken in a submarine deep below the surface of the ocean. Assistants then killed the babies one by one. At the instant of each baby rabbit's death, the mother's brain reacted.

A similar experiment was conducted in Russia at the Zooveterinary Institute at Kharkov in 1942. A female dog was first accustomed to having her puppies removed from her for short periods. Once she began to accept this without protest, her puppies were taken to a distant room where a pain stimulus was administered. At that moment the mother became uneasy, began barking, and turned her head toward the room where her puppies were.[7]

There is growing evidence to suggest that psi is a characteristic of all living things. Psi may be a quality of organic life.

Studies in animal behavior strongly suggest that many animals have something akin to psi ability. Dogs, cats, and pigeons have all shown incredible ability to find their way home even from great distances, suggesting a power similar to ESP.

"The collection of anecdotal material on exceptional feats of homing in these three species gives about as strong a case as anecdotal material taken alone can do," states J. B. Rhine. "Instances of particular interest were found in which the animal was reported to have followed and found its human companion in territory completely new to it and over distances ranging into hundreds of miles."[8]

For example, a dog was lost on December 1, 1948. The Burk family, who owned the dog, moved 1,200 miles away. On

November 27, 1949, the dog came to their new home.[9] It is difficult to explain this without recourse to psi.

In their fascinating book *The Secret Life of Plants,* Peter Tomkins and Christopher Bird have shown that plants can pick up and respond to the thoughts of those around them. In an experiment that has since made world history, Cleve Baxter, America's foremost lie-detector examiner, whose story is told in detail in Tomkins's and Bird's book, hooked up the electrodes of a polygraph lie detector to a common houseplant, *Dracaena massangeana.* Baxter thought of burning the leaf to which the electrodes were attached. To his amazement, just then there was a dramatic change in the tracing pattern on the lie-detector graph. This puzzling phenomenon indicated that the plant had somehow picked up Baxter's thought! After dozens of carefully controlled experiments, he concluded that there is some sort of primary perception inherent in all living things.

Psi may be a silent partner to the biological processes in living things. Though psi isn't studied in biology classes, it may be a hidden quality of organic life as real as protoplasm. One theory regards psi as a sort of organizing principle in nature. British Marine biologist Sir Alister Hardy has suggested that psi may play a key role in the lives of animals. In his paper, "Biology and Psychical Research," published in 1953 by the Society for Psychical Research (SPR) in England, he suggests that some animal species may share a "group mind holding the whole plan of structural form and particularly development . . . a sort of psychic blueprint between members of a species." Species may be linked to other species, life to forms of life, in a sort of cosmic mind. This may help to explain the behavior of migrating birds, the communal life of bees, and perhaps the extraordinary behavior of the British blue tit. All over England blue tits mysteriously learned almost simultaneously how to open the cardboard tops of milk bottles and get at the cream. This may also help to explain the prevalence of ESP in the parent-child relationship. According to Sir Alister Hardy, ESP may even be an integral factor in the very evolutionary process carrying information along the never-ending stream of life.[10]

FAR-REACHING IMPLICATIONS

Parent-child ESP often involves trivial events—thinking of your daughter the instant before she phones, for instance. But the implications of an ESP connection between parent and offspring are anything but trivial.

Learning more about ESP may help us better understand parent-child communication and child development. And it could very well affect every profession with any relation to parents and their children.

A transformation is taking place throughout the scientific world. Changes are occurring rapidly. In medicine a holistic approach is evolving that takes into account all aspects of a person—body, mind, emotions, spirit. We are becoming more aware of the power of healing methods such as therapeutic touch that remain inexplicable in terms of Western medical science. The age-old discipline of meditation has been shown to lower the incidence of stress-related illness. A "new physics" has developed whose philosophy sometimes resembles mysticism more than hard science. Mind stuff—the world beyond the reach of the senses—receives more press then ever.

A "new age" approach which emphasizes "inner experiences" is gaining popularity in a wide variety of fields. In sports, for example, many athletes train themselves for peak performances by playing the game in their minds. Though the new age approach does not necessarily imply the paranormal, it does reflect a broadening awareness of the importance of the mind. This awareness in turn heightens appreciation of parapsychological experiences.

ESP is, after all, an undeniable part of life. Research into the fascinating world beyond the senses is, therefore, an integral part of the study of human consciousness. It may give us a greater perspective on ourselves, our relationship with our children, and perhaps our interconnectedness with all organic life.

Learning about the ESP connection could open the door to a new dimension of the parent-child relationship. For many it may spark an interest in "psychic parenting"—paying greater attention to the ESP messages parents and children share.

Many believe that psychic ability is the special gift of only a chosen few—talented psychics, mystics, rare and unusual individuals. To a degree this may be true. Some are obviously far more psychically talented than others. Perhaps some have a hereditary predisposition for ESP. A few can make accurate predictions, solve crimes with ESP, and perform uncanny feats of telepathy almost as easily as other folks can mow their lawns. ESP is second nature to them. The clairvoyant Gerard Croiset, world famous for his psychic investigative work with the Dutch police, is a striking example.

Croiset's talent for the paranormal began to show at an early age. One day a teacher returned to school after being absent for a day. Croiset told the teacher that he had spent the day with a girl who wore a red rose and whom he would soon marry. The teacher had actually taken the day from work to see his fiancée in a distant area and she had in fact worn a red rose.

Croiset is often able to hold an object in his hand and recite uncanny details associated with the object, a form of clairvoyance known as psychometry. In one instance he used this talent to help solve a rape case. The police gave him two wrapped objects. He correctly identified the first as a tobacco box without opening the wrapping. He then described the house from which it came and two middle-aged brothers who lived there. These men, he said, were the rapists.

He then identified the second parcel as a sack associated with a cow. It turned out to be a cow blanket. He said the rape victim had been put into the sack after the rape took place. The brothers had argued over how to kill her—one wanting to bury her alive, the other wanting to drown her. Fortunately for the girl, the brothers couldn't make up their minds so she was allowed to live.

All this from holding a wrapped parcel in his hands! The bizarre story proved true and the two brothers were convicted.

Such a display of psychic talent is extraordinarily rare, perhaps even more rare than great musical genius. Few can develop their talents to this extent and solve a grisly crime by handling an object from the scene. But most people can probably learn to pay greater attention to a less spectacular form of ESP— *the parapsychology of everyday life.* ESP happens more often than we think. Studies have shown that ESP occurs in the lives of over half the American population.[11] It may be part of the lives even of those who don't wish to admit that what they experience might belong in the realm of the so-called paranormal.

Everyone probably has latent psychic ability. If animals have something akin to psi operative in their relationship with their offspring, why not people? This is the view of many parapsychologists. According to Professor W. H. D. Tenhaeff, who held the world's first chair of parapsychology as director of the Parapsychological Institute at the State University of Utrecht in the 1950s and who brought attention to the then-unknown Gerard Croiset and studied his amazing psychic feats, everyone has psychic ability to some degree.

Learning to be psychic may be largely a matter of "tuning in" to the inner sense. As Dr. Schwarz puts it: "When parents show an interest in the subject, they begin to see ESP operating in their own lives, to develop it and to recapture the wonderful gift they had as children."

Given the right conditions, many parents may be able to coax their latent psychic ability to the surface and experience ESP with their own offspring. In the final chapters of this book there are suggestions for attuning to the ESP connection that many may find helpful. For those who are interested in "psychic parenting," there are exercises to induce a state of mind/body relaxation to enable the mind to better focus on extrasensory perception, exercises to awaken intuition, and games to play with a son or daughter to test for and possibly increase ESP.

Paying attention to ESP can be either beneficial or not, depending on its use. Obviously ESP is not a substitute for other forms of knowledge and communication. ESP should not be developed at the cost of other aspects of the parent-child relationship—talking with one another, playing together, being together, showing love. ESP should never be used to invade another's privacy or to attempt to influence another person against his or her will.

Some parents feel that psi lends greater insight into their children's experiences. Some believe ESP occasionally alerts them to potential problems. For others, the ESP connection is simply an inexplicable part of the parent-child relationship, something without immediate practical application, perhaps, but something to be acknowledged and respected.

"Telepathy is the primitive way of transmitting knowledge and concepts," says Dr. Schwarz.[12] Telepathic communication may play a role in the child's learning process on an unconscious level. It may be a "missing link in explaining how a child really learns to read." He suggests that the process may be dependent on "the emotional rapport of the parent and child and the result varies accordingly: a neurotic influence possibly yielding a reading problem." A sincere desire to impart knowledge on the part of the parent and teacher and to absorb knowledge on the part of the child may result in superior reading skills. A parent "might more easily impart the wish for reading knowledge when he is in a state of tranquil positive rapport"—the condition under which parent-offspring telepathy works best.

Telepathy may also affect the child's social, emotional, and moral development. It may help to account for the way a child learns to respond to his parents' feelings, to his parents' likes and dislikes. Paranormal communication may affect the development of a child's conscience, his sense of values, of right and wrong and so forth. Dr. Jan Ehrenwald, a psychiatrist who has done extensive research on parent-child ESP, believes that telepathic communication between parents and children could play a role in the genesis of certain behavioral disorders.

The effect of psi of the learning process and child development is highly theoretical. There is no proof that psi plays an integral role in these aspects of life. Many things work together in molding a child's character and emotional development. Telepathy may be one factor. And it may be a factor with far more influence than we have previously imagined.

Dr. Schwarz believes that extrasensory perception may be so important that psychology should turn to the problem of unexplainable parent-child communications. By ignoring the psi connection, child psychologists may be overlooking an important missing link in child development.

As Dr. Schwarz eloquently puts it: "The significant implication may well be that all of us are influenced for better or for worse by the often beguilingly trivial everyday telepathic events, which because of their far-reaching, subtle emotional effects can take us by surprise, be seemingly forgotten, and yet leave indelible imprints on our character, our behavior, and, for all one knows, even our destiny."[13]

2

Parents, Children, and ESP

Rarely does ESP spring into our consciousness in full evening dress. ESP is too primitive for that. More often it flits across the screen of our inner mind like a hawk, leaving us with the vague impression that we've seen something fleeting by but we're not sure what.

Take the example of your daughter on the phone—probably a form of ESP with which most everyone can identify. Thinking of your daughter from whom you haven't heard in six weeks is immediately followed by the telephone ringing with her on the other end of the line. The usual response to this sort of everyday ESP is: "What an odd coincidence! I was just thinking of you!"

Few would associate the thought of their daughter with the fact that she is presently telephoning and the phone is just about to ring—even though this may be what triggered the thought. Few mothers would say to themselves: "Aha! My daughter just popped into my head out of the blue. She is therefore telephoning me at this very instant. I must go over to the phone and wait for it to ring!"

The parapsychology of everyday life is often like this. We are conscious only of a brief flash if indeed we are conscious of the episode at all.

The same is true of crisis telepathy—the sort of ESP associated with an accident, injury, or death. A mother may get a distinct flash: My daughter was just in a horrible car accident. But it doesn't usually happen this way. More often than not the mother had a foreboding, perhaps a vague feeling, that something is wrong with her daughter. Something terrible has happened. Or she may perhaps have a pain in her own body in the very same place where her daughter was injured—*without knowing why* she feels the pain. What we perceive through ESP is usually a story half told or perhaps most often a mere preview. Why is this so? According to J. B. Rhine, "The most significant and revealing characteristic of psi is that its operation is entirely unconscious."[1] Information seems to be received in some primitive part of the brain and appears to be processed below the level of our awareness.

According to parapsychologist D. Scott Rogo: "ESP functions in two stages. The subconscious first assembles the ESP data and then transfers it to conscious awareness."[2] And the message that is transmitted to our conscious mind is often anything but clear. In fact, what we perceive extrasensorily is more often like a reflection in a fun-house mirror.

Psychic information is frequently combined with various things in the subject's conscious or unconscious mind. Parapsychologists refer to this phenomenon as "noise," which is a little like static on a radio broadcast.

As Dr. Schwarz points out: "Telepathy is related to the subconscious mind with all its propensities for symbolization, distortion, displacement, condensation, and other mental mechanisms."[3]

You dream of being cornered in an unpleasant place by a mad cow wearing a too-tight purple jersey. When you wake up, you could swear you've never seen that cow before but you remember that your mother-in-law wears that same jersey, which says little for her figure. Your unconscious mind has expressed an idea that you were perhaps too polite to put into words.

The distortion of telepathic impressions is easy to see with telepathic picture drawing—a game parents might want to play with their children to test for ESP and develop extrasensory talents. Person #1 goes into a separate room and makes a simple drawing, concentrating on what he has drawn. Person #2 tries to "see" the drawing in her mind's eye and makes her own drawing based on that inner image. Later the two compare the results. (For more on this see chapter 7.)

Upton Sinclair, the well-known writer, and his wife, Mary Craig Sinclair, experimented with this kind of telepathy. They recorded hundreds of examples with meticulous accuracy in the book, *Mental Radio.* Thanks to copious notes and a large collection of drawings, the Sinclair experiment has become famous in parapsychology. It attracted the attention of William McDougall at Duke University. Impressed by the Sinclair's results, Dr. McDougall was inspired to establish the now-famous department of parapsychology at Duke University, where Dr. J. B. Rhine and his colleagues did the most extensive tests in the U.S. proving the existence of ESP in a scientific lab.

Sinclair made a drawing of an object and concentrated on it. In another room with the door closed, his wife, Mary Craig, lay peacefully. She mentally gave her subconscious mind the suggestion that she would see, in her mind's eye, whatever was on that drawing. She would then draw her telepathic impression or describe it. Her perception and the original drawing were compared.

Hundreds of drawings were strikingly similar if not practically identical, ruling out all possibility of chance. For example, a sailboat was drawn. Mary Craig wrote down the word "sailboat." In another example, something resembling a horn of plenty was drawn. Mary Craig made an astoundingly similar drawing and called it a "trumpet flower." In yet another example, three overlapping circles were drawn. She reproduced the drawing precisely.[4]

Some of the drawings were complete misses.

Most interesting, however, are the partial successes. Some drawings showed telepathy at work but the image conveyed was distorted. Comparing such drawings gives us an idea of how elusive ESP is.

In one example, Mr. Sinclair drew a sort of jack o'lantern face. His wife drew a cresent-moon–shaped object resembling the mouth, a star above the cresent which resembled the nose, and —of all things—an upside-down eye. In one case there was a realistic drawing; in the other, a highly abstract one.

It is surprising that ESP sometimes carries a message while utterly distorting its meaning. For another example, a sketch of a volcano with smoke pouring out was drawn. Mary Craig drew a practically identical drawing. Yet she didn't realize it was a volcano. She called it a black beetle (the smoke resembled the beetle's body while the sides of the volcano resembled the beetle's feelers). Her mind picked up the picture accurately yet distorted or perhaps never received the meaning.

One would assume that if anything were conveyed telepathically, it would be the idea, the subject matter, not the details of the drawing. It is reasonable to expect Mary Craig to have drawn another perhaps dissimilar-looking volcano or just to have thought of a volcano, rather than drawing the identical volcano and calling it a beetle.

But frequently psi is anything but reasonable.

To make matters more frustrating, psi has no hard and fast rules about what it will distort or how. In another drawing, Mrs. Sinclair got the idea but missed the drawing. Her husband drew an oil lamp with a flame. She drew an object that did not resemble the lamp yet commented, "flame and sparks."[5]

As if this were not sufficiently confusing, there is yet another puzzling thing about the way messages were conveyed in the Sinclair experiment. It gives us more insight into the peculiar way ESP works. Upton Sinclair writes: "Again and again we find Craig getting, not the drawing she is holding under her hand, but the next one, which she has not yet touched."[6]

When the phenomenon appears, half the time it dons the strange attire of our unconscious mind. It tells a story in symbols, in distorted messages. The other half of the time it delivers an incomplete message.

An example of everyday ESP that occurred between my wife and me makes this point. One morning shortly after my wife, Jan, got out of bed, I had a vivid dream. I was looking at a painting of the crucifixion. It was a grim scene. They were driving the nails. Later when I got out of bed, I noticed that Jan had taken the album for Bach's *St. Matthew Passion* from our record shelf but had not begun playing it. The cover of this album depicted a grim painting similar to the one I had seen in my dream—the crucifixion. They were driving the nails.

There is little doubt that the dream represented a telepathic episode. Had ESP told me a straight story, I might have woken and made the logical connection: "Aha! Jan is looking at Bach's *St. Matthew Passion!*" But as usual it was a story half told.

The fact that ESP often conveys trivial information, and doesn't even tell the story well at that, may seem annoying. It tempts us to ignore our extrasensory connection with our children, to write off our ESP experiences as so much trivia. After all, if it can defy the laws of physical science and leap across space as if space weren't there at all, we might imagine that it would get the story straight. Nonetheless it is remarkable that the story is told at all.

Perhaps by whispering a garbled message in our ears, ESP does not always meet our standards of effective communication. However, its half-told stories often bring an important message, especially when it comes to our children.

ESP may be behind may sudden hunches, flashes of intuition, and "gut" feelings. In fact, ESP and intuition sometimes look and act so similarly that the casual observer mistakes one for the other. But there is often a big difference between the two.

Intuition or *intuitive perception* is the immediate knowledge of something without the conscious use of reason. According to Carl Jung, intuition is not in opposition to reason but rather another dimension of knowing.[7] Intuitive perception is rather a tame bird because it is often based on subliminal impressions—perceptions just below the threshold of consciousness. Unlike its sister ESP, who prefers to do business outside the realm of space and time and all the other structures we use to describe the physical universe, this form of intuitive perception obeys the rules. It follows all the laws of science and psychology, though it is somewhat subtle about doing so at times.

For example, a mother has a sudden intuitive perception or "hunch" to check on her baby in another room. She may have heard something out of the ordinary. The baby is more quiet than usual. She may not be consciously aware that she notices anything different. But her unconscious mind has picked up a difference— a subliminal perception. She acts on the hunch and saves her baby from choking.

Like intuition, ESP is also the immediate knowledge of something without the conscious use of reason. But ESP ignores all the rules of logic and science. She leaps right across the space-time barrier to make her announcement. For example, a mother has a sudden hunch that she should drive a different route while bringing her child home from school. The mother acts on her hunch and drives home by an alternate route. Later she discovers that there has been a serious accident on the road she usually travels. The scene of the accident has not come to her conscious awareness. But the extrasensory story half told has reached her in the form of a "hunch" and she acts accordingly.

The distinction between intuitive perception and ESP seems so basic that we ought to be able to tell the difference. One travels in the familiar space-time continuum like everything else brought under scientific scrutiny. The other flits about in a spaceless, timeless no-man's-land and refuses to be analyzed.

But they are not so easily identified. For one thing, they exchange names frequently. The word "intuition" is often used to describe ESP. And the expression "ESP" is often used to describe intuition.

And as if that weren't enough, they often exchange clothing.

Consider the following case reported by Constance Young, Professor of Nursing at the University of Bridgeport, Bridgeport, Connecticut:

A patient who had been admitted to the coronary care unit complained of what the nurse caring for him described as routine chest pain. A pain medication was administered. Normally the nurse would wait until the medication had a chance to take effect and then check on her patient. However, the nurse vividly recalled that after about fifteen minutes something made her go back to the patient's room, where the patient was having a seizure as a consequence of cardiac arrest.[8]

Intuition or ESP? The intuitive nurse may just sense the "vibes" or feel a certain type of energy. She may not even know why she reacts.

To make matters even more confusing, intuitive perception and ESP often work hand in hand to deliver a message. Often subliminal impressions and ESP are combined.

AN UNSOLVED MYSTERY

How does ESP work? Why does a mother think of her daughter the instant before she calls? Unfortunately there are no simple answers. The way psi works is as much of a mystery as is its origin. And even the best theories are anything but satisfying.

Could an as-yet-unknown form of energy be transferred from brain to brain like radio waves? Some have considered this possibility. In the 1940s Hans Berger, the physiologist who invented the electroencephalograph, realized that the electrical rhythms in the brain were altogether too weak to account for telepathy. However, he theorized that electrical energy in the brain could be transformed into "psychic energy" that travels through space in a wavelike manner and could be diffused over any distance, even passing through physical barriers without weakening and finally upon reaching another brain be transformed back into electrical energy. This energy in turn could produce neural patterns and hence thoughts, images, or feelings—*voilà!* telepathy.[9]

Several parapsychologists have suggested that ESP may be explicable in terms of some sort of as yet-unknown form of electromagnetic energy. An experiment conducted by Dr. Charles C. Tart of the department of psychology at the University of California at Davis showed that ESP may be enhanced if the percipient (person who receives the telepathic message) remained inside a copper wall Faraday cage that was electronically connected to the ground. The Faraday cage is a solid wall and shielded enclosure named after Michael Faraday, a pioneer in the field of modern electrical science. The device is commonly used to shield sensitive electronic equipment from radiowave interference.

Dr. Tart placed students inside the enclosure. For ESP test material, he used Tarot cards for their striking visual and psychological appeal. The student was to arrange the Tarot cards in an order communicated telepathically by another student in a non-adjacent room. Dr. Tart found that students did somewhat better on the test while in the Faraday cage than elsewhere.[10]

This suggests but does not necessarily prove a link between ESP and some form of electromagnetic energy. It could be a major scientific breakthrough if more research were to confirm that ESP were associated with known laws of electromagnetic energy.

Some Russian parapsychologists consider psi part of a new physical energy field or "psi-field." This may be analogous but not identical to the electromagnetic field.[11]

However, if some sort of mental radio waves—electromagnetic or other—are responsible for ESP, the psi energy is unlike anything known to science. Telepathy seems to work equally well whether the two persons sharing thoughts are in the same room or on the other side of the world. In addition, experiments have shown that no barrier prevents the information transfer—not even a lead shield.

Dr. L. L. Vasiliev, a professor of physiology at the University of Leningrad and a well-known Russian parapsychologist, isolated subject (percipient receiving the telepathic message) and agent (person sending the message) in an enclosed room fully constructed of thick lead slabs with mercury to seal the joints. The room completely screened off electromagnetic energy. Yet telepathy worked just as well as if there were no screening at all, even when subject and agent were separated by a distance of 1,700 kilometers (approximately 1,056 miles). Hence, despite former theories, it appears that psi is not based on electromagnetic waves.[12]

However, ESP experiences may be related to environmental stimuli, say some parapsychologists. Dr. George Schaut and Dr. Michael Persinger of Laurentian University in Ontario hypothesize that spontaneous telepathy may be associated with geomagnetic activity. Analyzing cases published in Fate Magazine between 1960 and 1970, they found that telepathic experiences involving sickness and death occurred on days when the geomagnetic activity was significantly lower than on days immediately before or after the experience.

Whatever psi energy is and however it reaches us, it must affect our brain somehow in order to become part of our knowledge. To every physical sense we can ascribe an appropriate organ—to sight our eyes, to hearing our ears, to smell our nose. What is the organ of the sixth sense? Elusive as it is, psi must affect us *somewhere.* Some part of us must function as a "receiver" for psi impressions. And just as a definite place in the brain is associated with vision, hearing, and smell, some part of the nervous system must be associated with extrasensory perception. Psi must have, as Dr. Ehrenwald puts it, "a neural foothold." But where in our biological organism is psi's neural foothold? According to Dr. Ehrenwald, it is most likely in the brain stem and in the brain cortex.

Some neurophysiologists think that the limbid-midbrain system is involved in the processing of subliminal stimuli and that this part of the brain may also be associated with extrasensory perception.

Many parapsychologists agree that the right hemisphere of the brain is involved in processing ESP impressions. The right hemisphere, sometimes called the "heart brain," is associated with creativity and intuition, while the left brain is associated with reason and logic. Tuning out the left hemisphere temporarily, turning inward, and paying more attention to our intuition may be the first steps in fine-tuning our minds to psi. Deep mind/body relaxation, meditation, and some of the exercises in this book can help many parents tune into the right hemisphere and perhaps evoke their latent ESP.

One odd hypothesis called the "filter theory" suggests that ESP incidents are the result of some sort of biological accident. The brain may act as a filter screening out impressions of dubious value for biological survival or practical use in our lives. Without this filtering we might be bombarded with useless, irrelevant impressions. The reticular formation of the brain stem facilitates or inhibits the two-way flow of sensory stimuli to the higher centers from both inside and outside the body. Dr. Ehrenwald suggests that this primitive part of the brain may also act as a sort of defense, keeping extrasensory perceptions from our awareness.

Others have suggested that the frontal and temporal cortex play an important part in the selective filtering of input from the outside world.[13] Dr. Ehrenwald suggests that correct hits in ESP studies may be the result of a flaw in our screening or inhibiting functions of the reticular formation and higher cortical centers. This flaw in screening "results in the intrusion of a few . . . capricious bursts of psi incidents—conscious or unconscious—into a subject's scoring pattern."

This theory is by no means satisfying. Major psi events such as crisis telepathy "involve," Dr. Ehrenwald admits, "mental events of a highly complex nature and cannot be explained in terms of the random firing of a few unruly motor cells in the brain cortex or by reference to a bunch of neurons in the reticular formation caught napping at the job of blocking the entrance to consciousness of some wholly irrelevant ESP or clairvoyant impression."[14]

Many have suggested that we are all really connected, that all humans share a common collective unconscious mind. As writer William James puts it, "There is a continuum of cosmic consciousness against which our individuality builds but accidental fences, and into which our several minds plunge as into a mother sea."[15]

Oxford University professor of logic Henry Habberly Price, past president of the Society of Psychical Research, speculates that a part of our mind—the "collective unconscious"—is somehow connected on some level with all other minds. He suggests that there are no clear-cut boundaries between one mind and another. The unconscious of one mind may interact with another. The collective unconscious, which he considers more a "field of interaction" than a specific entity per se, may connect all apparently individual minds and be responsible for telepathy. He says—analogous to the filter theory—that the individual mind has developed a repressive faculty which suppresses the continual flow of telepathic impressions from one mind to another.

He also suggests that a part of our unconscious mind may be capable of perceiving everything, however remote, because it may be in contact with all things—an idea somewhat similar to Eastern religious thought that suggests that all minds are ultimately interconnected and part of the One.[16]

Dr. Price's theory of the interconnectedness of minds may apply especially to parents and their offspring. Family therapist Edward Taub-Bynum has developed a fascinating theory that may help to explain some of the puzzling mysteries of family life such as parent-offspring ESP and the fact that siblings who, though they may live in distant locations and have no contact with one another, often develop the same personal mannerisms and even choose the same pets. Dr. Taub-Bynum has many times observed extraordinary forms of communication among family members: crisis telepathy, shared dream images, and so on. In one family he was treating, the parents were in the midst of separation. The mother and her nine-year-old son claimed to be able to read each other's minds at times. The laws of psychology offer no satisfying explanation for such phenomena.

Dr. Taub-Bynum theorizes that in addition to our personal unconscious there is yet another level of mind which he calls the *family unconscious,* a region that lies between the individual consciousness and the collective unconscious. The family unconscious represents a "shared inner landscape"—a sort of group mind that links all members of the family together in a spaceless, timeless dimension. The family unconscious may act as a medium for the extrasensory transmission of information. Dr. Taub-Bynum calls the family unconscious an "enfolding field" and discusses psi in terms of quantum-relativistic theory in which the division of space and not-space is by no means clear. The idea of the family unconscious is by no means a definitive theory. However, more research regarding this possible dimension of the human mind may help to explain the great number of ESP episodes within the family.

Perhaps the most satisfying theory and one that will probably appeal to the majority postulates that we are more than biological organisms, more than mere flesh and blood. A part of us—call it the mind, the spirit, the soul—is nonphysical, immaterial. According to this theory, the mind is not identical to the brain but rather interacts with it. Though they do not speak of psi, several neurophysiologists including Sir John Eccles, Nobel Prize–winner in 1963 for his discovery of the chemical means by which impulses are communicated by nerve cells, believe that the mind is nonphysical. They have even proposed elaborate models attempting to explain the interaction between the nonphysical mind and the biological brain.

If the conscious mind (spirit or soul) is nonphysical, then presumably it is not subject to the same laws that govern our physical beings. Perhaps the love bond we share with our children has an extraphysical dimension outside the finite world of space and time. For that matter, we may be linked somehow to the life force of all living things, indeed, to the very universe.

Perhaps our nonphysical mind communicates directly with other minds. Our mind may intuit information "clairvoyantly" without the aid of the five senses. The information our nonphysical mind perceives is then conveyed to our physical brains in the form of a flash of ESP.

But how? The idea of a nonphysical mind doesn't explain how psi works. It simply tells us there is a part of us that we don't understand—a psi faculty. It tells us what we already know, and that is that we don't know how psi works.

Which brings us back to where we started.

PSI: A REPRESSED FACULTY

Meanwhile, because it is so elusive, psi is like a rejected ragamuffin orphan, a child with no proper home either in science or religion. It has knocked on almost everyone's door at one time or another, played a role, minor or major, in almost everyone's life, including the bit part of telling a mother who is on the line when her daughter phones. Yet even when it stands right before us demanding our attention, many of us turn our head away, ignore it, as if by so doing we can pretend that it isn't there at all.

People throughout the world, both scientists and laypersons, have noticed, commented on, recorded, and confirmed the reality of psi. Hundreds of carefully controlled studies have proven the existence of ESP in the laboratory. After reviewing the evidence objectively, we can no more deny the reality of ESP than we can deny the reality of dreams. Indeed, it takes a greater leap of faith to deny the existence of psi than it does to accept it.

Yet many otherwise rational-minded people do just that. They refuse to give psi a second glance. About ESP many believe that "it doesn't happen because it can't happen." This belief, conscious or unconscious, colors everything they hear about psychic phenomena. At worst they assume all this ESP business is a big fraud; at best, a delusion. Of course, there is fraud in ESP research. There are charlatans and fake psychics. But who among us is willing to imagine a fraud spanning decades; a fraud involving some of the world's most eminent scientists? And delusion? Who is capable of imagining a delusion of such magnitude that it involves every nation in the world? A delusion experienced by hundreds of thousands of parents and their children yearly? There is only so far one can carry the fraud accusation without seeming utterly ridiculous. When the telephone was first demonstrated to them, French experts argued that the demonstrators had had a ventriloquist under the table.[17]

"We've been brainwashed to believe that psi isn't here," says Dr. Berthold Schwarz. "It's like the story of 'The Emperor's New Clothes' in reverse."

It's a well-known tale. Once upon a time there was an emperor who was excessively vain and fond of clothes. A clever tailor claimed he could make a suit of clothes of unimaginably beautiful fabric. But there was a catch. The clothes would remain invisible to anyone who was not fit for the office he held or who was simply dull-witted. Vain man that he was, the emperor simply had to have a suit of unimaginably beautiful fabric so he could wear it on the occasion of a great procession through his kingdom. So he commissioned the tailor to do the job.

The tailor made a great to-do about weaving a suit out of fabric, which, alas, remained invisible to the emperor. But the emperor, who wasn't about to consider himself dull-witted or unfit for his office, wouldn't admit that he couldn't see the clothes when the tailor helped him dress. And neither would anyone else.

According to Hans Christian Andersen's tale, when the emperor walked in royal procession the people shouted: "How beautiful are the emperor's new clothes! What a splendid train! And they fit so perfectly!"

Nobody would let on that he couldn't see the clothes the emperor was wearing. Who would wish to admit he was a fool or unfit for his post?

No one but a little child. "But he has nothing on!" cried the child. That's when the word spread. One person whispered to the other what the child had said until all the people cried: "But he has nothing on!"

"Brainwashed!" says Dr. Schwarz. "Many of us are just like the people who wouldn't admit that the emperor was riding through town naked!" We won't admit the reality of psi even when it stands right under our nose.

Dr. Ehrenwald suggests that our society has a "cultural repression" of the paranormal. This keeps many parents from acknowledging—even to themselves—their own possible ESP experiences. Many parents laugh off possible ESP episodes or dismiss them as mere coincidences. Others who are aware of ESP experiences with their children don't discuss them with others for fear of ridicule. They may be labeled "kooks." Cultural attitudes can eventually condition the parent to repress possible ESP experiences. One shuts the door to psi before it even knocks. The entire range of psychic phenomena, from knowing who is on the line when the phone rings to seeing a vision of a loved one at the moment of his death, seems to be the random occurrence of freak, inexplicable events that defy the laws of nature.

Psi is unruly and unpredictable. We can't control it. Even the most gifted psychics often have difficulty and seem to lose the ability from time to time.

And unlike most everything else in nature we can name, psi seems to have no specific purpose. It is simply there, hanging about in the ether, popping in and out of our lives like a wayward magician. And, as parapsychologist D. Scott Rogo points out, science resists innovation and abhors anomaly if "breakthroughs or events are not consistent with the current vogue of scientific thinking."[18] Perhaps when a new framework is conceived which makes room for psi, it will be more welcome to join the rank and file of things acceptable to science.

Psi is unsettling. If we acknowledge the reality of ESP, we are left wondering: How does psi work? Why does psi work? Psi threatens our view of the physical world. It introduces an unknown and inexplicable dimension in our lives. This applies particularly well to precognition. There's no phenomenon where the "it doesn't happen because it can't happen" argument seems more applicable. Everyone likes to rest assured that tomorrow is tomorrow and what happens then cannot be intuited yesterday. The very idea of knowing that something is going to happen before it happens, as if it already did happen, is enough to make anyone's head spin. For this reason alone, it is easier to shut the door before psi knocks than welcome it into our home.

In addition, psi has an unsavory reputation. Many justifiably connect it with the lunatic fringe of society—drug freaks, strangely garbed occultists, self-styled magicians. Judging psi by the company it keeps, many often unfairly accuse it of not being a legitimate child of nature.

No. We can't explain it. We don't have the answers about ESP and perhaps never will. But if we close our eyes and block our ears, we may be denying a part of ourselves, a part of nature that we can't explain but nevertheless a real part of nature. And more than that. We may fail to see that psi opens the door to a new way of thinking that affects the deepest part of our being—our interconnectedness with our children.

FAVORABLE CONDITIONS FOR PARENT-CHILD ESP

Under what circumstances are parents most likely to experience ESP with their children? Certain states of mind, certain life events tend to be psi-conducive or favorable for the occurrence of ESP.

Dreaming is considered the ideal state for spontaneous ESP. More telepathic communication and precognitive episodes occur during dreaming than at any other time. (More on this in chapter 7.)

During waking life, well-known psychics enter an altered state of mind that appears to help them think in visual images during ESP sessions. Most agree that the ideal frame of mind for ESP is a relaxed, passive-alert state. Meditation and relaxation exercises can help bring about this state. In 1970 Dr. Gertrude R. Schmeidler of the City College of the City University of New York tested college students before and after having them meditate and do breathing exercises. ESP scores proved higher after meditation.

A psi-conducive condition may be created by just thinking about ESP. Odd as it may seem, one who is on the lookout for ESP is more likely to experience it. Similarly paying attention to dreams seems to yield a richer, fuller dream life. This is partly because dreams are more easily remembered when one pays attention to them.

By paying attention to possible ESP episodes, one becomes more attuned to the parapsychology of everyday life. A parent may begin to notice ESP experiences with her child that seem so trivial, the little "coincidences" that often pass unobserved, that most parents wouldn't give them a second thought. Thinking about psi may also be a way of fine-tuning the mind to ESP's "frequency," much like turning a radio dial to the frequency of a particular station.

A positive attitude about psi also seems to increase the probability of ESP experiences. In fact, many parapsychologists agree that this is one psi-conducive condition that can be repeatedly verified by means of scientific tests.

If you dial your daughter's telephone number, her phone will ring regardless of your attitude toward the phone company. ESP is unlike that. Psi works most effectively for those who appreciate it and acknowledge its reality, and least effectively for those who don't believe in it. It is as if psi were a very sensitive house guest all too willing to make itself scarce at the slightest provocation.

In an often-quoted study, Dr. Schmeidler tested students at both Harvard University and City College of New York. Students were separated into two groups—sheep, that is, those who believed in ESP; and goats, those who did not believe. Not surprisingly, the sheep scored significantly higher on ESP tests than the goats.[19]

Several researchers performed similar tests with similar results. This became well known in parapsychology as "the sheep-goat effect"—ESP works best when one believes in it.

Actually when it comes to skeptics, psi often has the last laugh. Those who disbelieve in ESP not only have fewer correct hits on ESP tests than those who do believe. They sometimes miss so many answers that it cannot be explained by chance alone—demonstrating psi in reverse! The idea is that the law of averages determines that chance will produce some correct answers. Therefore one would have to use ESP in order to consistently answer incorrectly. Parapsychologists call this phenomenon "psi-missing."

When ESP is taken for granted, it is much more apt to be a part of our lives. On the other hand, some have suggested that ESP rarely occurs in everyday life as a result of our cultural conditioning. Since ESP is an unconscious process, the mind may prevent it from entering our conscious awareness or distort the extrasensory perception so that it becomes unrecognizable.

As Dr. Schwarz points out, "A culturally favorable environment appears to be helpful. If the parents don't pooh pooh and denigrate any budding psychic ability in their children, or for that matter the presumed psi exchanges between themselves, the phenomena are accepted for what they are: facts of life, and not suppressed and later repressed by ridicule or the like."[20]

Other factors that some claim influence psi are abstinence from alcohol, adherence to a vegetarian diet, and so forth. However, these conditions are what Berthold Schwarz calls "prissy preconceptions." Expectation is probably behind all of these notions. If you expect a certain style of life or a certain habit to have a negative or positive effect on psi, it probably will.

Gardner Murphy, one of the world's most prominent parapsychologists, has suggested that psi phenomena are primarily the result of processes that depend on the relationship between people.[21] Tying in with this idea is a point that Renee Haynes makes in her book, *The Society For Psychical Research: 1882–1982: A History*: "The time, the place, and the loved one may produce one result where a different time and place and person may well produce another. A laboratory at ten in the morning, with a detached and unfamiliar figure operating incomprehensible machinery is not always good at evoking faculties rooted in the process of keeping alive as an individual or as a species, and in primordial emotions."[22]

Perhaps the ultimate psi-conducive condition is to be found in peak experiences occurring within the parent-child relationship. The parent-child ESP connection is the strongest of all psychic bonds—and, if we accept the theory of some parapsychologists, the prototype of all psychic experiences. Our relationship to our offspring and to those who gave us life may be our link to the paranormal. Certain high-energy states within the parent-offspring relationship seem to trigger psychic experiences: greeting a newborn baby and forging the lifelong parent attachment bond; crisis situations such as an accident or serious injury; death. These life-altering experiences seem to open a gateway to the realm beyond the senses. They allow many of us to become temporarily psychic—to experience ESP that we otherwise associate with mystics and the gifted few.

There is yet another high-energy state that all parents experience, one that may open a doorway to the paranormal and trigger more psychic experiences than any other. It occurs when parents become part of the never-ending stream of life. This is the period when the offspring undergoes the most miraculous change of all. When mother and child share the closest of all human bonds. When they are not only one mind, but one flesh.

In the womb.

3

The Parapsychology of Pregnancy

If anyone should be able to pull the proverbial rabbit from the hat, it is the pregnant woman. Her ability to create new life in the depths of her belly is indeed magical. The changes that take place during pregnancy stagger the imagination. Her entire being undergoes a psychobiological revolution that may very well carry psi on its wings.

And it all begins with a single cell smaller than the dot at the end of this sentence. The cell grows to million upon millions of times its original size. From it come the baby, the amniotic fluid, the fetal membranes (sack in which the baby and fluid are contained), the curly white umbilical cord, and, with a contribution from the uterus, the placenta.

As the fetus floats about snug and secure in a sea of crystal-clear water, its own private universe, amazing changes take place in the mother's body. Every organ and system experiences changes—some small, some tremendous—to meet the needs of the developing new being. Even the maternal blood is altered.

The remarkable uterus—baby's temporary home—grows to contain a full five hundred times its prepregnant capacity. Its weight increases a full twenty-fold. The neck of the uterus, or cervix, once as hard as the tip of the nose, becomes as soft as an earlobe, so that it can open like a blossoming flower on the day of birth. The breasts expand and begin to produce baby's only perfectly manufactured and fully nutritious food. And of course there is that change that every pregnant woman knows only too well. The abdomen expands. Pregnancy becomes apparent to all.

Yet one of the most remarkable changes that occurs takes place not in the expectant mother's body but in her mind. The mother may begin to forge the lifelong psychic connection with her child developing within. And throughout the life-creating prenatal months, she may find herself unusually intuitive. For the first time in her life, she may discover that she has extrasensory perception. And so may the expectant father.

CONCEPTION INTUITIONS

"I don't have a strong belief in psychic stuff," says Dr. Jerrold Lee Shapiro, clinical psychologist and author of *When Men Are Pregnant,* "but right after we made love one afternoon, I said to my wife, 'We made a baby this time!' I can't describe how, but I knew. Later, when I was being interviewed by a writer for the *San Jose Mercury News,* I told him about my experience. There was a moment of intense contact between us. His eyes became bright and moist. He broke into a big smile and said that he had never really discussed it with others, but he had been aware of the moment for his own child."

The *conception intuition* is one of the most common forms of prenatal psi. In case after case, parents sense the moment of conception. They know they are pregnant before even the most sophisticated tests of medical science can confirm their intuition.

Erica's story is a classic example. On the morning following the beginning of each of her pregnancies, she woke up with a quiet certainty that a child had been conceived.

"It was a healthy, peaceful, exciting feeling," she recalls. "And it left no doubt in my mind. The morning after our second child was conceived, I told my husband, 'I'm pregnant!' Later the same day I called my physician to make an appointment."

Erica's first child was only three months old at the time. She hadn't even had a period yet. The likelihood of conception was extremely slim. But she was still sure. "I got pregnant last night," she informed the physician. "I know."

"How can you know?" the physician asked skeptically.

"I don't know how I know. I just know," said Erica. She insisted on making an appointment.

Her doctor told her that it was impossible to test for pregnancy only a few hours after conception. And it was certainly impossible for her to know she was pregnant. But Erica wouldn't be put off. Finally, to humor her, the physician made an appointment for three weeks later. He was astounded when the test came out positive. "You really *are* pregnant!" he exclaimed.

Amy and Joe's experience is another striking example. The moon was full on the night of St. Patrick's Day, 1987, when they returned to their chartered forty-foot sloop anchored off one of the Caribbean Islands. They were on vacation, island hopping, and had been on the beach partying all evening. They made love when they got back to the boat. And when they did, they both sensed something special had occurred.

"It was almost a supernatural experience," recalls Amy. "We both knew something really heavy-duty had happened."

Joe recalls: "I knew that we had conceived on that boat. I remember joking about it. 'It's just our luck that it's going to be twins.'"

Amy had the same feeling. But she wasn't joking about it when she visited her midwife for her first prenatal appointment nine weeks later. She told the midwife that she was carrying twins—one boy and one girl.

Her midwife informed her that it was not unusual for a mother expecting her third child to imagine she was carrying twins, but that it was highly unlikely since there was no history of multiple births in her family.

But Amy was certain. "I don't know if it's a spiritual intuition or if I am just feeling more attuned to my body, but I know there are two babies."

Two months later, when Amy kept referring to her unborn child as "them," her midwife suggested an ultrasound—a procedure that gives a picture of the fetus in utero. The test showed that there were indeed two babies. One was a boy. The test couldn't identify the sex of the other.

It wasn't until she gave birth that Amy's intuition was fully confirmed. The other was a girl.

Many who can't recall another single psychic experience in their lives have conception intuition. Penny, a mother of three living in Laconia, New Hampshire, knew without a doubt that she was pregnant with her third child even though medical evidence told her she wasn't. "Every pregnancy test was negative," she says. "But I knew they were all wrong. They had to be. I was sure I was carrying a child."

Perhaps Penny's tests were done too early. Perhaps the lab made a mistake. Penny tried yet another test. This one was positive. She had been pregnant all along.

Lisa, who lives in Swansea, Massachusetts, says: "I knew within twenty-four hours that I had conceived. I felt a heaviness, a concentrated weight in my lower abdomen which lasted about forty-eight hours. I was wholly convinced it was pregnancy." From a strictly physiological point of view, her intuition and accompanying feeling of heaviness in the lower abdomen make no sense. There is no physical reason for such a feeling a mere twenty-four hours after conception. The developing embryo is still a mere speck in the mother's Fallopian tube. It doesn't travel to the uterus until several days after conception. And ordinarily the mother does not begin to notice physical changes for at least two weeks from the time sperm and egg unite.

Many know during lovemaking. This is the way it was with Anne in every one of her three pregnancies. "There was no doubt in my mind. During lovemaking I knew a child had been conceived."

Dr. Peter Hope, a family practitioner in Laconia, New Hampshire, has heard the story over and over again. "I've had a number of patients tell me, 'We made a baby last night,' before any medical tests could detect it. Of course there are numerous infertility patients who *wish* they had conceived. But it's quite another matter when one has the intuition that one *has* conceived—especially when that intuition proves correct."

Even the most sensitive pregnancy test can give results only eight days after conception. At this time the developing embryo produces human chorionic gonadotropin (HCG), a hormone which can be detected in the mother's blood and later in her urine. Yet thousands of mothers and fathers-to-be feel something during lovemaking that can't quite be put into words—a sense of inner knowing.

But there is an enigma here. The sudden inner certainty that a child has been conceived during lovemaking contradicts everything we know about the human body. It contradicts the laws of physics itself and flies in the face of all reason. Knowing that a child has been conceived during lovemaking is scientifically, biologically, and psychologically impossible. For during lovemaking sperm and egg *have not yet united*. A child is not conceived until several hours after intercourse.

Impossible. Yet the simple fact remains—conception intuitions during lovemaking occur every day.

How can this be? The implications are staggering. To know that one has conceived before conception, some part of the mind would have to transcend time.

Impressive as this seems, many parapsychologists might doubt that conception intuitions are extrasensory perceptions at all. It can be argued that the mother is simply responding to subtle changes in her body.

When she is most fertile, dozens of physiological mechanisms take place of which presumably her unconscious mind may be aware. For instance, the cervical mucus becomes more sticky. A drop placed between two fingers will form a strand when the fingers are pulled apart. If a woman doesn't notice the altered mucus or the other physical changes accompanying her most fertile period, she may feel a subtle difference in her lovemaking. It might be argued that the father too notices subtle changes in his mate's body or in lovemaking. Perceiving such physiological changes on a subliminal level could explain conception intuitions.

Perhaps. But that doesn't account for the mother's or father's sense of complete inner certainty.

Take the example of Milton, a message therapist in Albuquerque, New Mexico. He had conception intuitions when both of his children were conceived. Recalling the first pregnancy, he says, "After we made love, there was something qualitatively different about the way I felt, and the thought went through my mind—'There's another being here. We are pregnant!'"

He and his wife, Lyn, both had an intuition that she was pregnant when their second child was conceived, though they didn't discuss it at the time. Shortly afterwards, Milton went on a business trip. When he returned home, Lyn was finding it difficult to break the news because they hadn't planned this pregnancy. But before she could finish telling him, he interrupted her. "If you're trying to tell me that you're pregnant, I've known for some time. And I think it's great!"

This happens so frequently and to so many men and women that a large number of midwives have come to take conception intuitions for granted.

What can we make of conception intuitions? It is almost impossible to verify such reports. However, there is little doubt of their veracity. How do parents know they are pregnant at the very beginning of pregnancy, or even before the child is conceived?

Does the baby announce his or her arrival to the deeper mind? Some people think so. They believe that the baby chooses his parents, the time to be conceived, and the time to be born.

Those who believe in reincarnation may find this a probable explanation.

It is not very satisfying to others, however. Most likely we can explain conception intuitions in two ways. Many, perhaps even the majority, may result from subliminal impressions. The mother perceives subtle changes in her body and senses that she is—or is ripe to be—pregnant. To explain other intuitions, it seems that we must look to clairvoyance or even precognition.

Indeed, the conception intuition may be the first experience in a hitherto unexplored dimension of the childbearing drama—the parapsychology of pregnancy.

PRENATAL ESP

The whirling vortex of psychobiological forces that coalesce to create a new being seems to draw psi like a magnet. Whether you call it intuition, instinct, the voice within, attuning to the deeper mind, or simply ESP, it seems to occur more often during pregnancy than at any other time.

Time after time, expectant mothers report the same phenomenon. "I feel more psychic than usual," says Miriam, a business executive, in the second trimester of her first pregnancy. "It's as if my radar were becoming supersensitive and I'm more able to pick up on things."

It is a common experience during pregnancy. Most prenatal ESP belongs in the category of *everyday ESP.* Suddenly intuiting who is on the other end of the line when the telephone rings, sharing the same thought at the same time with her partner, having a intuition about her labor or her baby which later proves to be true—these are the sorts of things that the pregnant woman's "supersensitive radar" most frequently picks up.

Many expectant mothers begin to have ESP experiences for the first time in their lives. Joanna, a woman from Concord, Massachusetts, expecting her first baby, is a typical example.

"I've never had ESP before," she says, "but since I became pregnant, I've felt more attuned somehow."

Many pregnant women feel "more attuned." "I would contact someone for the first time in months, to find out that the person had just left a message on my answering machine," one expectant mother says. "Or I would mail a letter to a friend, to later discover that she had just mailed a letter to me."

Clairvoyant dreams, discussed in chapter 7, become almost commonplace.

Many mothers- and fathers-to-be may find themselves thinking the same thoughts at the same time. As pregnancy progresses, the expectant mother becomes increasingly vulnerable and dependent on her partner. She may think of him more often, wonder about his safety. This may be one factor triggering increased ESP between the parents. Sharon, an expectant mother, says: "Nothing like this has ever happened to me before. It is uncanny. I feel plugged into an awareness beyond myself. I often find myself thinking of my husband at the every minute he calls. I think that he should be phoning now even though it isn't the time he usually calls. Then the phone is ringing. . . . "

An accurate intuition of the unborn baby's gender is a very common form of prenatal ESP. Many expectant mothers and fathers correctly intuit their child's sex months before birth. At the Northern New Mexico Midwifery Center in Taos, New Mexico, expectant mothers in their third trimester were asked what gender they thought their unborn child was. Over 75 percent accurately intuited the sex.

An intuition about the baby's gender frequently comes in the form of a "naming" episode, that is, the expectant mother or father suddenly flashes on their child's name as if it were being given to them from a source outside themselves. For example, during her first pregnancy, Kathy, a mother in Manchester, Connecticut, had chosen only a girl's name. She recalls: "One evening during the seventh month, all of a sudden I knew his name was Kyle and that he was a boy." She later gave birth to a son.

Kathy had a similar experience during her second pregnancy. During the seventh month the name "Janine" came to her. Her second child was a daughter.

An intuition of the child's gender frequently comes in dreams. Many expectant parents envision their child's gender either realistically or symbolically in a dream. The following story is a striking example:

During her second pregnancy, Peggy O'Neill, director of research for the Institute for Higher Healing in Richmond, Virginia, had been hoping for a girl. One night she dreamed that she had decided to give the child away and that it had been transplanted to another woman's uterus. Later in the dream she decided she wanted the baby back. She says: "I was told that if I could identify the child I could have it back. I was then taken to a hospital room full of boys about 14 months old. At first I was really shocked that they were all boys. Then I realized my baby must be a boy. I saw a beautiful child with blond hair and blue eyes and was struck by how much he looked like his brother. I knew he was my child and was overwhelmed with love for him. I took him home with great joy.

"I realize the reason I had given my child up," continues Peggy, "was that I wanted a girl. But now I knew it didn't matter."

Peggy later gave birth to a son who at 14 months old did appear as he had in the dream and looked precisely like his older brother.

Shortly after her son was born, Peggy had a dramatic naming experience. She and her husband, Al, were determined on an Irish name but decided to put off naming the baby until they came across a name that "felt just right." On the third day after the birth, she, her husband Al, and a friend, Ivette, were all taking naps, each in a separate room. Peggy dreamed that she should name her son "Jonathan." While she was taking a bath shortly after waking, Al came into the bathroom and said, "I just dreamed we should name our baby 'Jonathan.'"

Later in the afternoon, their friend Ivette, who had since gone home, called and asked if they had chosen a name. She was quite surprised when she heard the name they had chosen, for she too had dreamed they should name the child "Jonathan," but didn't mention it because she knew the parents were committed to an Irish name!

Many parents have vague or specific impressions about the baby in utero. Says Sylvia Klein Olkin, director of Positive Pregnancy and Parenting Fitness and author of *Positive Pregnancy Through Yoga*, "A friend of mine had a strong intuition that something was wrong with her baby. She went to her doctor, who told her nothing was wrong. Yet the mother still sensed something was wrong and tried to convince her physician to do a cesarean section. However, the physician thought she was crazy and would not operate. Later the baby was stillborn."

The mother may have an impression about the baby without even realizing that it is an intuition. While driving along the highway during her seventh month of pregnancy, Marsha, a mother of two from northern New Hampshire, suddenly told her husband Al, "I don't think this baby will be anything." She didn't know why she said that. "It was just an idea that popped into my head," she said. About two weeks after Marsha had that premonition, she gave birth to a baby boy. Two and a half hours after birth, the baby died.

Cybele of Orange County, California, had a similar experience. "During most of my second pregnancy I kept feeling that something was wrong. At twenty-six weeks the baby died in utero."

Though intuitions about pregnancy and the baby can prove true, it is important to bear in mind that most all women have dreams, thoughts, fears, and forebodings about complications such as giving birth to a deformed child. Such feelings are a normal part of pregnancy. Usually they are best ignored. If, however, a foreboding is unusually vivid or overwhelming, it might be wise to consult a physician or midwife.

Another mother had an intuition that her baby was alive and healthy though her doctor repeatedly told her it was dead. "I was a battered wife during the first trimester when I was pregnant with my second child. My husband beat me very badly in the abdomen. For the next two months I was bleeding off and on, with five periods of heavy bleeding. My physician told me I would definitely lose the baby; miscarriage was inevitable. Rather callously, I thought, he gave me a choice: I could either go upstairs in the hospital and complete the abortion or go home and let the miscarriage occur naturally. In either case, he said, miscarriage could not be prevented. Suddenly I knew that he was wrong. With remarkable certainty, I knew that I would not lose that baby—that the baby was alive and healthy."

Nor did she lose the baby. Her daughter was born alive and healthy right at the time of her due date.

In her book *ESP In Life and Lab* Louisa Rhine records the following episode of *crisis telepathy* which occurred during her second pregnancy:

"My husband and I were living in Youngstown, Ohio. I was pregnant with our second child. Our first was in a home for retarded children in Dayton, Ohio. He was ten months old, and I had seen him only twice. From that time neither my husband nor I saw nor heard of him.

"My second pregnancy was a very happy one. I didn't have a blue day and was happy as a lark. That is why . . . one night in March during my sixth month the terrible gloom that descended upon me was so unexpected. We had been out to dinner, arrived home early, and were getting ready for bed when this heavy unhappy feeling began filling my heart. . . . That night was a mixture of tears, tossing, and turning. When the morning finally came that horrible heavy feeling was still with me. My husband was reluctant to leave me and made me promise to get out of the house and be with someone. . . . At two in the afternoon I dragged myself to the grocery store to buy food I didn't need. I remember vividly standing by the meat counter when all of a sudden I had a glorious feeling as though a great weight had been lifted from my shoulders. It was exactly 3 P.M.

"That evening I told my husband everything. We had just

finished eating when we received a long-distance phone call. It was from the home our baby was in in Dayton, Ohio. Our baby had been very sick the night before and had passed away that afternoon at 3 P.M."[1]

Heightened intuition often continues and sometimes peaks during labor. "Mothers often show remarkable psychic ability during labor," says Houston, Texas, midwife Pat Jones. "I often ask a woman how far dilated she is [that is, how far the cervix has opened, an indication of labor's progress]. If she really thinks about it and gets in touch with her intuition, she can often tell me exactly how much she has dilated. Sometimes I ask when she will give birth and many can tell the time the baby will come."

Pat Jones has also noticed that the mother and father will sometimes refer to the baby by the correct gender at the moment of birth before the baby has fully emerged. "Look! He has opened his eyes!" a mother might exclaim. Or, "Here is her head! She will be born any minute!"—without realizing she has intuited the baby's gender.

During pregnancy and labor, the inner mind often uses symbolic language to convey information unknown to the conscious mind. ASPO/Lamaze teacher trainer Suzanna May Hilbers visited a friend, Helen, in labor to find a nurse shaving her belly in preparation for a cesarean. The physician suspected cephalopelvic disproportion (a condition in which the baby's head is believed to be too large for the mother's pelvis).

Suzanna sat on the edge of the bed and tried to comfort the frightened mother. "Your baby will soon be able to see the blue sky," she said.

"All he can see is black," said Helen.

"What do you think the baby would like to see?" asked Suzanna.

Closing her eyes, Helen thought for a moment. "I think he wants to see me."

As she talked about what she wanted to show her baby, Helen began to relax. Her fear melted. Apparently, turning inward was just what she needed to help her labor progress.

"What color can your baby see now?" Suzanna whispered.

Helen's eyes widened. "The baby can see blue! He can see the blue sky!"

Just then a nurse came in to wheel the mother to the operating room. But it was too late for surgery. The cervix had fully dilated. Helen's baby was born vaginally within ten minutes.

The baby inside the uterus couldn't really see the sky. But Helen was nevertheless relating a real event in symbolic language. Her inner mind was aware that the gateway of the womb had opened.

Many intuitions which appear to be ESP episodes are actually the result of subliminal impressions.

One mother reports: "I knew something was wrong during my second pregnancy. I felt that the baby wasn't developing properly. It was an ingrained feeling. During each prenatal visit, I kept commenting that things weren't right. However, the midwife assured me I was worrying needlessly. The pregnancy was perfectly healthy. The baby's growth was normal. There was no reason to be concerned. But I still felt uneasy. Something wasn't right. Finally I felt as if I stopped being pregnant. A few days after having this feeling, the baby died in utero."

While the feelings foreshadowing this tragic event appear to have an element of paranormality (and may very well be a case of ESP), there is another possibility. The mother, who had been pregnant before, may have noticed a difference between the fetal activity during this pregnancy and her former one. This could account for her ingrained feeling that things were not well with the baby.

One might assume that because the mother is carrying the child, she would be the one to experience prenatal psi. Yet this is not always so. Fathers, too, experience heightened intuition during the prenatal months.

During their first pregnancy Penny began to notice that her husband had suddenly become remarkably intuitive. "Charlie doesn't ordinarily have ESP," she said. "No. It didn't begin until the pregnancy. We had been doing massage for each other for some time. Suddenly Charlie seemed to have an intuitive sense of what was happening in my body. He could sense exactly where I was feeling muscular aches and pains. Many times he would put his hands on the spot where my back hurt. He felt something like heat or radiation coming from the spot. Never had he felt anything like this before pregnancy."

Though it may seem uncanny, the father's knowing, sensing, and even experiencing what is happening in the mother's body is by no means unusual.

The father's prenatal psi experiences usually involve either his partner or unborn child—the two persons most often in his mind. Sylvia Klein Olkin recalls a striking intuition that her husband had during the eight month of their pregnancy. "One evening my husband said: 'Sit down. I just got a thought about the baby. I think we will have a baby boy. He will have very dark hair and blue eyes.' I was quite surprised that he said this because I was expecting a girl. However, we did have a boy with blue eyes and pitch black hair."

It is perplexing that the father should also become more prone to ESP during the prenatal months. But even more perplexing is his experience of physical symptoms of pregnancy.

The following story was reported by a nurse. While at work, a man was bothered by morning nausea. When this began to interfere with his work, he telephoned his wife.

"Call the doctor," he told her.

"Why?" she asked.

"I think you are pregnant."

His wife told him the idea was ridiculous, but to humor her husband she made an appointment. Her pregnancy test was positive.

Nine months later, the expectant father began experiencing back pains during work. Again he telephoned to ask his wife to call the doctor. When she asked why, he said: "I think you are in labor."

Their child was born within twenty-four hours.

The father had experienced his wife's symptoms.

British psychiatrist W. H. Trethowan calls this phenomenon *couvade syndrome*. Short of demon possession, couvade syndrome may be the most unusual of all widespread complaints recorded in medical literature. It includes a variety of physical and emotional symptoms: unintentional weight gain, morning nausea, and other gastrointestinal discomforts, irritability, nervousness, excessive fatigue, and other symptoms associated with pregnant women.

Many men experience pregnancy symptoms. Joseph, an architect in Cambridge, Massachusetts, experienced prenatal symptoms along with his wife Julie. "I'm not particularly predisposed to this sort of thing," he is quick to point out. "I tend to view such phenomena with a skeptical attitude. However, when it happens repeatedly it is difficult to deny. Julie and I seemed to share sympathetic symptoms more often as the due date neared. For example, I would feel tired when she did, which is most unusual for me."

The most dramatic episode occurred when Julie went into labor. Joseph was at work at the time. "All of a sudden I felt very nauseous, my stomach was racing. I lay down on the couch in the reception area, I felt so bad. I wondered if it might be a sympathetic feeling. I phoned Julie but she had been sleeping at the time and said she felt fine. But I still felt that this might be the big moment and had a strong feeling that I should be with her. I left work immediately. By the time I arrived home, Julie was starting to feel labor contractions."

According to Dr. Trethowan, whose research in the 1960s has since been backed by the observations of dozens of health professionals, approximately 11 percent of all expectant fathers—more than one in ten—experience couvade syndrome. And strange as it may seem, more often than not the expectant father is *unaware* that his symptoms have any relation to the pregnancy.

Couvade syndrome was named after a curious practice called *couvade* (from a French verb meaning "to hatch" or "to brood").

Common to many peoples throughout the world, couvade refers to a group of male childbirth rites and taboos varying from one society to another. The father sometimes observes a strict diet, sometimes follows behavioral guidelines, and may during childbirth even take to bed and mimic labor. In some societies ritual couvade is practiced to deter evil spirits from the mother. However, the rite may also have a powerful psychological purpose: to serve as a passage rite ushering the father across the oneway bridge to parenthood.

Like ritual couvade, the couvade syndrome may also represent the expectant father's sharing pregnancy on a deep psychological and perhaps even psychic level.

"I had several pregnancy tests and they all came back negative," recalls Karen, a mother of three. "Yet my husband David and I both knew I was pregnant! It seemed very strange to us that David seemed to progress through pregnancy with me. He had morning nausea along with me for the first three months and shared other symptoms as the months went on."

Robert Plott writing in 1677 observed: "The pangs of the woman in the exclusion of the child . . . sometimes affected the abdomen of the husband."[2] During World War II medical officers observed transient abdominal upset in soldiers about the time their wives were in labor.

The cause of pregnancy symptoms in men is by no means clear. Anxiety, ambivalence about the pregnancy, unconscious envy of the mother's reproductive ability may all contribute to a complaint such as morning nausea. Such symptoms, therefore, are usually thought to be psychophysiological (mind/body) reactions.

Anxiety and perhaps buried feelings may explain some cases of couvade syndrome. But do they explain all? A psychophysiological reaction doesn't explain why the father sometimes develops prenatal nausea *before* he realizes that his wife is pregnant.

Perhaps the answer to couvade syndrome is not to be found in psychophysiology but in *parapsychophysiology.* Prenatal symptoms in men may very well be telesomatic reactions ("tele," from the word "telepathy," "somatic," of the body: ESP of the body). The telesomatic symptom is a psi-mediated physiological response. The mother's bodily symptoms may be picked up telepathically and on an unconscious level.

There is another bewildering aspect of couvade. When the father experiences prenatal nausea, for example, the mother usually does not. This is most strange. It is as if the father (telesomatically) took on his partner's symptoms—as if he were somehow able to share the burden of her pregnancy.

But how? Indeed, it is a good question.

There are several cases recorded in parapsychological literature in which the mother's own mother or someone else close to her experiences signs of pregnancy or labor. For example, one expectant mother in Minnesota went into premature labor three and one half weeks early, records Louisa Rhine, renowned parapsychologist who has collected thousands of psychic experiences. That night the expectant mother's younger brother, who lived with the woman's mother three hundred miles away, came home to find his mother pacing the floor. "Ann is having the baby," the mother said. She had been suffering with back pains.[2A]

Physical changes in expectant fathers and others close to the mother remain one of the unexplained mysteries of childbearing. To understand telesomatic and other psychic experiences during pregnancy, we must adopt a broader view of the prenatal drama. We need a model of pregnancy—however theoretical—that will help to explain this.

Pregnancy is not just a biological state of having a gestating child in the womb. It is also the condition of expectant parenthood that both mother and father share. The consciousness—or perhaps the "family unconscious"—of both parents is affected.

Perhaps pregnancy creates a *prenatal energy field* embracing mother, father, and unborn child. Perhaps as pregnancy progresses, the prenatal energy field grows to encompass everyone in the expectant mother's family and those who are directly involved in her pregnancy, including her caregiver.

Which is to suggest that the expectant mother may expand in more ways than meet the eye.

NESTING

Prenatal ESP seems to become more common as pregnancy nears its climax in labor. Triggered by causes which remain hidden to science, a change occurs toward the end of pregnancy. The mother shares a characteristic with every animal that makes a home for her young. Inspired by hormones, instinct, psi, or all three, many animal species begin nest-building shortly before delivery of the offspring. The human mother also experiences a *nesting period,* which occurs during the final weeks and days of her pregnancy.

Her inner life revolves around a new axis. Everything is the baby. Her emotions embrace the unborn child. There seems to be a growth spurt in the development of prenatal parent-infant attachment. Both parents' thoughts and plans turn to their unborn child. Will the baby be a boy or a girl? What will he look like? Whom will she resemble? How will life change when the child is born? They may worry about the baby. Increased dreams about the expected family member are common. The parents may also have a feeling of communicating with the unborn child in a language beyond words. And prenatal psi may increase as mother, father, and baby prepare for the awesome passage rite of birth.

During the nesting period the expectant mother's thoughts frequently turn to homemaking. Her preoccupation with family life may overshadow other activities. This is what one expectant mother was surprised to discover. Up until her nesting period, Karen loved her job. Then there was an about-face. "I'm beginning to lose interest in my work," she says. "I just want to get out of here and concentrate on my husband, my baby, and my home."

Jeanne, another expectant mother, felt similarly. "My career self feels under the threat of annihilation and is fighting desperately for survival."

The father too may become involved in activities centering around the pregnancy and the unborn child. Many of his actions are socially conditioned—outgrowths of the way fathers are expected to approach pregnancy in our society: taking childbirth classes, preparing for labor, shopping for the layette. Others seem to be triggered by the father's developing relationship with the baby—his own nesting period. He may begin a long-term project like building a cradle or redoing the baby's room. He may become more concerned about his partner's well-being and express his nesting urge by working longer hours and adopting a protective role toward his mate.

The parents may share nesting behavior such as choosing a name for their child and speculating about the baby's gender and personality. Coupled with increased emotional preoccupation with the unborn child, nesting activities may assist the development of prenatal attachment.

From where comes the nesting urge? Is it the result of physiological changes, including altered hormone levels? Does psi play a role? Instinctual nesting behavior may very well be a meeting ground of physiology and the paranormal. During nesting as in many other life situations, psi and physiology may interpenetrate.

Usually from one to several days before the expectant mother goes into labor, the nesting urge peaks. A nesting instinct may come as a subtle inclination tugging her to make last-minute preparations before birth, or it may sweep over her with an overwhelming urge to clean the house and prepare a place for the baby. *This instinct is one of the first signs of impending labor.*

Such *labor intuitions* are common. Either or both parents may have a sense about when labor will begin, whether it will be late or early.

One mother, Joanna, had an intuition of her labor a full six weeks before her due date. She and her husband Tom were planning a two-week vacation in Europe before the birth. Suddenly, two days before her departure, she had an overwhelming urge to cancel the flight. "I sensed the baby would be born soon and I knew I wasn't just being overcautious. My doctor told me pregnancy was progressing normally and I had a long time to go. But I knew the baby would be born any day." She canceled her flight just to be sure. Three days later, she went into premature labor.

Knowledge of labor's onset may come in the form of vague or precise impressions and dreams. Like Joanna, the mother may sense that birth is imminent, regardless of her due date.

Houston midwife Pat Jones has observed that parents often have a labor intuition without realizing it. "The mother or father may tell me when the baby will be born without thinking it through. Speaking of an upcoming family gathering, one mother said, 'Oh, the baby will be born before then.' Or the week before the mother gives birth, she will neglect to make an appointment or even cancel an appointment already scheduled."

This is just what happened toward the end of our own first pregnancy. I felt that the baby would be born the following weekend. This was peculiar, since my wife, Jan, had none of the signs of impending labor. However, at the time I was so certain of the intuition that I canceled our Monday appointment with the physician. On Saturday night, Jan's mother called and asked if the baby had arrived yet. I said, "No. Call tomorrow morning. The baby will be here then." At the time I was joking. But in fact the baby was born the next morning.

Fathers and sometimes others close to the mother often have intuitions about labor's onset. Penny, one new mother, recalls: "The morning I went into labor, my husband Charlie woke up and said he knew this was going to be the day. I had already felt some contractions but hadn't told him yet."

As with many prenatal perceptions, it is not always possible to separate the paranormal from the subliminal. Many labor intuitions probably result from subtle messages from the body. Physical changes often—but not always—occur during the days preceding labor. For first-time mothers, the baby's head drops further into the pelvis and is said to "engage" in the bony architecture. As a result of this, the mother carries her baby lower and further forward. She also experiences "lightening" (less pressure on her ribs) and decreased shortness of breath (which bothers many mothers throughout the third trimester). Whether or not she's a first-time mother, she may discharge a thick, often blood-tinged glob of mucus, the mucus plug that sealed the cervix—a sign that labor will probably begin within forty-eight hours. An increase in mild uterine contractions is another common sign. Prelabor diarrhea is yet another. The bowels empty prior to birth so that there is more room. The mother may notice a decrease in fetal activity—as if the baby were resting up for the big day. Finally, she may have a spurt of energy.

The father as well as the mother may notice these signs. He may observe a subtle change in his partner's behavior on an unconscious level. This may surface to his conscious mind or manifest during dreams in the form of a labor intuition.

But this by no means explains all labor intuitions.

Consider the example of Molly Connelly, a midwife with a very hectic daily schedule. She is a busy psychotherapist, one of the most prominent midwives in New England, the director of the New Hampshire Childbirth Education Association, coordinating the activities of childbirth educators statewide, and a popular speaker who travels through the U.S. And she is also the mother of twelve children.

One night after lecturing to a gathering of professionals in Chicago, while she was sleeping in her hotel room, Molly was suddenly awakened. She sat straight up in her bed with an overpowering feeling. The thought came to her: "Susan's having her baby!"

Susan was one of her midwifery clients in New Hampshire who would, of course, be attended by the midwife giving care in Molly's absence. However, it was still two weeks before Susan's due date.

Molly told herself that the impression was ridiculous and went back to sleep.

The following morning she called Susan to inquire about her pregnancy. But Susan was no longer pregnant. Her baby had been born in the middle of the night.

Mothers often go into labor with no premonitory signs. In addition, labor intuitions sometimes occur in persons who are miles from the expectant mother, persons who have no way of sensing the signs of imminent birth.

No way but ESP.

One is tempted to imagine that the mother's heightened intuition is somehow able to spill over and affect others.

Perhaps a tentative explanation for labor intuitions and other forms of prenatal ESP affecting persons close to the mother is to be found in the prenatal energy field. The pregnant woman elicits an almost magical response from those around her. Every eye turns to her as if she were surrounded by a vibrant, magnetic aura. Her family shows concern. Friends offer help. Even strangers seem compelled to speak with her. Everyone knows she's special. When she passes, everyday life seems to take a moment off to celebrate the magic blossoming in her womb.

Something inexplicable happens just before a mother goes into labor. A certain prebirth atmosphere foreshadows the miracle. There is a dynamic tension in the air, the center of which seems to be the soon-to-be-birthing mother's energy field. The mother's home is tinged with a vital current—an unnameable force, pulsating, brooding. The effect is like the feeling in the atmosphere just preceding a dramatic change in the weather—like the air before a storm. It affects the mother, her partner, sometimes the entire family, and sometimes the midwife or physician planning to attend the birth—whether or not they are nearby. The mother's family and friends become a little more "hyper," more excitable. Problems seem to come to a head.

Houston midwife Pat Jones has noticed this energy. She says: "I often know when the mother is getting ready to birth. I have a sense about it. I can feel the energy building, building, growing stronger and stronger." She is rarely wrong.

"Occasionally I have missed births and while driving on the freeway have known that the birth has just occurred," she says. "All of a sudden there is something different about the energy."

It may be this difference in the energy—a change in the prenatal energy field—that awakens her from a sound sleep so often. "Many times I have woken in the middle of the night just before the phone rang and knew it was about to ring with a client in labor on the other end of the line."

The dynamic prebirth atmosphere might also explain an experience of Ontario midwife Heather Keffer. She slept fitfully one night, tossing and turning, unable to get a particular client off her mind. At 7:30 A.M. the client phoned to tell her that she had been up through the night in labor.

These experiences are by no means rare. Nancy Holroyd, a registered nurse and childbirth educator practicing in Duanesburg, New York, often finds that, for no explicable reason, she will begin thinking of one of the women from her class. "All of a sudden I just can't put her out of my mind," she says. "It's like a presence I can't explain. Invariably she will find that the mother was in labor or had just given birth at the time she was thinking of her. This has occurred with ten out of the eleven parents she has taught within the last year. One of the women in her class had a November due date. However, during the first week of September while Nancy was on vacation, she began to think of the mother intensely. When she returned home, she found that the mother had gone into premature labor during her vacation.

Nancy's own pregnancy was marked by a psychic premonition. Long before she became pregnant, she had a strong feeling that she would bear a child with Down Syndrome (a genetic abnormality that results in altered physical appearance and varying degrees of mental retardation). She discussed her fear with her husband, insisting that the only way to prevent her fear from being realized was not to have any children. In spite of this she decided to become pregnant. In June 1985 her first child, Andrea, was born with chestnut-colored hair after Nancy had had a dream of a baby girl with chestnut hair. Her second child, Sheila, was born in April 1987. "This was the child I knew I was supposed to have," she recalls.

Two nights before she conceived Sheila; she dreamed that she and her husband were in a cafeteria with a small dark-haired elfinlike child with a cardiac condition. Now, at one year, Sheila is small, elfinlike. She had open heart surgery at six months of age. Her hair is dark. And she has Down Syndrome.

Today Nancy is quite in love with Sheila and is satisfied with her daughter just the way she is.

Many physicians and midwives receive distinct impressions when a client goes into labor or gives birth. Dr. Peter Hope, for example, often wakes in the middle of the night at the time a client is beginning her labor. "I have often waked, noticed the time, then later received a call from a woman whose labor began at the time I was awakened."

This may be the most common form of ESP among those caring for childbearing women. When she goes into labor, the mother may unconsciously send a telepathic message to her caregiver to be sure of receiving help.

Dr. Thurmond Knight, a physician in Randolph, Vermont, has an interesting variation of the labor intuition. He is often awakened from a sound sleep with stomach cramps when one of his clients is in labor. This *sympathetic pain* may be a *telesomatic symptom*. In the case of Dr. Knight it is a pretty neat trick since he is a man and has no uterus! Yet this has happened to him so often that now when he wakes with cramps he knows the phone call will inevitably follow.

Inexplicable though they are, telesomatic symptoms coinciding with labor's onset are not uncommon. There are several documented cases recorded in parapsychological literature of mothers experiencing labor pains at the time their daughters were giving birth. One woman in Israel gave birth to a premature baby five weeks before her expected due date. On the day she gave birth, her mother, who lived in London, experienced severe stomach pains for about three and a half hours. She had no reason to expect that her daughter would have a premature birth.[3]

Dr. Berthold Schwarz records the case of a woman in New Jersey who began bleeding when her first daugher in California went into premature labor seven weeks before her due date. Another time she began bleeding when her second daughter—with whom she had no immediate contact—went into labor. Another time she began bleeding when one of her daughters who was hundreds of miles away was hospitalized for a threatened abortion.

Louisa Rhine, who has collected thousands of cases of spontaneous ESP, reports a mother-daughter birth story with an unusual twist. The pregnant woman's mother experienced back pains at the time her daughter, living in another community, had an unexpectedly premature labor and birth. The mother had severe pain throughout the night. Yet her daughter didn't experience any pain at all during labor.[4]

Ontario midwife Heather Keffer has discovered, much to her surprise, that her menstrual periods synchronize with the onset of her clients' labors. The first time her period began at the same time a client went into labor, she thought it was a strange coincidence. However, it kept happening—including once when a client went into labor while she was in London. The connection was difficult to deny.

On one occasion a client called to tell Heather that her labor had begun after an obstetrical exam. "Oh well," said the midwife to her associate, "there goes my theory about synchrony between my period and the onset of labor." A client had gone into labor and Heather was not having a period. Or so she thought until she changed her clothes to attend the birth. After changing she smiled at her associate. "Guess what?" she said. Her period had just begun.

Oddly, Heather's clients all give birth around the same time of the month—during the days of her menstrual period.

Other midwives have similar experiences. Dawn King, a midwife in Ontario, has also noticed a close correspondence between her menstrual cycle and the onset of labor in her clients. Over fifty percent or her clients give birth during her menstrual period. On one occasion a mother went into labor at the onset of Dawn's period. Five days after her period ended, the client's neighbor, another woman for whom Dawn was providing midwifery care, began her labor. Dawn began bleeding again. "I've never had two periods in a single month at any other time," she says.

It is uncertain whether the mother regulates her time of birth to coincide with the midwife's menstrual cycle, or whether the dynamic prebirth energy that seems to stem from the expectant mother's prenatal energy field somehow triggers the menstrual period.

Many childbirth professionals have noticed a perhaps related phenomenon. Births on a given maternity unit frequently occur in clusters. Often the laboring women on a busy labor and delivery unit will all begin to progress in labor at approximately the same time or give birth at the same approximate time. It is as if individual mothers respond to an ebb and flow of psychic energy.

As with all potentially psychic experiences, some labor intuitions may be coincidences, others ESP. A physician or midwife has only so many clients expecting to give birth in any given period. It is only natural for the caregiver to think of those clients around their due date. One might even expect the caregiver to wonder if a client is in labor upon awakening, or perhaps hear the telephone ring and wonder, "Is that Mrs. Newborn in labor?"

However, this doesn't explain the precision timing of so many labor intuitions—the fact that the caregiver may flash on the client just as she is going into labor. Nor does it explain telesomatic reactions.

Psychic experiences among childbirth professionals may be the result of increased energy emanating from the mother, the result of the caregiver's own psychic sensitivity, or both. Those who are drawn to the profession are often psychically sensitive and have had psychic experiences throughout their lives, independent of their work with childbearing families. For example, the head nurse of a maternity unit in a rural hospital says: "Sometimes during a fetal activities test, even weeks before a mother's due date, I will touch her belly and get a sudden feeling that she won't be able to make it vaginally but will have to deliver by cesarean. This intuition has never failed to prove correct."

Though psychic sensitivity is by no means rare in the medical profession, there seem to be a greater number of intuitive persons in childbirth than in other areas of medicine (with the exception of psychotherapy).

Are intuitive persons unconsciously drawn to the childbearing-related professions because that is where they will be best able to use their extrasensory abilities? Many midwives do feel they are "called" to work with childbearing families. Or does the pregnant mother bring out the health professional's intuition?

In either case, those with a natural approach to childbirth and those who respect pregnancy and birth as natural processes seem to be most likely to experience intuitions about pregnancy and labor.

If the pregnant woman could be considered magical, the laboring woman should be compared to a goddess. Her prenatal energy field seems to reach the peak of its power. Many have commented on the "birth energy"—the vital, electric current that seems present when a child is born. It is as if the laboring woman were surrounded by an aura of energy whose outermost boundaries embrace the universe.

She becomes "larger than life." Participating in the miracle sometimes enables her and her mate to experience a state of mind otherwise associated with meditation or religious experience.

Though labor is undeniably painful for most mothers, it encompasses a broad spectrum of experiences from agony to ecstasy. Many mothers describe their labors as fulfilling, deeply meaningful, which no one would say of the pain of a toothache. And for many mothers and fathers, the elation that crowns birth is unforgettable, one of the very high points of their lives.

The mind often experiences a profound and dramatic change. The boundaries hemming in everyday life seem to temporarily dissolve, allowing a glimpse of a larger, richer world. The laboring mother may find herself immersed in a cosmic awareness—a feeling of being one with nature, with God, with all organic life, or with all women who have ever given birth.

Transpersonal psychologist Leni Schwartz, Ph.D., beautifully describes the mystical dimensions of childbirth in a passage of her book, *The World of the Unborn:* "We are becoming increasingly aware that childbearing can precipitate transcendant, ecstatic emotional states, similar to those caused by other intense experiences such as orgasm, or the creation of art, contact with nature, or a spiritual experience. Women experience a feeling of being one with what is taking place as in the fusion of the lover with the loved one, the mother and father with the child, the artist with the work being created. One transcends the ordinary familiar sense of self, to achieve an extraordinary understanding of being one with the cosmos. Women sense the autonomy, at the same time they experience being part of all that is, ever has been, ever will be. These experiences move beyond ordinary space and time. Ego boundaries seem to dissolve. They are states that we read about in mystical literature and are accessible to each of us. This expansion and deepening of our personal awareness is one of the unexpected and wonderful aspects of having a baby."[5]

Psychologist Abraham Maslow refers to such mind states as "peak experiences." Peak childbearing experiences seem to be more likely when the mother births naturally, in a peaceful environment, with caring attendants and persons she loves.

When she was in labor with her first child, my wife Jan's contractions swept over her, surging and ebbing like waves of a stormy sea. She bore down to give birth with a sense of vast primitive strength. She recalls the experience as one of the most ecstatic moments of her life. "I felt that I was being taken over by a power greater than myself. There was nothing I could do about it. It flowed through me like a stream rushing down a mountain. I was absorbed, totally absorbed in the power of birth, one with all existence."

Another mother describes her labor as follows: "All through labor it was like climbing a mountain—difficult but never more than I could bear. When I got to the summit, I felt like I was at the top of the world and could stoop down and lift the whole earth in my hands. Never in my life have I known such elation. When the baby came I laughed and cried at the same time."[6]

The father too may have a peak experience. Tom, a physician quoted by Leni Schwartz, recalls: "The awesome quality of the life force . . . there was so much life energy in the room . . . birth energy . . . so much beauty . . . it was powerful."

Though peak experiences do not occur at all births, they are by no means unusual. Many parents have described their birth experiences in terms of mystical ecstasy.

"Giving birth can be a deeply intimate experience for both parents," writes Dr. Schwartz. "It can be a window to intrinsic patterns of the universe, to the cycles of life and death that have existed since the first matter crossed that indefinable boundary line and took the form of living cells."[7]

It comes as no surprise that labor and birth open the door to a heightened state of consciousness. After all, giving birth is one of the most significant events in the lives of a couple—the beginning of their family. And it is more than that. It is a miracle as awesome as the creation of the earth in the very beginning. Should we not expect it to be magical?

PREGNANCY: A PSI-CONDUCIVE CONDITION

Apparently the miracle taking place within the womb somehow opens a doorway in the mind, making the mother, indeed, the father as well, privy to knowledge beyond the realm of the senses. But how? There are several reasons the expectant mother may be the ideal candidate for ESP. In fact, everything seems to orient her to psi.

A Possible Physical Basis

Her bodily changes may provide one possible explanation. A pattern of delicately interwoven processes unfolds to support the growing baby and to prepare the expectant mother for the miracle of birth.

Hormones are responsible for many of the incredible changes that take place throughout pregnancy. The activity of hormones is responsible for the first missed menstrual period that spurs the expectant mother to ask herself the big question. Within a week or so after conception, the developing placenta—at this time a tiny mass of fingerlike projections called chorionic villi—produces the hormone human chorionic gonadotropin or HCG (the basis of pregnancy tests). HCG causes the ovaries to produce elevated levels of estrogen and progesterone until the placenta later takes over the production of these hormones. Increased estrogen and progesterone suppress menstruation and insure that the uterus is a welcome home, rich in nutrients, for the tiny embryo.

Hormones also cause the cervical softening that prepares the cervix to open a gateway for the baby at birth. Hormones cause increased vaginal secretions and even change their color, odor, and taste. Hormones initiate the hyperplasia (growth) of the breast tissue in preparation for creating baby's perfectly nutritious food.

Could hormones perhaps also be responsible for the expectant mother's increased ESP? Do prenatal hormones affect whatever parts of the brain and nervous system receive and send extrasensory perceptions?

This is an intriguing question. Science has not yet come up

with an answer. Research in this area, however, would prove fascinating.

If future research does show that prenatal hormones influence the mother's psychic perceptions, another fascinating question arises. Do the hormones that help prepare the mother for parenthood also help forge the psychic bond that she has with her child?

Another mystery.

Changing hormones probably offer little in the way of explaining the expectant father's increased intuition. We do not know what, if any, hormonal changes the father experiences during the prenatal months. However, in many cases his body is certainly affected by pregnancy.

The fact that pregnancy is a *normal life crisis* may offer another clue to increased prenatal intuition.

While it may be a time of excitement and joy, pregnancy is also one of the biggest stress-inducers there is. Childbirth is a turning point, a crisis in the lives of even the most prepared expectant parents. During the prenatal months, a man and a woman confront and come to terms with the awesome fact that they will soon be crossing the one-way bridge to parenthood. Soon their roles will change irreversibly.

It is well known that ESP is more common during periods of great stress. Therefore it is reasonable to assume that the stress of pregnancy may trigger psi experiences.

But whatever role the prenatal life crisis might play in increased intuition, the psychic life of the expectant mother cannot be reduced to stress alone.

The Expectant Mother's Altered State of Consciousness

The most convincing explanation for prenatal psi is undoubtedly to be found not in the expectant mother's body but in her radically altered state of mind.

Just as dreams seem to occur more frequently when one observes them and perhaps writes them down soon after awaking, ESP experiences seem to happen more often when one turns inward. This may be one reason the pregnant woman has a greater propensity for ESP. She turns inward.

As the prenatal weeks roll on, the expectant mother develops a rich inner life. She becomes more introspective and contemplative. From the time she first learns she has conceived, she tends to become preoccupied with her pregnancy. During the early weeks she may repeatedly want to confirm the miracle. She may view her body over and over again in the mirror though the changes are still slight. Many women check their weight gain several times a week. Just to be sure.

It happens to every mother. It happens to hundreds she passes on the street. Pregnancy. An everyday occurrence. But that doesn't make it any less special when it happens to her. With all of its drawbacks (for instance, who but a philosopher would find poetry in prenatal nausea?) pregnancy is indeed a magical state of being.

From time to time the expectant mother may even feel that her body is being taken over by a force greater than herself, beyond her control. Pamela, one expectant mother, put it this way: "At times I felt I wasn't my own person any more. It was frightening."

But though the expectant mother may find pregnancy frightening now and then, at other times she may also find it ecstatic. Any time from the fourteenth to the twentieth week after her last menstrual period, she may notice a sensation deep within her that feels a little like the wings of a baby bird cupped in the palm of her hand. This, her first perception of fetal movements, is called *quickening*. A milestone in the prenatal drama, that delicate butterfly motion is a woman's secret joy. The magic of a universe is born within her womb.

Is it any wonder that she seems more attuned to what we call the paranormal? Rather we should be perplexed if she weren't.

Compared to what is happening within her body, ESP seems small stuff indeed.

And while her body nurtures within her the seed that becomes the child she will soon hold in her arms, past, present, and future merge. She dwells on her past. Frequently she thinks of her own mother, her childhood. She thinks of the present—her relationship with her partner, her already changing interests. And she thinks of the future—the baby soon to be born, the role she will soon assume. As she turns inward, she may find that she is suddenly attuned not only to her own past, present and future, but also to a realm of mind that transcends space and time.

Meanwhile, her husband may have noticed another aspect of his partner's altered state of mind that might contribute to her prenatal psi: her greater sensitivity.

In fact, there is hardly an expectant father who hasn't noticed that his partner is not quite herself. Though he may not have heard the classic request for pickles and ice cream, he has most assuredly noticed that his mate is moody. She is happy one moment and on the verge of tears the next. Her emotions may change for inexplicable reasons. She may cry over seemingly trivial details. Even the casual remark of a friend or relative may affect her deeply. As one mother put it, "Things make me cry very easily, even the most minor things—a particular phrase, an image, a thought, a tone of voice—things that don't normally make me upset."

The technical term for the expectant mother's rapid emotional swings is "emotional lability" (changeableness). Various factors may contribute to the pregnant woman's labile emotions—hormonal changes, her dramatically altered body, perhaps physical discomforts such as prenatal nausea, and the mother's preoccupation with her soon forever altered role. This greater emotional sensitivity and greater openness may contribute to extrasensory ability.

Yet another and perhaps one of the most significant causes of greater maternal intuition is to be found in the expectant mother's altered brain activity. This goes hand in hand with her altered state of consciousness. As pregnancy progresses she seems to become more oriented to her right brain hemisphere. The right hemisphere, sometimes referred to as the "*heart brain*," is associated with emotion, intuition, creative artistic endeavors, and so forth, while the left hemisphere is associated with logic, rational thinking, reasoning. As a result of her right brain orientation, the mother becomes less rational, more emotional.

Many parapsychologists have pointed out a relationship between the right hemisphere and psi. Greater right hemisphere orientation may in itself contribute to a higher propensity for extrasensory experience.

There is another virtually unexplored dimension of the expectant mother's altered state of mind. "Not only are pregnant women closer to their own unconscious processes," observes transpersonal psychologist Leni Schwartz, Ph.D., author of *The World of the Unborn*, "but they appear to be connected to the deepest levels of the collective unconscious."[8]

As a result, many expectant mothers find themselves identifying with the creative power of nature in the form of mythic images. Earth mother figures and other archetypal images symbolizing fertility and fruition may have special meaning to her.

For example, during her first pregnancy Evelyn, a mother living in central Vermont, had a mythic dream announcing her labor. "While dozing I could feel and see an Earth Mother figure hovering close to me. She looked very much like the ancient symbols—large, pendulous breasts over an enormous bulging belly ready for birth. I realized my instincts were telling me I would soon be giving birth. I accepted the Earth Mother as my new self-image." Shortly after waking from this dream, Evelyn's labor began.

Such mythic identifications in dreams or in waking life don't necessarily imply paranormality. Rather they indicate that in some part of her mind the mother (and perhaps the father) is beginning to see herself as larger than life. It is in this state of mind that psi seems to flow more freely.

Taking part in the miracle of creation seems to link the

expectant mother more closely with the creative live force in the universe. She is somehow intimately conjoined with the root of all being, the intrinsic source of life forms beyond appearances. Such partnership with the infinite may be the source of her vibrant prenatal energy field that seems to embrace all those with whom she is close. Perhaps we all have roots connecting us with all life, with all conscious beings. But the pregnant woman seems to be closer to those roots.

Meanwhile, the developing prenatal bond may cause another transformation in both parents' state of mind. Dr. Ehrenwald's cradle of ESP theory could be adapted to pregnancy. According to him, the early mother-infant relationship is the source of extrasensory perception. However, maternal-infant attachment begins during the prenatal months. Perhaps the parents experience increased ESP as a result of the developing bond with their child—or in order to better develop that bond. This may be the most important factor in explaining the parapsychology of pregnancy—and for that matter, all psychic experiences.

Whatever explanation we adopt, the innumerable cases of ESP parents report may be just the tip of the iceberg. If we look deeper we may discover that the role psi plays in pregnancy is bigger than we commonly imagine. Indeed, psi may be a silent partner to the life-creating miracle for every parent who has ever given birth.

If we permit ourselves to entertain such a notion, the implications are staggering. It could open the door to an entirely new field—the parapsychology of pregnancy. A closer look at an often ignored part of the prenatal experience—ESP—could very well revolutionize the way we look at parents and their developing child.

Needless to say, paying attention to ESP is no substitute for sound prenatal care. However, closer attention to her inner voice may help an expectant mother enjoy a healthier pregnancy. For example, she may get an impression that she should eat something missing in her diet. Some believe that the unusual food cravings felt during pregnancy are messages from the body or from the baby highlighting something needed for optimal fetal growth. Heeding such impressions may make the difference between complications and a healthy pregnancy. Of course, all intuitions should be examined in the light of common sense.

Psi may be an integral component of the love bond expectant parents form with their developing child. The growing baby within seems to take part in pregnancy's energy field. At times mother, father and baby seem to share a "family unconscious" evidenced by the seemingly "paranormal" communications that pass between parent and baby. Tuning in to the baby in utero may help the parents better prepare for parenthood. It may enhance the lifelong love bond parents and child share before the baby is born.

Many midwives and physicians have noted the remarkable intuition of the expectant mother. In her day-to-day practice, New Hampshire midwife Molly Connelly is constantly reminded of it. She has come to the conclusion that "during pregnancy the mother becomes more finely attuned to her mind and body."

Both ESP and greater receptivity to the body's subtle signals are involved in the mother's intuition, she believes. But, as she puts it, "It is always worth paying attention to maternal intuition, whatever the source, for it often reveals valuable information."

Don Creevy, M.D., of Palo Alto, California, a prominent and popular obstetrician, makes it a policy to pay attention to prenatal intuitions. In his words, "I always operate on the assumption that the pregnant woman's intuition is correct. Some may think it's a lot of bull and sometimes intuition may prove to be incorrect. But it is so often true that I find it a better policy to react as if it were valid."

Sylvia Klein Olkin recognizes that "the expectant mother is far more intuitive and clairvoyant than she is at other times of her life." She believes that this is the result of an increase in inner energy during the prenatal months. In her lectures she implores all parents and professionals to pay greater attention to prenatal intuition.

Why? Paying more attention to prenatal intuition may prove a useful diagnostic tool warning parents and caregivers of impending complications. ESP may alert the health care provider to potential problems *before* they can be detected by medical tests.

Providing a new—or perhaps age-old—diagnostic tool is just one of the benefits obstetrics can reap from paying attention to prenatal psi. Parapsychology may have much more to offer the field of obstetrics. Parapsychology might very well lend obstetrics a deeper insight into the inner life of expectant parents—a vast and incredibly rich world we haven't even begun to explore.

It could also shed light on the interconnectedness expectant parents and the caregiver share—a subtle relationship brought into relief by such phenomena as labor intuitions and telesomatic symptoms. Understanding this relationship might help both caregiver and client create optimal birth experiences for women. It could even prove to be an important factor in reversing one of the results of modern technology that hangs over every expectant parent's head like a dark cloud—the rising cesarean rate.

If nothing else, a closer look at the parapsychological dimensions of pregnancy reveals that there is more to childbearing than meets the eye. Perhaps parapsychology and obstetrics could join hands in a fruitful marriage. The two fields might very well give birth to the dawn of a new age of obstetrics: *paramidwifery*, the clinical counterpart of psychical research in childbearing. And this is only the beginning. The possibilities are endless.

4

The Secret Bond: ESP Between Parent and Unborn Child

Nothing in any of the world's mythologies is more incredible than what takes place inside the body of a pregnant woman. An awesome inner drama unfolds that one might well imagine was linked with the paranormal. A strange being implants on the wall of the uterus just seven days after sperm and egg unite in microscopic matrimony. It is not recognizable as a human being yet. No, at one point it appears more like a fish. At another, it is like a salamander, complete with tail. But it grows rapidly, undergoing millions of complex transformations. From fish to amphibian to cute baby who looks a little like Grandpa and whom Mom and Dad photograph for all their relatives and friends.

Ontogeny recapitulates phylogeny. This is probably the most philosophical three word sentence in all of scientific literature. One might imagine it to be a sentence whispered by a high priest to an initiate crossing the threshold to a bold new knowledge of his place in the universe.

But it isn't. It's an expression out of high school biology class. But what does it mean? The development of the individual being repeats the history of the development of the entire animal kingdom. Millions of years of evolutionary history are replayed on fast forward in the depths of the womb. The developing fetus relives the upward-striving drama of organic life since life began.

And some say there is a part of the human mind that is aware of it all—a sort of race memory amplified to include not only the species, *Homo sapiens*, but all forms of life—a memory linked to all creatures that ever lived, a universal consciousness of which we are all a part.

We are connected, perhaps, by a psi-ordering principle that links life with life from the time when crystal birthed cell and cell birthed "I think, therefore I am." Outrageous? Perhaps. But no more outrageous than what takes place between the thickening walls of the uterus.

Our interconnectedness with all life, our part in the universal consciousness explains, some believe, how extrasensory communication with others can be part of our own consciousness. But at what point does our own consciousness come into being? When are we first capable of communication?

The idea has intrigued the minds of philosophers for millennia. Does awareness begin when the mother first perceives her child's movements? At birth? At conception? Before?

There is mounting evidence that the newborn is fully conscious and able to perceive details at birth. Some young children can give accurate accounts of their own birth—much to their parents' surprise. Young children—particularly before the age of five—may talk about their birth memories. Many adults also have remembered their own birth, particularly in the course of psychotherapy.

Dr. Stanislav Grof found that some of his patients remembered their births when using LSD in a psychotherapeutic setting. Dr. Grof was able to verify the accuracy of some of the memories, indicating that they were not simply fantasies.

David B. Chamberlain, Ph.D., psychologist, and author of *Babies Remember Birth*, has done extensive research on the subject of consciousness at birth. Using hypnotherapy in his clinical practice, he found that birth memories kept cropping up.

This triggered his interest in what later led to extensive research on consciousness at birth and before. He found that children could correctly remember many details of their own birth, including time of day, locale, persons present, instruments used, position of delivery, behavior of nurses and doctors, even room layouts and details of their discharge from the hospital and arrival at home.

To verify the reliability of birth memories, Dr. Chamberlain hypnotized subjects in mother and child pairs and compared their separate recollections. All the children were between nine and twenty-three years old. All the mothers claimed they had never shared details of their child's birth with that child.

After her baby was brought from the nursery to her, one mother reported: "I pick her up and smell her. I smell her head. I look at her toes and say, 'Oh God! She has deformed toes!'" The mother then called the nurse, asked about the toes and was reassured that they were normal. About this event the child, also under hypnosis, recalled: "She's holding me up, looking at me. She's smelling! And she asked the nurse why my toes were so funny. The nurse said that's just the way my toes are and that they weren't deformed."[1]

It is a mystery how a newborn can remember precise or even approximate words spoken at the time of birth since the baby does not yet understand language. Yet accurate birth memories show that the meaning of sentences spoken are apparently understood at some basic level. Some of the mystery may be reduced, Dr. Chamberlain suggests, if we remember that "formal language is not communication itself but only a vehicle to facilitate it. Communication, when you get right down to it, does have mysterious dimensions! Much communication is wordless, telepathic."

Dr. Chamberlain believes that psychic communication between parents and unborn children or infants both precedes and goes beyond language. "Children," he says, "may actually be better at this psychic aspect of communication than adults because they have such a *need* to know."[2]

Dr. Chamberlain's research with the cognitive newborn comes as a shock to many. How much more of a shock it would be to discover that the *unborn* child is also conscious and able to communicate with his parents. The idea seems fantastic. Yet as Dr. Chamberlain points out: "If a newborn is really conscious of what is happening at birth, it seems unreasonable to assume that this consciousness springs to life magically and full-blown at the instant of arrival."[3]

Indeed there is evidence to suggest that the unborn is conscious weeks, perhaps months, before birth. Conscious and capable of extrasensory perception and perhaps extrasensory communication with its parents.

Psychotherapist Dr. William Emerson, the clinical director of Inner Resources, a center for psychotherapy, inner growth, and the development of human potential in Petaluma, California, believes that the unborn child is not only conscious and capable of extrasensory perception, but "able to respond the deepest values and belief systems of his parents." Dr. Emerson specializes in regression therapy and prenatal psychology. In his practice he takes clients on an inner journey and helps them relive birth and prenatal memories. In many instances, he has found striking evidence of prenatal consciousness.

Dr. Emerson and his wife, Myrtle, during their own first pregnancy, had a chorionic villi sampling test (CVS) when the fetus was eight weeks old, to rule out the possibility of genetic defects. In this test, a thin catheter is inserted through the vagina and cervix and a small amount of chorionic villi, the rapidly developing cells that form the placenta, are aspirated. The material is then analyzed in a laboratory. CVS is accompanied by an ultrasound scan to guide the insertion of the catheter into the uterus. Using high frequency sound waves, the ultrasound scan projects an outline picture of the fetus onto a video screen.

During the test, Dr. Emerson noticed an amazing phenomenon. At the beginning of the test, when his wife was first hooked up to the ultrasound, he saw the fetus on the screen moving about the uterus in a relaxed, flowing manner. But as soon as the physician and nurse came near with the catheter, the fetus became rigid. It stopped moving. When the catheter was inserted, the fetus curled up, which was to be expected since the fetus was probably responding to a change in intrauterine pressure. When the physician and nurse left the room with the sample, the fetus started moving again. And as soon as the physician and nurse returned to the room, the fetus once again stopped moving. Dr. Emerson concluded that the fetus sensed the physician's presence.

This does not necessarily imply fetal ESP. The unborn child may have been reacting to the mother's feelings at the sight of the physician, communicated to the unborn child via hormones. But it does imply an extraordinary sensitivity on the part of a fetus eight weeks old.

Barbara Findeisen, a psychotherapist in the San Francisco area, also helps clients remember their births, and sometimes prenatal experiences, in the course of therapy. While reliving his birth memories, one client felt he was a breech. He asked his mother about his birth and was assured that he had been a normal vaginal delivery. Finally, unable to shake off the idea, he asked his mother again if he had been a breech. She admitted he had been but that she hadn't wanted to tell him earlier because she had been told that breech babies often have more problems.

Another client, while regressing in memory to the prenatal stage, became suddenly frozen with terror when he thought of the fifth month of his intrauterine development. He later discovered that during that month his father had gone outside to kill some kittens. Accidentally his father shot himself. His mother rushed outside and found her husband dying. Somehow the unborn child, at five months' gestation, remembered this terror.

Some people have reported remembering attempts at abortion even during *early pregnancy*. One twenty-four-year-old woman came upon such a memory while in therapy. She recalled feeling threatened with destruction.

Findeisen has suggested that women with unwanted pregnancies attempt transuterine communication with the consciousness of their unborn child and explain their position. She reports that spontaneous miscarriage often occurs after such communication takes place. Psychotherapist Clara Riley, Ph.D., of the University of California in Irvine, also suggests that her clients who have a conflict about their pregnancy discuss the dilemma with the fetus.

Part of an extended, tearful dialogue that one woman, Sally, had with her unborn child follows: "I feel this isn't the right time for you to be there, growing . . . I couldn't give you what you want . . . You would be miserable. You should have warmth and love surrounded with happiness, and I can't give that to you. I want you to go away . . . There is no other way. I don't want to have to do what I have to do tomorrow. Please go away on your own. . . . I really am sorry."

The following day Sally miscarried.[4]

Dr. David Cheek of San Francisco has collected several mind-boggling descriptions given as though the unborn baby were *outside* the mother's body or somehow perceiving through the mother's eyes. For example, one thirteen-year-old girl recalled under hypnosis a remarkable memory of something that occurred while she was still in the womb: "Mother is sitting on a couch. She'd knitting something. Daddy comes in and is asking why she is knitting something for a girl. Mother says, 'It's a girl, I know it's a girl. It *has* to be a girl . . .'"

The hypnotized girl then described what her mother was wearing at the time. "She has on a green plaid dress. I can't see any other color. I think it is dark."

The girl's mother recalls: "I had a green and black plaid dress on, and I can remember when that was. I had just begun feeling Debbie kicking. It was in April. I gave that dress away right after my pregnancy. I would have been almost five months along. That's incredible!"[5]

It certainly is. It means the baby—at five months into the pregnancy, no less—is somehow able to see outside her mother's body and recall the memory! This indicates either an out-of-body experience or incredible clairvoyant ability. Rather astounding for a person whom many regard as not quite a person yet.

Early prenatal memories are particularly incredible. Many of the recorded memories concern events that took place *before* the brain was sufficiently developed to permit memory. How can this be? As Dr. Chamberlain puts it, "We are apparently somebody capable of communication even before we have all our equipment."

Arnold Buchheimer, Ph.D., proposes the unique theory that "memories, specifically memory storage, are part of the cellular chemistry of the body."[6] He suggests that memory storage is not isolated in the brain but rather exists throughout the body. Even if this is so, how can the unborn child perceive an event occurring outside the mother's body?

Dr. Cheek gives a tentative answer. He suggests that "the fetus in utero has highly developed clairvoyant abilities" and that "pregnant women also seem to have heightened sensitivities regarding their infants."[7] Apparently the ESP connection reaches back into the womb, when parent and child seem to share a secret bond long before the child is born.

HIDDEN COMMUNION

If you watch her unobserved, you may see the expectant mother with her hands on her belly, a contemplative look in her eyes, gently rocking her baby. You would almost expect the inseparable pair to be sharing communication beyond the senses. After all, telepathy is more common among those who are close. And who can be closer than one flesh? Mother and child are as one being occupying the same physical space. The same food nourishes both. From time to time they may even share the same thoughts.

While the unborn child develops from a pulsating point of protoplasm to the being mother will soon cuddle in her arms, he lives in his own private universe, separate, it seems, from the rest of the world. But perhaps not so separate as one might imagine.

People in many primitive societies believe that maternal impressions can mark the unborn child. Contact with certain animals is thought to cause disfigurement or birthmarks. Some people believe that if the mother eats porcupine during pregnancy it can cause a humped back in the child[8] or if she sees a hare, a harelipped child will be born. With the development of medical science we have cast this sort of belief away. If asked, most obstetricians would assure their clients that the mother's feelings and experiences do not and indeed cannot affect the unborn child. But there is every evidence that they may be wrong. Though accidentally encountering a hare during pregnancy may not cause a harelip, the mother's impressions may indeed affect her unborn child.

To study the fascinating world of the unborn child, pioneer psychiatrist Dr. Thomas Verny of Toronto founded the Pre- and Perinatal Psychology Association of North America (PPPANA), an organization consisting of individuals from diverse backgrounds. One of the aims of PPPANA is to learn about the effects of the pregnant mother's behavior, thoughts, and feelings on the physical and psychological development of the unborn and newborn child.

Dr. Verny believes that the mother's thoughts and feelings reach the baby in utero and even influence prenatal development. Theoretically it may even be possible for a child to be marked by his mother's having sighted a particular animal—*if* the mother believes strongly enough in this superstition to cause prolonged stress.

Strong emotions alter the mother's blood chemistry and, by way of the placenta, the baby's as well. Stress is the prime example. Though brief, short-lived maternal stress probably has no long-term effect on the baby, prolonged stress certainly does.

Dr. Lester Sontag of the Fels Research Institute in Yellow Springs, Ohio, has done landmark research on maternal anxiety and its effects on the unborn baby. He has discovered that distress in the mother produces a marked increase in fetal activity. Severe maternal fatigue produces the same effect. Violent emotional upsets increase fetal activity up to tenfold. When the mother is stressed, a class of biochemicals called catecholamines, which include epinephrine and norepinephrine, is released. These hormones act as transmitters, causing the unborn child to sense the mother's anxiety.

A Scottish study revealed an unexpected correspondence between maternal stress during pregnancy and later problems in children. Dr. D. H. Stott explored the relationship of a wide range of possibly noxious factors in pregnancy to later ill health of the child. One hundred fifty-three mothers in the Glasgow area were randomly selected. Information was obtained about their pregnancies. A nurse visited the home of the mothers periodically until the child's fourth birthday and obtained information about the child's health, development, and behavior. Physical stress, including accidents involving injury, heavy and tiring work, and dental operations during pregnancy, had no effect on the child's health.

However, a striking relationship appeared between psychological stress and illness in children. Stress involving continued personal tension—particularly marital discord—was associated with ill health, neurological dysfunction, developmental lag, and behavioral disturbances in the offspring. According to Dr. Stott, there was "virtually a one-to-one relationship in those cases where interpersonal tensions were reported."[9] Studies with rats and mice have shown a similar relationship between prenatal stress and later illness in the offspring.[10]

Two Finnish psychiatrists, Matti Huttunen and Pecka Niskanen, showed that the father's death during pregnancy had a terrible effect on the child, as might well be imagined! The psychiatrists researched official records and gathered the names of 167 children whose fathers had died before they were born and of 168 children whose fathers had died during their first year. They then examined the children's medical records for a thirty-five-year period. All of the children grew up without their biological fathers. Yet the number of children with behavior disorders and psychiatric problems (including schizophrenia) was more than twice as high among the group whose fathers died while they were still unborn.[11]

Maternal stress hormones may have been communicated to the baby via the placenta. Or perhaps the baby has a direct memory of the event. Violent upheavals in the mother's emotional life may affect the baby just as surely as exposure to cigarette smoke.

It is well known that the unborn child reacts to cigarette smoking. The mother's smoking endangers its health. If the mother smokes heavily, the baby may be born underweight and be susceptible to a number of complications. Innumerable studies have proven this. But Michael Lieberman has gone one step further. In a medical study he showed that the baby is affected when the mother even *thinks* of smoking. The fetal heartbeat increased when the mother was shown a cigarette.[12] However, it is difficult to say whether this is the effect of psi or of maternal hormones released at the thought of smoking.

The role of stress hormones by no means rules out a parapsychological connection between mother and unborn child. Hormones in no way explain the clairvoyant experiences of babies in utero. Apparently the mysteries parent and child share cannot be reduced to biochemical terms alone any more than can love. According to Gerhard Rottmann in Germany, telepathy may be one of the ways the mother's feelings affect the baby's development in utero.[13] In fact, the parent-child ESP connection is probably an integral part of the lifelong love bond that begins to develop while the baby is still in the womb.

The expectant mother cannot control all the stress factors in her environment—the death of a close friend or relative, for instance. But positive feelings about the baby may somehow offset the stress. In his book *The Secret Life of the Unborn Child*, Dr. Verny states: "While the external stress a woman faces matters, what matters most is the way she feels about her unborn child. Her thoughts and feelings are the material out of which the unborn child fashions himself. When they are positive and nurturing the child can . . . withstand shocks from almost any quarter.[14] . . . Her thoughts, her love or rejection or ambivalence, begin defining and shaping his emotional life."[15]

But how does this happen? As Dr. Verny points out: "Nothing we know about the human body can explain how these feelings affect the unborn child."[16] Do the mother's and father's feelings become part of the "family unconscious" and therefore part of the baby's experience as well? Perhaps this is just another way parents and their unborn children share a hidden communication that no words can adequately describe.

Katy, an expectant mother in Cleveland, Ohio, says: "Throughout pregnancy my husband John and I have felt we were communicating with the baby. We sometimes carry on a dialogue with her. I believe that in her own way she understands us and responds with little kicks. When John calls me from work, the baby often kicks excitedly as if she too can hear his voice and recognize that it is Daddy." Katy's experience is typical of many parents who feel they communicate with their unborn child in a language beyond words.

For most parents the ESP connection remains unconscious. Occasionally, however, extrasensory communication springs unannounced into the everyday waking mind. Through dreams, reflections, and sudden psychic flashes, parents sometimes glimpse the baby's gender or aspects of the baby's personality.

An expectant father in Pennsylvania had a most unusual reaction when his wife announced her first pregnancy. For several hours he said nothing. Then he accurately described the baby as a girl with red hair and blue eyes (neither he nor his wife has red hair). While expecting his second child the same father had a dream accurately describing the child. Three days before the second child's birth he told his wife, "I really wish this was going to be another girl, but it will be a boy with brown hair and brown eyes." It was.

His wife too had a psychic flash about her unborn child. "I felt something was not quite right," she says, recalling her second pregnancy. "I wish I could explain it more but I can't. I just knew something was not right about the baby." Her son was born with a cleft lip and cleft palate, which were later corrected via surgery.

Cybele, a mother who lives in Orange County, California, had the distinct impression that her baby was a breech throughout her entire first pregnancy. "Several midwives assured me the head was down," she recalls. "But I still felt the baby was breech, though I can't explain why." Her child was born in the breech position.

Early in her fourth pregnancy Cybele sensed she was having twins. She consulted several different midwives who all assured her that there was no evidence of twins. "I'm not going crazy!" she insisted. "I know there are two!" She did in fact give birth to twins.

Robbie E. Davis-Floyd, Ph.D., of the department of sociology/anthropology at Trinity University in San Antonio, Texas, reports: "In 1979 when I was pregnant with my first child, I *knew* the baby would be a girl. I *knew* that, without a flicker of doubt. I bought only little girl clothes and furnishings at the baby store and I planned to name her Peyton Elizabeth—my mother's maiden name plus my middle name. People laughed at me when I told them, no, I had not had an amniocentesis, I just knew that she was a girl.

"When I became pregnant again four years later, I *knew* the baby was a boy. I bought only little boy clothes. There were other things I *knew* this second time—that the baby boy would weight exactly 10 pounds (he did) and that my labor would be three days long (it was)."

As she puts it, "There is an inner knowing in all of us. It's here and all we have to do is be silent and listen."

It is difficult to say how often an intuition stems from true communication with the baby, from the mother's own unconscious and perhaps extrasensory abilities, or simply from the mother's fantasy. Even distinct impressions about the baby are difficult to verify. For example, sometimes the mother senses her child is a girl and this turns out to be correct. However, she did have a fifty percent chance of being right.

However, psi impressions involving the unborn are often accompanied by a certain feeling of connectedness, an inner sense of validity. Though research in the area is difficult, to the parents it makes little difference whether or not their impressions can be demonstrated as valid in a laboratory.

For many expectant mothers, guided imagery can provide a powerful means of enhancing psychic communication. Dr. Davis-Floyd used guided imagery during her second pregnancy to take an inner journey to greet her unborn child and solve a potential complication. The results of the imagery were striking. At the time Dr. Davis-Floyd was living in Austin, Texas. Her friend Rima Star, a therapist, served as her guide through the imagery.

"For the last few weeks the baby had been posterior," Dr. Davis-Floyd recalls, "that is, with the back of his head toward my back instead of toward my front. I knew that he would have to turn soon if he was going to, and I wanted to encourage his turning because the posterior position often makes for a more difficult labor. As soon as I felt I had contact with the baby, I received a clear sense of distress involving the umbilical cord. I got worried because I couldn't seem to visualize him clearly enough to find out what the problem was. I felt stuck, but Rima encouraged me to breathe more deeply and smoothly.

"After several minutes I could see the baby clearly. It was as if my consciousness was in the womb with him. I felt some fear from him, and I saw that his head was deeply engaged in my pelvis. The cord went from the placenta across the back of his neck and over his left shoulder down to his naval. He was afraid that if he turned anterior, the cord would cut across his throat and choke him, since he could no longer slip it over his head.

"Rima had the idea that he could take hold of the cord and just slip it down off his left shoulder after he turned. I made this suggestion to him, and received an immediate sense of acceptance and relief. Soon after that he did turn, and was born one week later *tightly holding the cord, with both hands, just below his left shoulder.*"

Possible extrasensory communication with the unborn is not limited to parents. The *prenatal energy field*, which includes the mother and baby at its hub, seems sometimes to encompass also the midwife or physician like some sort of ever-widening psychic umbrella.

A few childbirth professionals occasionally feel a psychic connection with the unborn child of a client. "It is a feeling I can't explain," says Pat Jones, prominent midwife in Houston, Texas. "Yet I can sometimes tell when there is a problem with the baby before medical tests have picked the problem up, and I often know whether the child is a boy or a girl."

Ontario midwife Dawn King sometimes feels that she and the unborn baby of a client are attuned and that she can perceive the baby's emotions. "My connection with the baby is strongest when my hand is on the mother's abdomen."

On one occasion she helped an expectant mother through a guided visualization to help her explore emotions associated with a past cesarean section. Guiding the mother step by step, she helped her relive the birth process in her imagination. When the mother remembered the operation, the baby became extremely agitated. In order to reassure the child, Dawn put her hand on the mother's abdomen. The baby immediately stopped kicking.

Through the remainder of the visualization, which lasted close to two hours, the baby was quiet, until Dawn guided the mother through a visualization of the child's birth with positive suggestions. As she began to describe the beautiful journey the baby would make down the birth canal, the baby began moving in the uterus. This time, says Dawn, "he was like a cat purring."

It appears that the baby is anything but a silent passenger during the life-creating months. The unborn child has far more input into the prenatal drama than science has until recently supposed. The baby chooses the position in which it will lie in the womb—often the same rather awkward-looking position the child assumes just before falling asleep after birth.

The baby may actually begin learning in utero. Infant behavior patterns, particularly speech, may begin before birth. Dr. Henry Truby of the University of Miami, Florida, says that infants can overhear the mother's conversations during the latter half of pregnancy and may begin to develop speech patterns as a result.[17]

New Zealand physician Albert Liley, researcher in the sensory functioning of the unborn child, says the unborn baby establishes the endocrine balance during pregnancy and causes all manner of changes in maternal physiology so that the uterus is a suitable environment. "It is the fetus who determines the duration of pregnancy," he says.[18] But what causes the onset of labor? No one knows.

Many believe that the baby "decides" when he or she will be born. At the optimal time the fetus increases secretion of certain pituitary and adrenocortical hormones, which trigger an incredibly complex process involving the mother's uterus, cervix, pituitary gland, placenta, and the baby's hypothalamus, pituitary gland, and adrenal cortex. All this happens to open the door so the baby can leave the uterine environment and join its parents.

The mother may influence her labor either unconsciously or consciously. European psychiatrist W. Ernest Freud suggests that negative feelings may affect the baby's part in the hormonal reactions that initiate labor. "Would the fetus, after being exposed to certain amounts of a mother's ambivalent [feelings]," he speculates, "become entrapped between contradictory messages, so that eventually his cooperation at the time of labor and birth is impaired?"

In some cases the mother or baby or both may even unconsciously choose the time of birth. In 1962, 601,222 normal labors were analyzed to determine the peak incidence of birth. The highest frequency of births occurred between 3 and 4 A.M., when the mothers were most likely to be in a peaceful emotional state.

Women often delay labor until the midwife or physician is available. Donald Creevy, M.D., a prominent west coast obstetrician, has seen examples of this over and over again. "I remember once coming back from vacation and having one of my patients smile at me and say, 'I waited to go into labor until you were here.'" Dr. Creevy has had a number of similar experiences. Mothers often immediately go into labor when he returns home from vacation.

Sloane Crawford, certified nurse-midwife in Brookline, Massachusetts, often tells her clients when she is planning to be away for a weekend and laughingly requests that they do not go into labor during this time. The odd thing about this is that it works! "I don't know how," says Sloane, "but women somehow program themselves to avoid labor when I am away."

Some midwives believe that suggestion can influence the time of labor's onset, perhaps via psychic communication with the unborn child. Midwives Heather Keffer and her associate Michele Kryzanauskas of Ontario, Canada, often attend home births that require driving one to two hours over rural roads. To avoid driving during stormy weather and risk missing the birth, they advise clients to ask the baby not to be born if the weather report predicts a storm, if one of the midwives' children is sick, if one of them has a cold, and so forth. "We say it in a joking manner," says Heather. "Please tell your baby not to choose this date to be born. Then we explain why. However, though we may give this information jokingly, we do have a serious intention. By letting the baby know her wishes and expectations, the mother may be able to influence the time of birth."

This does not necessarily imply psi, though it may. The mind influences labor on a psychophysical level. Animals as well as humans can hold back their labors until they feel it is safe to give birth. However, it is difficult to explain how a mother can influence labor's onset a week or more in advance.

The psychic connection between parent and unborn child and sometimes between childbirth professional and unborn child is an aspect of the parapsychology of pregnancy that deserves more research. In addition, paying greater attention to nonphysical communication with the unborn could perhaps find a place in *paramidwifery*, the field that could be born if obstetrics and parapsychology joined hands.

ESP may provide valuable clues in diagnosing potential problems and perhaps in emotionally supporting the baby through times of great stress. Some suggest that the psychic communication with the unborn may also have a practical role in contributing to a safe, peaceful birth.

For example, Igor Tjarkovsky in the Soviet Union specializes in water birth with a paranormal twist. The mother labors and gives birth in a tank of water. For many patients and babies, the primal experience of birth is enhanced when it takes place underwater. This relaxing and soothing childbirth method is now gaining popularity.

In Dr. Tjarkovsky's unique version of water birth, in addition to a physician and nurse assisting during labor, there is a "sensitive"—a person with parapsychological abilities—to report possible impending danger. The role of the sensitive is to perceive the bioenergy, sometimes called biofield or "aura," surrounding the human body. It is, perhaps, this energy that is affected by Chinese acupuncture. According to Dr. Tjarkovsky, even if sensitives weren't physically present during the actual delivery, "they were able through use of their bioenergy, to keep the situation under control. Because they can perceive people's biofields, they were able to see or sense whether certain factors were unfavorable and advise me against continuing the delivery underwater."[19]

Dr. Tjarkovsky is well aware that a telepathic connection is most strong between mother and child. The unborn child is affected by what the mother thinks, feels, and experiences. Tension in the delivery room can contribute to problems just as much, if not more so, than bacteria. On the other hand, positive thoughts directed to mother and baby may contribute to a more rewarding experience for both.

Even a casual glimpse of the varieties of apparent paranormal experiences with unborn babies is eye-opening indeed. It is enough to convince us that the inner tapestry parents and unborn children share is a rich world of extrasensory experiences that to all outward appearances seems incredible.

CLAIRVOYANT DREAMS

Incredible as they are, the psychic experiences that occur during waking life may be a mere fraction of those that parents and unborn children share. The most fascinating may take place during sleep.

A vast inner landscape unfolds in expectant parents' dreams. The dream world of pregnancy is rich with symbols and vivid scenes: images of fertility, growth, and birth. But pregnancy dreams may prove to be more than a mine of psychological insights. They may also open the door to the uncharted world of extrasensory perception.

That's the view of Patricia Maybruck, Ph.D., a clinical psychologist in San Francisco. In a fascinating study of prenatal dreams, she collected 1,048 dreams from 67 mothers and examined them in detail. She made the extraordinary discovery that six percent of these dreams may have been genuine psychic dreams—a high percentage when one considers that it means six out of one hundred prenatal dreams may be paranormal! If this is so, *clairvoyant dreams*, which some believe are communications from the unborn, are probably the most common form of psychic experience in pregnancy.

By the time she finished her fascinating study, Dr. Maybruck had a "definite sense that many dreams were reflections of unmeasurable qualities, including communications with the unborn, images of both *past and future* times in the dreamers' lives and possibly echoes of their 'past lives.'" Such dreams are particularly common during the third trimester.

It has already been suggested that parent-child bonding, before and after the baby is born, may take place during REM sleep, (rapid eye movement, the sleep state associated with dreaming) which is a psi-conducive condition. After birth the baby remains in REM sleep much of the time while the mother is active. Before birth, the baby is often active while the mother is in REM sleep. During both these periods, the ESP connection may be a wide-open channel for hidden communion between the two.

ESP dreams during which the mother glimpses the baby's gender, physical traits, and personality characteristics are perhaps the most common. A vivid dream showed Katy, a first-time mother in Cleveland, that her unborn baby was a girl. "In one of the dreams the baby told me her name was 'Molly,'" recalls Katy. Weeks after this dream Katy had an amniocentesis performed to rule out a possible complication. In this test a needle is passed through the abdomen into the uterus, where a small quantity of amniotic fluid is drawn off to be analyzed for abnormalities. The amniocentesis revealed that the baby was healthy and, in fact, a girl. Katy and her husband John decided to keep the name "Molly."

A vivid dream showed Meg Grindrod, a midwife in Rochester, New York, that her own child in utero was a boy. She had been hoping and planning for a girl and this dream helped her make the emotional adjustment to a male child. "My belly became as clear as glass," she recalls. "I could see through it and there was the baby, rear end up and clearly a boy. I started crying and crying. When I woke up I felt purged of the disappointment and accepted that my baby was a boy."

Other expectant mothers have reported similar dreams. During such a dream, the mother is able to see through her belly and see the child's gender and sometimes physical appearance. One mother dreamed she was having an ultrasound that gave her a vivid picture of the baby's gender, eye color, hair color, and facial features, including a downward curve to her lips, all of which later proved to be astoundingly accurate.

One must, of course, be cautious about attributing psychic significance to all dreams revealing the baby's gender or other characteristics. Some may reflect genuine ESP. Others are "just dreams" and may "predict" the wrong information.

During her pregnancy, Meg Grindrod had a precognitive dream about a friend's birth, though at the time of the dream she thought she was dreaming of her own.

"I dreamed that I was lying down flat on my back, which I've never done during labor, and somebody delivered my baby and lifted it up over my belly toward me. I saw that it was a girl. I thought it was myself giving birth, because when I am assisting at other births, I see the baby born from a different perspective—from the view of the mother's birth outlet, not her head. Later, however, I was at the birth of a friend, just keeping her company. I was lying beside her on the bed with my head on her pillow when the obstetrician delivered the baby. When the doctor lifted the baby girl up, I had a strong sense of déjà vu. I was witnessing the same scene I had seen in my dream!"

Déjà vu (from the French meaning "already seen") refers to the peculiar sense of having been in a particular place before or having lived through a scene when in fact one has not. Some parapsychologists believe that many déjà vu experiences can be explained in terms of precognitive dreams. The dreamer has actually glimpsed the future scene during sleep.

Dreams sometimes predict pregnancy's outcome. The parents may precognitively glimpse aspects of the birth and the period after birth. Dr. Thomas Verny records the following incident in *The Secret Life of the Unborn Child*: "The night before one of my patients had a spontaneous abortion, she shouted herself awake several times, yelling, 'I want out, let me out!' She is convinced that was her child speaking through her."[20]

This dream may have been an example of ESP or it may have resulted from the mother having noticed subtle changes in her body—mild uterine cramping, perhaps. Perceptible physiological changes almost always precede a miscarriage.

Expectant mothers usually have a heightened receptivity about their physical changes. This results partly from increased attention to the body and partly from the pregnant woman's propensity to turn inward. The mother's dreams frequently pick up subtle impressions she may not have noticed in her waking life.

Dr. Robert Van de Castle, director of the Nocturnal Cognition Laboratory and professor of behavioral medicine and psychiatry at the University of Virginia Medical School, calls dreams that result from subliminal impressions *prodromal dreams*. Such dreams often reveal information about a physical condition before it can be detected via other means.

True *precognitive* or *clairvoyant* dreams, he points out, cannot be explained in terms of subliminal impressions. Often precognitive dreams are particularly intense and vivid. For some they are quite unlike other dreams and are etched clearly in the mind. They may also have a lingering quality.

Even so, it is often difficult to tell the precognitive from the prodromal dream. For example, one mother dreamed her baby would be stillborn. This later proved to be true. In this case, the mother may have unconsciously noticed less fetal activity preceding the intrauterine death.

However, it is hard to imagine how subliminal impressions could have accounted for the following bizarre dream from Dr. Van de Castle's extensive collection of pregnancy dreams: The mother dreamed that her child would be born with six fingers on both hands. The child was actually born with six fingers on one hand.

In another striking dream in Dr. Van de Castle's collection, the mother dreamed that her child was encircled by a snake. It turned out that the umbilical cord was wrapped around the baby's neck.

One mother had a dramatic clairvoyant dream just prior to the grim outcome of her pregnancy. She dreamed that the baby told her: "I must be born now! I must be born now!" The mother had no doubt in her mind that this was a true psychic message and not simply a nightmare. She insisted that her doctor give her an ultrasound to determine the status of the baby. However, the physician refused. He told her that the baby was fine and there was no reason for ultrasound. Shortly afterwards the baby died in utero. The cause of death was asphyxiation resulting from a knot in the umbilical cord.

There is yet another form of ESP dream in pregnancy. Those who believe in reincarnation feel that clairvoyant dreams can reveal information about the baby's "previous lifetime." This type of dream is called an *announcing dream* because it presumably announced the arrival of the incoming personality.

Ian Stevenson, Ph.D., of the University of Virginia School of Medicine, who has studied reincarnation cases among the people of many countries, says that announcing dreams are a common feature of reincarnation cases.[21]

Announcing dreams may reveal elements of the baby's personality and physical characteristics such as birthmarks or deformities corresponding to wounds presumably received in a previous lifetime.

The baby most typically announces his arrival toward the end of pregnancy and often just before birth. At this time expectant mothers and sometimes the fathers, relatives, or close friends of the family may have a clairvoyant dream. "Occasionally also two or more members of the family will have such a dream," says Dr. Stevenson.[22]

Among the Tlingit Indians announcing dreams are quite common. The typical Tlingit dream, Dr. Stevenson says, includes details of arrival scenes. The mother may dream of the incoming personality coming to her house with a suitcase, getting off a ship, and so forth. In the Turkish variety of announcing dream, the personality often simply reveals himself, sometimes with wounds acquired in a previous life that correspond to a birthmark in the baby, and communicates his desire to be reborn in the family of the dreamer.

Ordinary dreams include *day residue*, that is, impressions of the previous day woven into the dream in a distorted manner. Uncanny as it seems, prenatal dreams seem sometimes to include *future day residue*, impressions of events that have not yet occurred, which appear subject to the same dream mechanisms of distortion.

Beverly, one expectant mother in Dr. Maybruck's study, dreamed that her physician put her in the hospital on a program in which women nearing their due date were all placed together in a large room full of beds and women. The doctor was going to try to induce labor with something that was going to cause vomiting. During the dream the mother kept saying to herself: "It's the second, the second! I'm not even due until the fifteenth!"

It turned out that Beverly's daughter was born two weeks before her due date. At the time the hospital was being remodeled. Consequently Beverly was taken to a combination labor/recovery room with a group of women almost all of whom were being induced as in her dream. Many were nauseous from drugs.

Did Beverly's dream pick up details from a future day and weave them into a dream image, as dreams recall incidents from the past? Was it a genuine precognitive dream or merely a coincidence? It is impossible to say. However, the sheer volume of dreams that seem to include details from future events suggest that many are precognitive.

Another possible precognitive dream that Dr. Maybruck recorded may have picked up future day residue. Norma dreamed that while she was fishing with her husband and some friends, a tidal wave rose and knocked her unconscious. When she regained consciousness, she was in labor and in pain. Her mother told her the baby was too big and couldn't come out. The mother said she was going to cut Norma with Norma's husband's fishing knife but that it wouldn't hurt. The baby was born with no vernix, the cheesy, white emollient cream-like substance that protects the baby's skin in utero.

Actually, as a result of toxemia symptoms (a pregnancy disease characterized by swelling, high blood pressure, and protein in the urine), Norma's labor was induced the day after she had this dream. She did have a cesarean and her baby was born with almost no vernix on the skin.

If Norma's dream was precognitive at all, which is by no means certain, it was a highly distorted version of what actually occurred.

It is important to realize that nightmares about stillborns and deformed babies are common. No mother should become upset and take her nightmares too seriously. Almost all mothers have nightmares about their babies. These reflect universal concerns and fears during pregnancy. *In the overwhelming majority of cases such dreams do not foreshadow actual events.*

On the other hand, prenatal dreams should not simply be shrugged off as having no importance. Dr. Maybruck suggests that obstetricians pay attention to expectant mothers' dreams and give them nonjudgmental attention. The pregnant woman's occasional psychic dreams may serve as useful warnings indicating undetected complications. Therefore they may have significant value as diagnostic tools.

More research and greater attention to precognitive dreams is yet another example of how the parapsychology of everyday life could affect obstetrics, and by so doing, affect parenting.

5

The Root of All Psi: The Psychic World of Babies

The womb may provide our first encounter with psychic phenomena. There, in the depths of the primordial universe from which we all sprang, the parent-offspring ESP connection is forged. Or so it seems. Mother and child communicate in the most intimate of all ways. They are as one flesh.

Then, at pregnancy's climax, the miracle occurs that never ceases to evoke awe. A child is born. And a family too is born. A woman and a man cross the one-way bridge to become mother and father. Their lives are forever altered.

Birth is the greatest of all passage rites. The one becomes two. The baby becomes a separate being, no longer one flesh with the mother. When the baby leaves the womb for mother and father's waiting arms, a series of life-altering transformations takes place with almost lightning rapidity. The newborn takes its first breath. Its circulatory system is rerouted. It is no longer conjoined to that of mother. The baby no longer depends on the umbilical cord and placenta for oxygen and food. It is now able to take food from mother's breast.

The umbilical cord is cut. But the ESP connection that mother and father share with the child is not severed, perhaps cannot be severed. The experience of innumerable families suggests that parent and infant remain linked as if by a psychic umbilical cord that knows no barriers.

Many have commented on the high-energy atmosphere that seems present at birth. The prenatal energy field (discussed in chapter 3) seems to reach its peak during and immediately following birth. The elation that so often crowns the birthing drama is an all but palpable psychic current. Mother, father, and baby seem to be surrounded by a vibrant aura.

An amazing process takes place when parent and child meet face to face for the first time. Recent research has shown that most new mothers behave in a similar way with their infants provided that birth is natural and the mother unmedicated. Dr. Marshall Klaus and Dr. John Kennel found that the way the mother touches her newborn follows a pattern: First the mother explores the baby's head and extremities with her fingertips; then she caresses the trunk with an open palm; and finally she enfolds the baby in her arms.

Of course, every new mother reacts to her baby somewhat differently. However, the behavior of most mothers upon first greeting the baby is so similar that it is said to be "species specific"—members of the same species behave fairly similarly under similar conditions.

This behavior is believed to be an integral part of *bonding*, that is, the initial stage of parent-infant attachment. Bonding begins during the prenatal period while the baby is in the womb and continues after birth. In humans, the first hour or so following birth is a peak period in the bonding process. The energy field that seems to be such a living presence at birth may be part of this dramatic mother-baby interchange.

Fathers, too, experience a bonding process with their infants. Dr. Martin Greenberg, author of *The Birth of a Father*, refers to this as *engrossment*—"absorption, preoccupation, and interest in the baby." The new father touches and holds his baby. He focuses his attention on his child and often feels exhilarated.

What causes parents to interact with their babies in a similar way? Is bonding behavior encoded in the parents' psyche as the urge to migrate seems to be encoded in the brains of birds? Is it part of the parent-child ESP connection? Perhaps bonding behavior is an outward manifestation of the psychic relationship parents and child begin to share while the baby is still in the womb.

For reasons no one fully understands, prolonged contact between parent and child during the immediate postnatal period has a dramatic effect on the human psyche. Mothers who have spent the first hour with their infant often report feeling more confident about child care later.

On the other hand, interruptions to the "bonding period" may have long-term negative effects. For example, according to Helen Varney, associate professor and chairperson of the Maternal-Newborn Program at Yale University School of Nursing in New Haven, Connecticut, and author of the widely used text *Nurse-Midwifery*, maternal-infant separation during the initial postbirth hours is the major cause of "baby blues"—a combination of negative emotions, depression, tears, and irritability during the early postpartum period. Until recently, maternal-infant separation was routine in most American hospitals and is still a common practice in many. This may be the reason that an estimated 80 percent of American mothers suffer from baby blues.

It is of significant interest that baby blues are rare following home births. Is this because at home maternal-infant bonding is not interrupted by customs such as whisking the baby away for tests and observations?

Fortunately, human beings are flexible. The parent-infant bonding process is not a once and forever epoxy-glue phenomenon. It is an ongoing process. Those who are unable to remain with their infants during the immediate postnatal period still develop parent-infant attachment. Parents who adopt a child still bond with that child.

Yet there is no question that "bonding time" after birth does help parents adjust. But how can what occurs during the first postnatal hour affect what the parents feel days, perhaps months, afterward? How can this initial hour affect the mother's confidence or whether she feels depressed days or weeks later? The answers to these questions remain a mystery.

But the implication is that there is more to bonding than meets the eye. The parents' observable behavior appears to be a physical expression of the love between parent and child, and a "bonding period" may be necessary to help mother and father act out what is already occurring on an unconscious level. Bonding behavior may be rooted in a relationship beyond the senses. And it may be the first paranormal experience in the psychic world of babies.

Dr. David Chamberlain's research on birth memories and the cognitive abilities of the newborn, discussed in chapter 4, indicates that the psychic world of babies is far richer than was previously thought. He has shown that babies are not only conscious of birth but capable of remembering even the smallest details of their birth experience. Under hypnosis, many mothers and children whom Dr. Chamberlain studied agreed on a wide variety of details and rarely disagreed on a major point.

Psychic research is not Dr. Chamberlain's field. However, during the course of his research with infants, he repeatedly came across an odd fact. A striking recurrent theme appears in several birth and infancy memories that he and other researchers have recorded. Many people accurately remember important conversations that took place during the earliest moments of extrauterine life.

For example, in 1975 obstetrician David Cheek published an account of an extraordinary birth memory in the *American Journal of Clinical Hypnosis.* A man who was born prematurely was haunted by the memory of a conversation that took place during the crisis of a difficult birth. The doctor told the nurse: "Don't waste too much time; I don't think he's worth saving."[1]

To verify the accuracy of such memories, Dr. Chamberlain compared the separate recollections of mothers and children who claimed they had never discussed the details of the child's birth. One mother relates that she had repeated the child's full name and explained to him just why she had chosen it. The child recalls: "My name was repeated several times, proudly."[2]

Since infants obviously don't understand language, how do they understand the meaning of what was spoken? Dr. Chamberlain has come to the conclusion that babies have "an intuitive basis for communication apart from language, a knowing deeper than words."[3]

Another recurrent theme in Dr. Chamberlain's research casts more light on the psychic world of babies. He kept coming across memories of babies being inside the womb and accurately describing what their mothers were seeing outside the womb. It was as if the baby were either seeing through the mother's eyes or having an out-of-body experience. He couldn't avoid the conclusion that psychic phenomena were occurring in the parent-child relationship. As he puts it: "It seems that when you get close to newborns, you can't avoid confronting psi."

Apparent out-of-body experiences are fairly frequent in infancy memories. Says Dr. Chamberlain, "Often in birth reports people say they are perceiving themselves and events from a distance, viewing from a perspective above or to the side of their physical location."[4] This is understandably puzzling to the person having the memory, who can't understand why the perspective should be that of an outside observer.

One man recalls the period shortly following his birth: "At times I feel like I'm somewhere in the room witnessing what is going on, and at other times I am the child and seeing it from that point of view . . . I wonder how come I can see around behind him?"[5] Having such a memory is a good reason to feel puzzled, unless one is familiar with out-of-body experiences (OBEs).

One woman's very early infancy memory sounds like a classic description of an OBE: "I feel weightless, floating. Nobody knows I'm there; they can't even see me. I keep looking through the nursery window. It's weird. I can't be on both sides of the window!"[6]

We run into a similar phenomenon in prenatal memories. Some people recall an event from the viewpoint of being outside the body and outside the womb. One of Dr. Chamberlain's patients, Loretta, remembers in uncanny detail an event that occurred before she was born. The account is published in the book *Babies Remember Birth*:

"I can hear the water. I'm moving back and forth.

"My mother is standing on the deck of a boat. She doesn't like the boat; she's holding on tight and she's tense.

"My mother is standing on the deck, grabbing the side rail to hold on, leaning up against the railing to hold herself steady. She's looking at an island.

"There are other people looking over the water listening to someone tell them where they are going, explaining to them about the island.

"My father is standing by my mother . . . He's worried about my mother; he wants to know if she's all right. Her stomach is upset. The rocking of the boat is making her sick.

"She sat down and is rubbing my stomach. I feel the motion on the stomach, the rubbing. My mother was rubbing me and she was worried if I was all right."[7]

It is impossible to account for people's prebirth memories of their mothers' actions without recourse to either of two parapsychological explanations: either an amazing degree of parent-child telepathy exists in which children pick up their mothers' memories, or out-of-body experiences.

Vital energy seems to pass between mother and infant, and continues to occur throughout life. Adults frequently experience communication on a preverbal level. Two people who are in agreement and who seem to think the same thoughts at the same time often describe this as being on the same "wavelength" or "tuning in," as if some sort of mental radio broadcast were taking place. However, more than any other two people, mothers and infants may be on the same "wavelength." They may be connected somehow in the deepest part of the mind, "in tune" on a level that rarely even becomes conscious.

It is almost as if they were still sharing the oneness that they shared during pregnancy. In fact well-known anthropologist Ashley Montague, author of a number of books, looks at the early neonatal period as a continuation of life in the womb. Human gestation, he suggests, is only half complete by the time of birth. The latter half of gestation takes place *outside the womb.*

Dr. Joost A. M. Meerloo, psychiatrist and former associate professor of psychiatry at the New York School of Psychiatry, suggests that the telepathic relationship between mother and baby is a "temporary continuation of prebirth contact."[8] The normal symbiotic relationship between mother and child involves a mutual dependence on one another. According to Dr. Meerloo, it also includes an awareness of each other's outer and inner processes that goes far beyond human sensory contact as we know it. An extrasensory relationship may function on an unconscious level and trigger such actions as the bonding behavior that occurs during the first hour or so after birth.

Psychic communication is especially common during crisis periods, when the infant is in distress. This usually accounts for the most memorable ESP experiences.

The mother of an infant boy recalls: "I was in the living room when it happened. Josh was upstairs sleeping peacefully, I thought. Suddenly I had a hunch that I should check on him. When I went into his room, I found him choking on something he had picked up."

A most unusual tale of telepathy with an infant appeared in—of all places—the *Journal of Soil and Water Conservation.* It is told by Charles E. Little:

"Joe Garcia," Mr. Little writes, "a southern California vegetable grower of my childhood acquaintance, took his wife and infant son across the border between Sonora and Arizona in 1935, to walk into the blazing desert toward Los Angeles. After a time, the infant's breathing slowed, then stopped, and Garcia and his wife scooped out a shallow grave in the loose earth, covering it with stones—a gesture only, for the coyotes would come that evening and the little cairn would mean nothing to them. Joe and his wife walked on, into the slanting rays of the afternoon, which put the cholla and mesquite into sharp relief as the air cooled. Then they stopped. Something stopped them.

"'No es muerte,' Joe's wife said to her husband. 'He is not dead.' And she said it with such certainty that they turned in their tracks and without another word and at a half-trot hurried back the miles to the cairn. Pulling away the rocks, Joe Garcia lifted the tiny body, loosely swathed in cotton, and placed the infant's sandy mouth to his ear. A shallow breath. He was alive."[9]

Ina May Gaskin, author of *Spiritual Midwifery* and well-known midwife of The Farm, a spiritual community in Summertown, Tennessee, says that parent-infant telepathy is commonplace. "I tell all mothers to pay attention to their impulses because they are often right," she says. "Even if the baby is not actively crying, when the mother gets an impression, the baby may need her help. He may have wriggled into a corner and can't get free, have a blanket over his head, or whatever."

Communication beyond the senses may be an outgrowth of the parent-child love bond. Just as the love bond between mother and child is the first love relationship and forerunner of all future intimate bonds, the mother-child ESP connection may be the forerunner of all other psychic experiences.

THE CRADLE OF ESP

That's what Dr. Jan Ehrenwald, former consultant psychiatrist for Roosevelt Hospital in New York City, believes. Dr. Ehrenwald has had extensive experience with ESP. His work with psi distinguishes him as a pioneer in the burgeoning new field of parapsychiatry—the clinical counterpart of psychical research. And he has developed a provocative theory about psi which has astounding implications for both parapsychology and parenting.

He believes the origin of ESP is to be found in the mother-infant relationship and calls this the "cradle of ESP." In his book, *The ESP Experience: A Psychiatric Validation*, he refers to telepathy as "the embryological matrix of communication or information transfer which is later destined to be superseded by speech."[10] According to Dr. Ehrenwald, all forms of ESP—telepathy, clairvoyance, precognition, and clairvoyant dreaming—ultimately stem from this primordial cradle.

The mother is everything to her infant. She is his source of food. She changes his diaper, makes him comfortable, soothes him when he cries, holds him while he is so vulnerable, so wholly dependent. She is his world, his universe.

During the early postnatal period, the mother's and baby's ego boundaries have not yet been delineated. The newborn's ego is fused with the mother's. "Their respective egos or 'selves' are merged into one another," writes Dr. Ehrenwald. "The baby is a direct extension of his mother's body image. She does 'the doing' for him."

Mother and baby, he says, function as a "basic unit" much as they did while the baby was still in the womb. Their "dovetailing or interlocking behavioral attitudes are evidently a direct continuation of the embryo's and maternal organism's flawless biological cooperation."[11]

But how, asks Dr. Ehrenwald, "despite the physical separation of parents and offspring, is this biological unity and reciprocity being maintained? What is responsible for the perfect 'fit,' for their delicately balanced homeostasis and functioning in concert?"[12]

This is where telepathy comes in. While the baby is utterly helpless, Dr. Ehrenwald theorizes, telepathy "may indeed be a vitally important means of communication serving the integration and smooth functioning of the mother-child unit, and thereby its very survival as a viable unity."[13]

A telepathic rapport between mother and child—largely unconscious—facilitates the mother's caring for her child. This, according to one psychiatrist, is the purpose of telepathy, the phenomenon that has perplexed mankind for centuries.

Presumably, as the child grows and verbal skills develop, the more primitive preverbal world of extrasensory perception wanes in importance. Yet the psychic nexus that has been established in infancy remains a channel for possible communication beyond the realm of the senses.

Dr. Ehrenwald suggests that the cradle of ESP theory assigns "an important physiological function to an otherwise seemingly superfluous vehicle of communications—telepathy."[14] But it is difficult to swallow the theory lock, stock, and barrel, for the simple reason that mothers and babies do not have a "perfect fit," as Dr. Ehrenwald suggests. Far from it. A rare mother here and there displays incredible psychic sensitivity to her baby's needs that can only be explained by telepathy, but the majority feel unsure of their ability to care for their child—at least in the beginning. Most new mothers do *not* know precisely what their baby needs at every cry. Most have periods of frustration because they are unsure about how to respond to their crying child. Most learn to respond to their children and develop confidence in their mothering ability with experience—sometimes *long* experience.

However, we cannot discount Dr. Ehrenwald's basic premise that mother and infant do share a telepathic relationship. Psychic communication is probably common between mother and baby, but that does not imply that the maternal-infant relationship is the ultimate source of psi. The mother-child relationship may not hold the key to the origin of all extrasensory phenomena, but there is little doubt that it accounts for our first taste of psi.

THE PARAPSYCHOLOGY OF BREASTFEEDING

And our next taste may come with mother's milk. Breast-fed babies and mothers seem to share an incredible rapport. They may even share the same sleep patterns and dream in synchrony.

So believes William Sears, M.D., well-known pediatrician and author of several popular books, including *Nighttime Parenting*. He first latched onto the idea of maternal-infant sleep synchrony when his fourth child was born. He noticed a puzzling phenomenon. His wife would often wake just before the baby. It made him wonder: Were they experiencing something he hadn't learned about in medical school? Did they share some sort of sleep harmony? And if so, was this unique to his wife and child? He quizzed other mothers who consulted him in his pediatric practice and discovered that many of them related similar experiences. They would often wake a few seconds before their babies.

Edie Orr of Peoria, Illinois, a counselor for La Leche League International, has had this experience. (La Leche League provides information and support to breast-feeding mothers.) Edie says, "I often wake out of a sound sleep just before the baby wakes and begins to cry." After having heard similar stories from numerous nursing mothers she counsels, she discussed it with her colleagues. "We have been surprised by the number of mothers who report the same experience. Something in us seems to know when the baby is going to need us."

This may be a subtle form of mother-infant ESP that often passes unnoticed. Many parents have the experience but do not realize it until it is brought to their attention. As one mother put it: "I've always thought it was perfectly natural that I wake just before the baby starts crying for his feeding. But when you think it over, it almost seems like ESP."

The phenomenon may be rooted in synchronous sleep patterns. Dr. Sears says that the sleep patterns of nursing babies and their mothers tend to harmonize. According to one study he cites, mothers and babies actually tend to dream simultaneously during the night from twelve weeks postpartum until the baby is weaned.[15] Breast-fed infants, Dr. Sears continues, experience REM (rapid eye movement) sleep patterns (the state associated with dreaming) during sucking, and mothers also go into REM sleep when their babies nurse during the night. "This harmony of sleep cycles gives the nursing pair a heightened awareness of each other. Breast-feeding infants who share sleep with their mothers suck more often throughout the night, which also gives mothers and babies an increased sensitivity to each other."[16] Dr. Sears is currently working on a research project with mothers and babies to document the experience of sleep synchrony.

Shared sleep cycles triggered by breast-feeding may help prevent the dread Sudden Infant Death Syndrome (SIDS), says Dr. Sears. In cases of SIDS, the baby is found dead in the crib with no apparent cause of death. Dr. Sears suggests that SIDS is related to a diminished arousal response during sleep in some infants. He hypothesizes that the heightened sensitivity of both infant and mother stemming from breast-feeding may be an important factor in preventing SIDS. "I emphasize," he states, "that this is my own hypothesis based upon my pediatrician's intuition and not based upon any scientific studies that I am aware of." He hopes this idea will stimulate more scientific research in the area.[17]

Norwegian parapsychologist Jan Tolaas believes there is a link between REM sleep and psi during infancy in all mammalian species. The REM state, he points out, is a particularly favorable condition for the occurrence of ESP. Many parapsychologists agree.

The newborn spends much of his time in REM sleep. In full-term newborn babies, REM sleep accounts for about 50 percent of total sleep time compared to 20 percent in adults. Dr. Tolaas suggests that during the early postnatal period, when the baby's ego boundaries are fused with the mother's as they were in the womb, the REM state may serve a psi-communicative purpose. Perhaps the unconsciouses of the mother and baby are particularly close during the REM state.

Could the maternal-infant bond continue to develop during REM sleep? This seems likely when one considers the close relationship between REM sleep and breast-feeding, another process believed to enhance the maternal-infant bond. Of course, this is all highly speculative. One cannot blindly assume that ESP communication is occurring merely because a newborn baby sleeps a lot. However, this is a fascinating area for further research.

The relationship between REM sleep and maternal-infant psi, if indeed there is a relationship, may begin during pregnancy. In one study, fetal activity was monitored by means of speakers attached to the mother's abdomen. An association was found between the mother's REM sleep episodes and increased fetal activity. Mothers have higher amounts of REM sleep during the final months of pregnancy. Does this serve the purpose of helping her and her child forge the parent-child bond?

Psychic communication with the breast-fed infant is not limited to nocturnal ESP. "I know when my baby is going to be hungry," one nursing mother said. "It's an inner sense. I think most nursing mothers have this if they pay attention to it."

This by no means implies that bottle-feeding parents don't have just as strong a psychic bond with their children as do breast-feeding parents. The ESP connection can hardly be reduced to a matter of breast or bottle, any more than the love bond can.

However, breast-feeding may create a psi-conducive condition for parent-infant ESP. In addition to being linked with synchronous REM sleep, the breast-feeding mother tends to be more aware of her infant. Moreover, there may also be an extrasensory dimension to the breast-feeding relationship.

Nursing is a delicate blend of physical, psychological, and neurohormonal factors. When the baby sucks the breast, the pituitary gland in the brain releases the hormone oxytocin, which causes the milk to be ejected from the back of the breasts to the front and sometimes to leak or squirt from the nipples. This process was named "let-down" by dairy farmers who speak of cows letting down their milk.

Once the nursing relationship is established, the mother's breasts may let down milk when she hears her baby crying. This is a perfectly normal response to a psychological stimulus. It is analogous to becoming sexually aroused when thinking about sex. The sound of the baby's crying stimulates the physical response.

Many nursing mothers, however, seem to cross the border from this normal physical response to a psychological stimulus pattern to the realm of the inexplicable. Their breasts lets down milk when the baby cries *whether or not they can hear the baby crying.* In fact, when they are on the other side of town from the baby.

Edie Orr, quoted above, had this experience. On one occasion she fed her three-week-old infant and then went out shopping for a lamp. She says: "While I was shopping, my milk began to let down even though I had just nursed Sarah a half hour before. At the same time, I had a strong urge to call my mother-in-law who was baby-sitting. When I called she told me Sarah had just woke crying for me." This may be a physiological response to a parapsychological stimulus—parent-infant ESP on a body level—and it is a common experience among breast-feeding mothers.

A breast-feeding advocate, Dr. Sears has talked about the mother's experience of nursing with innumerable patients. He has heard many of them report that the let-down reflex has occurred when the baby wakes up crying at a time when the mother is several miles from the child. One mother told him that while she was away from her baby shopping one afternoon, her breasts suddenly felt full. She later asked the baby-sitter if her infant had woken up crying. The sitter told her he had. The time the baby woke up from a nap upset and crying coincided with the time her breasts started feeling full.

"I don't know what to make of it," says Dr. Sears. "But I feel there must be something going on that has so far eluded all the medical studies."

That something may very well prove to be a psi-mediated physiological response. The breast-feeding relationship is one of the most intimate of all human relationships. It is second only to the relationship of mother and unborn child in the womb, where the baby also depends on the mother's body for nourishment. In the womb, the child is nourished by mother's very lifeblood through the placenta. The breasts function as an external placenta, providing both nourishment and the security of the womb.

No interchange could better exemplify the maternal-infant symbiosis that Dr. Ehrenwald postulates is the basis of all ESP, the very substratum of psychic phenomenon. Indeed, next to pregnancy, the breast-feeding relationship may be the ultimate psi-conducive state.

Of course, many incidents that seem to be ESP can actually be explained in other ways. The mother who wakes the instant before her child may have heard the baby moving or making soft sounds in its sleep. Though the infant may be silent at the moment the mother wakes, she has no way of knowing that her infant didn't make some kind of sound prior to waking.

By the same token, much of the time there is nothing psychic about the mother's milk letting down at pretty much the same time her baby cries for food, whether she is in the same room or miles away. It isn't even a notable coincidence. The baby becomes accustomed to being fed at fairly regular intervals, or the mother may have thought of her child. It is quite natural for a mother to think of her baby while away from home. This is enough to trigger the let-down reflex.

But what of the mother who has just fed her baby, leaves her home, and suddenly thinks of her child and lets down her milk just as the child is crying? It would take a wide stretch of the imagination to write this off as coincidence.

Until more research sheds light on the paranormal side of breast-feeding, we can only guess how often such experiences occur. We can be fairly certain, however, that the ESP of breast-feeding touches the lives of a large number of mothers and infants. The oddest thing about it is that most of them aren't even aware that they've had a psychic experience.

THE LIVING BOND

Psi experience may be far more common in infancy than in later life. Mother and baby seem to share a living bond during the vulnerable months. Paranormal communication may very well be a natural part of the parent-infant relationship. Yet strange as it may seem, virtually no research has been done in this fascinating area. One might say that research about parent-infant ESP is in its infancy, or more accurately, yet to be conceived.

Many health professionals have run across evidence of psychic communication with infants yet refuse to acknowledge it. Some pediatricians, psychologists, and other health professionals who have noticed a parent-infant psychic bond—indeed, could hardly fail to notice it—behave as if they've taken an oath of secrecy about it. One reason for this may be that the psychic relationship between parent and child has not yet been validated in scientific studies. Another reason is the familiar emotional prejudice many have toward psi—the widespread tendency to ignore psi, to turn our heads and pretend it doesn't exist.

Most of our scant knowledge about the psychic life of infants does not come from parapsychologists, who oddly all but ignore the psychic world of babies. It comes from people like Dr. Chamberlain who stumble across psi experiences by accident, people who have no interest in psi research.

Another source of our knowledge of parent-infant ESP is the personal stories of parents. The experiences parents discuss, such as waking with a sudden need to check on the baby just when something is wrong, are all quite similar. They form a common pattern like ripples left on the sand by the waves. It is this orderly pattern—the similarity of experiences shared by so many parents—that is perhaps the strongest evidence in favor of the parent-infant extrasensory connection.

However, most probable parent-infant ESP experiences do not constitute hard scientific data. They cannot be measured, quantified, or analyzed, at least not as easily as laboratory ESP tests can be scored, but that does not make them any less real.

The living ESP bond a parent shares with a tiny vulnerable baby belongs to a realm of psychic phenomena that have not, and perhaps cannot, be measured in a laboratory. From the point of view of psychical research, the parent-infant relationship is a fascinating and virtually unprobed mine. Perhaps parapsychology will turn its attention to the unexplored psychic world of babies.

Meanwhile, a growing family of professions, from pre- and perinatal psychology to pediatrics, are exploring the world of the unborn and newborn child. They all share the same goal of happier, healthier babies, and they all encounter again and again the same puzzling phenomenon—evidence of parent-infant ESP. These experiences are utterly inexplicable outside of parapsychology.

Perhaps this family will expand and adopt parapsychology. If so, parapsychology may find a comfortable home and develop a compatible relationship with the pediatric-related fields. It may make a bigger contribution than we imagine. Parapsychology is like the traveler in an Arabian Nights tale who has discovered a trapdoor leading to a rich cavern, a magical world deep beneath the ground. It can travel in a world the other sciences have never dared to probe, indeed, never thought of probing.

Working hand in hand, parapsychology and the professions that explore the world of the unborn and newborn child have much to teach one another. They have much to share.

Will probing into parent-infant ESP show us that the root of all psi is to be found in infancy, as Dr. Ehrenwald suggests? Will it finally give us the answer to the ultimate question: Why psi? It seems unlikely. This will probably always remain a mystery, but a closer look at the psychic world of babies is bound to shed light on a subject very near our homes.

Our beginnings.

6

Phantasms of the Living

The very idea that our first taste of psi may stem from our relationship with those who gave us life could alter the way we look at parents and children, and for that matter, all human life. However, if our beginnings are suffused with psi, the ESP we experience is like a tale half told. The parent-infant ESP connection barely reaches beyond the threshold of consciousness except on rare occasions. Rather, parent-infant psi seems to be more like barely audible background music—an accompaniment perhaps to the parent-child bond. It is only during the later years that experiences are likely to occur which most people would consider paranormal.

Of course, psychic phenomena can and do occur in a wide variety of relationships. But the intimate relationship of parent and child, the love bond that is in itself a sort of psychic phenomenon, is fertile soil, perhaps the most fertile soil, for extrasensory experiences. Thousands of parents have experienced inexplicable events that suggest there is something more than meets the eye to the parent-child bond. Even the most casual glimpse of such incidents is eye-opening. Among them are some of the most astounding psychic phenomena ever recorded.

CRISIS TELEPATHY

In his autobiography, the famous painter Oscar Kokoschka relates a remarkable true tale of crisis telepathy involving his mother and his brother. His mother was having tea with his aunt in Prague, Czechoslovakia. Suddenly she jumped to her feet and announced that she had to return home immediately. Her youngest son was bleeding, she claimed. The thought had come to her out of the blue. Apparently not accustomed to having a tea interrupted in such a manner, the aunt tried to convince the mother that the notion was preposterous. However, the distraught mother heeded her intuition and sped home. When she arrived, she found that her son had cut his leg with a hatchet while chopping down a tree. Had his mother not arrived when she did, he would very likely have bled to death.

This unusual ESP experience, which may have saved a child's life, is known as *crisis telepathy*. Often dramatic, crisis telepathy occurs in connection with an accident, injury, illness, other crisis, or death. A mother is suddenly gripped with a feeling that her child is in danger. A child flashes on his father with a sense of sudden urgency. At that instant an accident occurs in the next room, or on the other side of town, or a thousand miles away. There are thousands of recorded cases of this type of ESP between parent and offspring. In fact, the majority of all recorded psychic phenomena probably fall into this category.

The experience of crisis telepathy may range from a subtle uncomfortable feeling to such spectacular psychic phenomena as hearing an audible voice with no speaker present or seeing an apparition. The latter psychic phenomena are quite rare. Those who do experience such things usually do so only once or twice in a lifetime, which for most parents is enough. However, experiencing an ESP-triggered uneasy feeling at the time of crisis involving a parent or child is common.

During the fall of 1986, my wife Jan had spent one Saturday driving and hiking in the beautiful Dixville Notch region of northern New Hampshire. Throughout the day she kept thinking of her mother Ruth, who lives several hundred miles away in Great Neck, New York. "I had a strong feeling I should call her," Jan recalls. "I couldn't get the thought out of my mind." Since she didn't arrive home until late at night, she called the following morning, but there was no answer. That evening a friend of the family phoned to say that Ruth had been having stomach pains throughout the day Saturday and had been admitted to the hospital.

An ESP-triggered urge to phone a parent or child is quite common. Molly, a New Hampshire mother of twelve children, often feels psychically connected with her children. On one occasion, one of her daughters was living over four thousand miles away in Alaska, where an earthquake was occurring. Worried about her daughter, whom she hadn't spoken to in weeks, Molly began praying that she would be safe. At the moment she was praying, her daughter phoned.

Threatened danger triggers a high number of memorable crisis ESP events. Ellen Vlok of the Cape of Good Hope, Republic of South Africa, gives a dramatic account of a telepathic impression she had when her daughter Elsa was undergoing a medical crisis. At the time Elsa was living near Cape Town, about eighty miles away.

"I suddenly became unusually uneasy over her," Mrs. Vlok recalls. "And no matter how I tried to fight the feeling down, the conviction that something was amiss with Elsa grew stronger and stronger."

Mrs. Vlok's husband and son, both attorneys-at-law, were startled when she burst into their office quite breathless to announce that something had happened to Elsa and begged them to take her to her daughter in Cape Town. They both ridiculed her, but seeing that she was adamant, her son eventually consented to leave the office to drive her to the Sea Point Hotel near Cape Town where her daughter was living.

"The nearer we drew to Cape Town, the more I urged my son to drive faster and faster, and when we reached the hotel at 11:00 A.M., I rushed up the stairs to the second floor where her bedroom was, my son following. On opening the door, we found her pathetically perched in a queer position on the edge of the bed, still in her nightclothes, numb with cold and unable to move at all, having slipped a disc in her spine as she was getting out of bed. Her calls for help had been futile, the maids only coming toward noon to do the rooms. Elsa had been in that taut position for more than four hours. We could not move her at all, so my son immediately rushed for a doctor, who could bring relief."[1]

Mrs. Vlok's story is among one of 35 dramatic cases of telepathic impressions investigated and documented by Dr. Ian Stevenson, professor of psychiatry at the University of Virginia School of Medicine. He is one of the most well-known psychical researchers in the field today.

Documentation by psychical research standards is fairly rigorous business. In many cases Dr. Stevenson engaged in extensive correspondence, often over several years, with his informants. Whenever possible he interviewed the percipients and other first-hand witnesses. He was always alert for details that might betray some evidence of normal communication or coincidence. If he found it, the case was discarded.

He is the first to admit that despite his meticulous research and best efforts, he may have overlooked some important details that might disqualify a paranormal interpretation in one or more cases. "But," he points out, "as the number of cases grows, this possibility becomes less and less reasonable as grounds for discounting all of them."[2] This possibility becomes less reasonable especially when one considers that there are enormous numbers of cases of similar psychic phenomena in the journals and files of both the American Society for Psychical Research (ASPR) and the Society for Psychical Research (SPR) in England.

One feature common to many ESP experiences is an inexplicable feeling of uneasiness. This may encompass a wide range of feelings, from a vague sense that something is wrong to overwhelming dread. One mother who has had numerous psychic experiences describes the feeling in this way: "When I sense something awful is going to happen, it's an inner turmoil, a fear, a sick-to-my-stomach kind of horror." The feeling of uneasiness often prompts the percipient to take some sort of action.

In the *San Diego Tribune*, November 26, 1987, staff writer Frank Saldana reports: "A Santee mother says her intuition may have saved the life of her two-year-old daughter after the girl was mauled by a dog."

Sue Christensen said she "sat down to watch 'All My Children' on television at noon Tuesday and began to feel uneasy."

Her intuition prompted her to call her daughter's name. When she received no answer, she began searching for her. She found her in the backyard lying flat on her back on the grass in shock after she had been attacked by a neighbor's young Alaskan malamute dog.

The girl was taken to an intensive care unit of a local hospital. She survived the attack. Whether or not the child would have survived had her mother found her hours later remains an open question. In any case, an ESP-triggered sense of uneasiness seemed to alert her to the problem.[3]

A sudden flash of ESP alerted one father to impending disaster. His taking immediate action may very well have saved the life of his son.

While at home one day he sensed that something horrible had happened to his twenty-year-old diabetic son, who was then in a semiprivate hospital room. He felt compelled to phone the hospital at 8:15 A.M. The patient in the adjacent bed answered the phone and said: "Joey is all right." But the father insisted that this was not so, that the nurses should wake Joey immediately. It was discovered that Joey was in an insulin coma. This situation had never happened to Joey in the hospital before.

However, this was not the first crisis ESP experience this

father had had involving his son. One time when he was in line with his wife at a New York theater miles from home, he suddenly said they must leave immediately and telephone their daughter to get help for Joey, who was in trouble. This proved to be true.[4]

Kris, a mother in North Dartmouth, Massachusetts, believes that acting on a sudden impulse once saved her daughter from drowning. She feels that she and her daughter Anna are very much attuned. For example, if she is going out for the evening, Anna will frequently wake up out of a sound sleep just as she is about to leave the house.

"We often go to the pool at my neighbor's house together," she says. "Anna couldn't swim very well at the time and wore a life preserver when she was at the deep end of the pool. She often used the slide and always used the preserver. One day she went down the slide without the preserver. I didn't realize she wasn't wearing it, but all of a sudden, I had the sense that something was wrong and dove into the water after her without thinking. By the time I reached her, Anna was struggling. She couldn't catch her breath. There is no question in my mind that I would have lost her if I hadn't reached her when I did."

The uneasy feelings so common with crisis telepathy suggest that a parent and child can affect one another in a rather profound way even when they are a great distance apart. Parent and child appear to be psychically sensitive to one another's difficulties. A highly emotionally charged event, imminent danger, or catastrophe that affects one may cause an uncomfortable feeling in the other.

Such psi-caused uneasy feelings are usually accompanied by the thought of a specific person, as one would assume them to be. A mother feels nervous and at the same time thinks of her son. She later learns that he had a narrow escape from a serious car accident at the time she thought of him. However psi, being so peculiar, doesn't always work this way. A person who feels inexplicably uneasy may have no thought of a specific individual. He may realize that the uneasy feeling is associated with a crisis to a loved one only later.

This was the experience of Nancy Hugger, a childbirth educator living in Vineyard Haven, Massachusetts. She has always felt a psychic connection with her mother. They often share ESP experiences. For example, when Nancy is helping a woman through labor, her mother, while at home, often picks up the time of birth and the sex of the child. The birth of a child often leaves Nancy with a feeling of elation and high energy. Nancy's excitement during this climactic event is perhaps conveyed to her mother telepathically.

On one occasion Nancy experienced a profound reaction apparently triggered by ESP while her mother was going through a severe crisis thousands of miles away. Yet she did not connect her reaction to her mother until later.

For several years her mother and father had been living in Iran where her father worked. Suddenly for no apparent reason Nancy, who was then a college student living in Vineyard Haven, became extremely upset. She was too upset to eat or focus her energy on anything, let alone to do school work. This lasted for three days.

Suddenly the problem vanished as mysteriously as it had developed. Within an hour after Nancy felt better, her father phoned from Iran informing her that her mother was on her way. Shortly afterward, her mother arrived in America.

Nancy later learned that during the period she was experiencing intense emotional distress preventing her from functioning in college, her mother had been going through a harrowing experience. There was trouble in Iran at the time. An American had been shot. To escape, Nancy's mother had had to run across a field in the dark to get on the airplane, which then left Iran secretly. She was left in Turkey from where she later had to get a flight to America.

It was only after leaving Turkey that she was finally able to relax, relieved to be on her way home—probably at the same time Nancy began to feel better.

Psychic experiences do not always spring into the mind fully hatched. Quite often an ESP experience grows and acquires more detail as time passes, as if it had to gestate awhile before revealing itself. For example, one may first have an uncomfortable feeling. A little later thoughts of the person to whom the feeling is related occur. Later still, the nature of the crisis may be sensed or an inner vision related to it may take place.

Sometimes a person who has an indefinite extrasensory experience—a vague uneasy feeling or a sense that something is wrong—may be able to acquire more details by quieting the mind and concentrating, perhaps asking the inner mind for more information. Sometimes more details come spontaneously. The psychic experience grows and seems to take on a life of its own.

Mrs. Joicey Acker Hurth, a newly married woman living in Cedarburg, Wisconsin, had this type of experience. Her moving story was investigated and documented by Dr. Ian Stevenson:

Mrs. Hurth writes: "I was still a happy bride of three months until that night in 1949 when my feeling of ecstasy suddenly turned into a mood of depression. There was no logical reason for it at the time. This day, as others preceding it, was filled with enthusiasm in relation to my adjustment to the community life of Cedarburg, Wisconsin, a delightful small city just north of Milwaukee.

"My husband and I were temporarily living with his parents . . . It must have been sometime after midnight, January 23, when I awakened with a feeling of deep sadness, an impression that something was wrong. I did not want to disturb my husband, so for a long while I stared wide-eyed at the ceiling of the bedroom, which was barely visible in a dim, shadowy light. I remember the terrible ache in my heart. I started to cry and sobbed softly into my pillow. My husband was immediately awake and asked many questions, to which I had no answers. I repeated over and over to him that I had a feeling that something was wrong. His efforts to console me were futile, and I did not sleep the rest of the night.

"The next morning when we went downstairs to breakfast my

in-laws were shocked at my appearance—swollen red eyes and haggard expression. They accused us of having had a 'lovers' quarrel,' but I assured them that this was not the case. I told them I had no explanation for my mood of depression. They were much concerned.

"I put bread into the toaster and while waiting for it I suddenly wheeled around and exclaimed, 'It's my father! Something is terribly wrong with my father!'

"I had no reason for my statement. My father was a man of robust health for his sixty-nine years and had known little illness in his entire life.

"Each one speaking in turn tried to tell me that it was my imagination. My mother-in-law reminded me of the letter I had received from my father only a few days before, and he had made no mention of an illness.

"'No,' I said. 'I'm sure. I must go home!'

"The telephone rang while I was speaking, and although this was a doctor's home where the telephone rang constantly, I knew this call was for me and answered it.

"My aunt spoke first, telling me that my father was in a coma and was dying. Then my mother took the phone and asked, 'Didn't you receive my letter? I wrote you that your father was very ill.'"

The letter had not reached Mrs. Hurth because the planes had been held up as a result of bad weather.

Her father had become suddenly ill. He had taken a sulfa drug, which had caused crystalization in the kidneys.

From whom did Mrs. Hurth's telepathic impression come? Her mother or her father? Mrs. Hurth remarks: "I still do not know whether my impression of my father's illness was telepathy between him, in his unconscious state, and me, or between my worried mother and me."[5]

Six years later in 1955, Mrs. Hurth had a rather awesome telepathic experience involving her five-year-old daughter Joicey. All of the details seemed to come into her mind at once.

When it happened, Joicey had just left to go to a Walt Disney movie where she was to meet her father.

"I returned to the dinner dishes still unwashed in the kitchen sink," Mrs. Hurth recalls. "Quite suddenly while I held a plate in my hand an awesome feeling came over me. I dropped the plate, turned my eyes toward heaven and prayed aloud, 'Oh God, don't let her get killed!'

"For some unexplainable reason I knew Joicey had been hit by a car or was going to be. I was quite conscious of her involvement in an accident. I immediately went to the telephone, looked up the number, and shakily dialed the theater. I gave my name and said, 'My little girl was on the way to the theater. She has had an accident. Is she badly hurt?'

"The girl answering the telephone stammered, 'How did you know? It, the accident, just happened. Hold the phone please!'

"While I held the receiver, waiting, the siren sounded and an ambulance went out. I was frantic. Soon a very calm voice, that of the manager, Ray Nichols, spoke, 'Mrs. Hurth, your little girl was struck by a car but she is all right. Your husband is with her now. She appears to be in good shape, only stunned. Your husband is taking her to Dr. Hurth [little Joicey's uncle] now for an examination. Incidentally, Mrs. Hurth, how did you know?' "[6]

Indeed, it is a good question. Ray Nichols, the theater manager, must have puzzled over that one for quite some time. One can only imagine how he felt when some thirteen years later he was contacted by Dr. Ian Stevenson, who got in touch with him to document the episode. He remembered the incident, and will probably continue to do so, for the rest of his life.

Sometimes a sense of uneasiness involves more than one person in the family. A husband and wife both sense that their child is ill or in danger. One or more siblings simultaneously feel their mother or father is undergoing a crisis.

A remarkable case of this type was written up in the *Journal of the American Society of Psychical Research* in 1914. It involved an entire family of eight persons who lived on a farm in northern

New York. All were simultaneously affected by a similar psychic phenomenon.

After breakfast they all left their home for the day's work on the farm, but none of them continued working very long. At about 10:00 A.M. they all ceased their daily chores and returned to the kitchen. A strange feeling crept over each of them, an intense awe, a dread foreboding that something awful was about to happen. Each thought it was some coming illness. And each thought the feeling was peculiar to himself. Only later did each person who had returned to the kitchen learn that everyone else in the family was affected in the same way.

What was the cause of the family's strange behavior? A son in the family had been killed accidentally in Michigan.[7]

The first collection of documented spontaneous ESP cases was published a century ago in 1886 in a massive tome called *Phantasms of the Living*, which includes seven hundred episodes. This was the first full-scale published work of the Society for Psychical Research (SPR) in England. Since the SPR was founded in 1882, its members have included some of the world's most eminent scholars: the famous psychologist William James, who served as president to the Society; the philosopher Henri Bergson, another SPR president; Alfred Tennyson; John Ruskin; Mark Twain; Lewis Carroll; and several Nobel Prize–winning scientists such as J. J. Thompson, who discovered the electron, and Lord Rayleigh, who discovered argon, among a host of others.

Phantasms of the Living was largely the result of the efforts of Edmund Gurney, a psychologist (who for thirty years was inspector of schools at Cambridge) and one of the first members of the SPR. Gurney collaborated with two other SPR men, Frederic Myers and Frank Podmore. It was Myers who coined the word "telepathy" in 1882 by linking up the idea of distance (tele) with "empathy." The SPR conducted a nationwide survey, seeking accounts of spontaneous ESP. After an astounding expenditure of energy and painstaking research, they managed to amass a veritable mountain of cases. Only those which could be fully verified were included in *Phantasms*. Myers wrote the lengthy introduction, Gurney wrote the voluminous text, and Podmore assisted in collecting and verifying the accounts. The first to include and examine spontaneous ESP, this book is one of the most important documents in psychic literature. In fact, the prestigious SPR considers it so important that in 1988 the Society honored the publication of the book with a centennial celebration. At this time another nationwide survey for spontaneous ESP was conducted.

Gurney, who had studied law, brought his legal training to bear on the cases he and his colleagues investigated. Each case in *Phantasms* is accompanied by affidavits, letters from witnesses, and other relevant material to corroborate it. In some reports the story is told three or more times by separate witnesses so the reader can compare their recollections. This doesn't make very exciting reading for the layman, but it does leave the reader with little doubt that the cases reported are genuine.

Very rarely a psychic experience involving a parent or child (or other loved one or friend for that matter) involves phenomena even more inexplicable than a strange uneasy feeling or sudden compulsion. In some cases the percipient does not merely think of the person in distress, who may be on the other side of the world at the time, but actually hears that person speaking. This sort of experience is what Gurney refers to as one of the "extreme examples of telepathic action."[8]

One mother had this experience while her six-year-old son was faced with terrifying life-threatening danger. The case is on record at the venerable American Society for Psychical Research, an organization established in 1885 by William Barrett, a member of the SPR.

The boy had been playing with his sisters six miles from home at a beach on Long Island Sound. Meanwhile the mother had a strong impression that he was drifting out to sea in a tiny boat. She heard her son calling, "Mommy! Mommy!"

She became very upset. But she was helpless. She had no car and no way to get to the beach. So she knelt down to pray earnestly that her boy would receive help. She prayed that he would stay sitting in the boat and not stand up.

Later that day the mother discovered that her son had been drifting out to sea in a boat just as she had perceived, but he was rescued. The persons who rescued him heard the boy calling, "Mommy! Mommy!"[9] They attributed his safety to the fact that he remained seated.

This mother's experience of hearing her son calling her when he was miles away is not unique. Other parents have had similar experiences. Sigmund Freud records an account told by a woman who had had many telepathic experiences. The mother writes:

"In 1914 my brother was on active service . . . It was ten in the morning on August 22, when I heard my brother's voice calling, 'Mother! Mother!' It came again ten minutes later, but I saw nothing. On August 24, I came home, found my mother greatly depressed, and in answer to my question she said that the boy had appeared on August 22. She had been in the garden in the morning, when she heard him call, 'Mother! Mother!' I tried to comfort her and said nothing about myself. Three weeks after there came a card from my brother, written on August 22 between nine and ten in the morning; shortly after that he died."[10]

It is not easy to explain this sort of experience in terms of mere "mental radio waves." How is the apparently nonphysical energy of psi translated into something as distinctly physical as an audible voice? The idea of hearing someone who is not there speaking defies all known laws of science. It defies common sense. It is even strange by parapsychological standards.

One is tempted to write off this kind of experience as a dream, just one person's fantasy, but that won't do. Too many people have had the experience. In fact, the voice is sometimes so distinct that the person hearing it responds. One woman who heard her name called by her mother, who at the time was dying eighteen miles away, described the voice as very loud, sharp, and impetuous. Thunderstruck, she ran out of the room to see if she could account for the voice.

Many other parents and children have reported experiences of hearing themselves called. Louise Rhine records several episodes. For example, one girl in Los Angeles heard her mother call as if from the next room. She turned to answer and then realized her mother was 3000 miles away. A few days later she had a letter from her mother that said, "I was so lonesome for you that I stood in the doorway of your room and called to you."[11]

The person who has such an experience is often unaware that the speaker is not present, that the voice is in fact a phantasm. In one *Phantasms of the Living* case, a father relates a tragic accident involving his eighteen-year-old son. He writes:

"I was in the baths at Llandudno, when I suddenly and distinctly heard my boy's voice calling loudly and in an agonized tone. So assured was I of it being his voice, that I hastily got out of the bath and looked out of the nearest window, thinking he must be on the rocks beneath me . . ."

His son was actually three or four miles away. He was killed by a fall from some rocks at the time the father heard his voice.

Mrs. Stella, a mother in Chieri, Italy, also responded to a phantasm voice. Her story was another investigated by the SPR.

It was May, 1882. She was sitting with other members of her family discussing household matters when she suddenly heard the voice of her eldest son calling, "Mama" three or four times impatiently. This was quite peculiar. For her son was in London.

She threw down her work and exclaimed, "There is Nino!" and went downstairs, to everyone's astonishment. No one was in the hall, and everyone laughed at her imagination. However, a few days afterward she heard that her son had been taken ill in London and had frequently expressed a wish that his mother could come and take care of him.[12]

How can a mother hear her son speaking when he is well over a thousand miles away? Does parent-child telepathy cause her to hallucinate the voice? Does she externalize an ESP impression in the form of sound? We know that the unconscious mind can play tricks. An idea in the mind can cause a genuine reaction in the sensory organs. This is a well-known phenomenon in ordinary life. Someone remarks: "I'm so hungry, I can just taste the flavor of prime ribs." A person walking through the desert sees a mirage.

The imagination is powerful. Perhaps imagination and psi work hand in hand to create the mother's experience of hearing her son's voice. The telepathic impression may be so vivid that she imagines she hears her son talking. An inner experience is transformed by some trick of the mind into a sensory perception. This seems to be the most reasonable hypothesis.

Except when two persons claim at the same time to hear the voice of a person who is thousands of miles away.

This was the experience of one couple living in England while their son was in America. He had left England two years before and married. He had always wanted to bring his wife home to see his mother.

About three-quarters of an hour after the parents had gone to bed one night, they heard their son speaking. The mother heard the voice. The father heard it too. He asked his wife if she was speaking.

"No!" she said. "Keep quiet!"

Their son's voice said, "As I cannot come to England, Mother, I have come now to see you."

The parents later learned that their son had died of a sudden illness on the very day they had heard his voice. Their son's widow said that before he died he had been anxious to get to England to see his mother. Apparently he did.[13]

Does that mean that the voice of their son was actually a physical reality in his parents' room? Did real, measurable sound waves travel to the parents' ears from . . . from what? Would a tape recorder, had it been running, have picked up the words? Or was it a case of collective telepathy?

The most satisfying explanation, which isn't very satisfying at that, is that there was no voice. The parents simultaneously had a vivid telepathic impression on an unconscious level, and that impression was translated into an audible hallucination.

Hallucination or not, the imagined voice often says precisely what the person many miles away is saying either verbally or in intent. And to that, we must give a nod.

Gurney and Myers referred to such phenomena as "veridical hallucinations." The hallucination, apparently triggered by psi, corresponds accurately to a real life event.

Even more "extreme examples of telepathic action" than auditory ESP are the cases in which the percipient has a vision from a distant scene or sees an apparition. Gurney and Myers refer to these experiences as "spectral illusions." They believe that the visual scene is a distinct hallucination of the sense of vision caused by telepathy.

Real life spectral illusions can be as uncanny as just about anything one is likely to stumble across in fiction. In fact, the TV serial "One Step Beyond," a popular half-hour thriller about uncanny experiences, consists largely of actual cases from the files of the SPR, dramatized, of course, for TV.

A few true-to-life cases don't even need embellishment to stand out as spectacular. For example, a psychic vision recorded in *Phantasms of the Living* (quoted from the *Memoirs of Georgiana, Lady Chatterton* by E. H. Dering, 1878) sounds more like something out of a Gothic novel than a typical parent-child telepathy case. However, it was investigated and documented by the highly cautious Gurney and Myers.

Lady Chatterton awoke with the moon shining brightly into the room. The white curtains around her bed were drawn to protect her from the draft coming through a large window.

"And on this curtain," recalls Lady Chatterton, "as if depicted there, I saw the figure of my mother, face deadly pale, with blood flowing on the bedclothes. For a moment I lay horror-stricken and unable to move or cry out."

Thinking it might be a delusion, she raised herself up in bed and touched the curtain. But the specter remained "as if reflected by a magic lantern," although the curtain moved to and fro. In great terror she got up and rushed to her mother's room.

"There she lay, just as I had seen her on the curtain, pale as death and the sheet covered with blood and two doctors standing by the bedside."

Her mother had been dangerously ill (Lady Chatterton does not say what the illness was) but by the time her daughter arrived, all danger was past.[14]

Louisa Rhine reports a similar story. After retiring to bed, a woman suddenly saw her mother slightly bent over, holding her left hand, and screaming: "Help me! Help me! Somebody help me!" Then the scene faded. She told her husband she was afraid her mother might have burned herself. But as it turned out, at the time the woman saw this scene, her mother had left the store where she worked and was unlocking the door to her car when she was attacked from behind by a man with a knife. In her attempt to grab the knife, the mother received a bad slash on her left hand. She screamed: "Help me! Help me! Somebody help me!" The man ran off.[15]

More often, visual psychic experiences are not quite so spectacular. Rather, they unfold before the screen of the inner mind like a waking dream. Such experiences are most apt to occur when one is just drifting off to sleep or otherwise in a relaxed state of mind.

Meg Grindrod, the midwife in Rochester, New York, had been up all night assisting at a birth. On the way home from the hospital, feeling exhausted, she felt she was hallucinating. "I kept picturing a state police car in my driveway and thinking that something terrible had happened to one of my children. I was obsessed with the thought all the way home. But when I pulled into the driveway there was no police car and everything seemed fine. As soon as I entered the house, my husband said, "If you had come home fifteen minutes earlier, you would have seen a sheriff's car in the driveway." Their youngest son had been lost for a couple of hours in the woods.

Ms. Grindrod did not see the police car as if it were actually right there in front of her. There was no question that what she perceived was on the screen of her inner mind.

The appearance or sensation of an apparition at a time of crisis may sometimes be the result of a vivid telepathic impression. Rather than registering in the mind as a thought or feeling, the impression seems to be dramatized as a hallucination, sometimes even a ghostly visitor.

A woman who prefers to be called Myra (not her real name) had a ghostly experience on the Jewish holiday of Yom Kippur. It happened in New York City. Myra had been fasting and was waiting for the holiday to end so she could prepare herself something to eat. The lack of food, she thinks, may have predisposed her mind to psychic phenomena.

The day was just shading into night. Myra was standing in the kitchen when she suddenly had the feeling of a presence nearby. She didn't actually see an apparition. She merely sensed a presence in the room with her. For no discernible reason, the Hebrew name "Chaim" sprang into her mind.

Two hours later it was dark. The holiday was over. Her mother called. She and her father had been in the synagogue praying. Her mother said she had been thinking of Myra all day.

"She called to tell me that a cousin by marriage whom we always called an uncle had died the day before," Myra recalls. "His name was Hymie which in Hebrew is Chaim."

Myra does not wish to believe she had seen a ghost, or even sensed one. She prefers to think that her sense of a presence in her kitchen was caused by her telepathically picking up her mother's thoughts. And she is probably right.

Presumably psi and imagination cooperated to produce a sense of an apparition in Myra's kitchen. A telepathic impression perceived on an unconscious level was externalized and made not quite flesh, which means that the apparition was more or less imagined and not an actual presence.

However, in many other cases the apparition is just as present to the senses as an ESP-perceived audible voice. In other words, the perceiver does not merely think of an apparition, but sees it. Such experiences occur most often at the time of the death of a loved one.

In another 19th century *Phantasms of the Living* case, Annie

Wright describes a vision of her daughter Fanny, which occurred just prior to Fanny's tragic death.

A few minutes after eleven, Fanny came running into the kitchen and asked her mother if she could go out to play. Soon after Mrs. Wright spoke to her, she went and fetched a pail of water from the bedroom. As she was walking across the yard with it, Fanny came in front of her like a bright shadow. Mrs. Wright stopped quite still, looked at her, and saw her vanish. A few minutes later, Fanny died in her arms. She had been run over by a baker's cart, which had broken her neck. Mrs. Wright had never had an experience like this on any other occasion.[16]

Did the mother telepathically perceive her daughter's death and externalize the psychically perceived information as a vision, or did Fanny actually appear to her in her astral body?

Gurney and Myers view this sort of experience as a form of externalized telepathy. That is to say, the telepathic impression is real, but the apparition, like an ESP-perceived audible voice, is a product of the imagination. But there is another possibility. Several dramatic apparition cases suggest that the percipient did not simply externalize a telepathic experience but actually saw the person's astral body. The apparition, therefore, may actually be the person perceived having an out-of-body experience, which implies that the person was present in spirit in the most literal sense of that term. Sometimes the apparition—or is it astral body?—appears in such distinct detail that one believes the person is actually present in flesh and blood.

On rare occasions, a distinct apparition is perceived by more than one person in the family. The following story is another from *Phantasms of the Living*.

Between 8 and 9 P.M. on August 21, 1869, a seven-year-old boy came running into his aunt's bedroom in Devonport, England.

"Oh Auntie!" he cried. "I have just seen my father walking around my bed!"

"Nonsense," said the aunt, who was the father's sister. She

pooh-poohed her nephew's statement because her brother was in Hong Kong. "You must have been dreaming."

But the boy was insistent. "No, I have not!" he said, and refused to go back to his room.

The aunt put her nephew to bed in her own room and between ten and eleven o'clock went to bed herself. She happened to look toward the fireplace in her room, where she distinctly saw her brother seated in the chair. What struck her most was the deathly pallor of his face. She was so frightened that she put her head under her bedclothes. She then heard his voice calling her three times.

The next mail from China brought her the tragic news of her brother's sudden death from heat apoplexy. As one might guess, he died on August 21.[17]

ESP OF THE BODY

Marvin, a twenty-three-year-old man who had had the first successful "blue baby" operation to correct a heart defect when he was a child, was left with a weak heart. After performing in Los Angeles in the second act of the play, *Dark at the Top of the Stairs*, he received seven curtain calls. The excitement was apparently what triggered his fatal heart attack. He died almost immediately.

At the time of Marvin's death, his mother, Ruth Mason, was at home fifteen miles away. At five minutes to ten that night, she screamed out for her husband. She had a horrible pain in her abdomen, unlike any pain she had ever experienced. She thought she was going to die. At first her husband thought she was suffering from an attack of acute appendicitis. He pressed her abdomen for tenderness, found none, and concluded that appendicitis wasn't the problem. He gave his wife a couple of aspirins, put her to bed, and she soon fell asleep.

She woke up at midnight when she heard her daughter

screaming: "Oh no! No! No! It can't be!" Her daughter had just received the telephone call informing her of her brother Marvin's death. The time of death was 10:00 P.M.

There is virtually no question that the mother's sharp abdominal pain was directly related to her son's heart attack. The grim news was carried to the mother in the form of a psi-mediated psysiological reaction. ESP of the body.

This is known as a *telesomatic symptom*: experiencing the physical symptoms or physical changes of another. By some process no one understands, ESP is translated into a bodily symptom. It is one of the strangest of all psychic phenomena. Yet it occurs frequently between parent and child. Psi-triggered physical symptoms are most common during times of illness, injury, serious accident, or death.

Betty, a middle-aged woman who lives in Florida, had a constant dull headache. Nothing she took would relieve it.

Fifteen hundred miles away in New York City, her son Dennis woke up with a severe headache. To the horror of his wife Jamie, he was soon unconscious. Minutes later an ambulance rushed him to the hospital, where he was treated for a cerebral hemorrhage. Fortunately, he recovered fully.

When Jamie called her mother-in-law in Florida to give her the frightening news about the hemorrhage, Betty's headache suddenly lifted. Betty recalls: "I would often have a strange feeling if Dennis was uncomfortable or in any kind of trouble. It is unexplainable. But this time I didn't have that feeling." Instead she experienced the headache, which is even more unexplainable.

A sudden accident to a child may sometimes be linked to symptoms of the injury in a parent. A nurse reports a dramatic psychic experience apparently triggered by her daughter's car accident. She actually sustained minor injuries in her body corresponding to some of her daughter's more severe injuries.

"I was driving with a friend Friday night. We passed a configuration of snow on top of a car. I don't know why, but this triggered something in me. I said to my friend, 'My God! Cookie is going to have a very serious accident!'

"The next day Cookie went out with some friends. I went to Mass, as I usually do on Saturday afternoon. The snow was now cleared off the streets and sidewalks and melting. While walking into the church, I fell and bruised my right hip and left knee. The very last prayer I said before leaving church was to ask God to help me accept whatever was in store for my daughter.

"Just as I opened the door upon my arrival home, the phone was ringing. It was the mother of the boy that was with my daughter. The hospital had called her. I knew it was about the accident.

"'Are they alive?' I asked.

"'I don't know,' she said.

"I soon learned that my daughter had been taken to emergency surgery. Among her other serious injuries, including a ruptured liver and a damaged heart, she had torn off her left kneecap and fractured her right hip—the same places I had bruised in church that day."

In this event the mother perceived that her daughter would be involved in a terrible accident. However, in many cases of telesomatic reactions, the person having the psi-triggered physical symptom is not aware that ESP has occurred. The parent or child does not link the physical symptom to the person injured until later. The psychic communication seems to take place on an unconscious level.

For example, Dr. Berthold Schwarz, expert on parent-child ESP, relates a curious story in his book *Psychic Nexus: Psychic Phenomena in Psychiatry and Everyday Life*. Out of the blue, a middle-aged mother began to think about having a problem with her leg at the same time her son was injured. The mother recalls:

"I saw stones and twigs while walking down the street and said to myself, 'Nellie, be careful.' I was trying to figure out why I was worrying about walking. I looked down on the path and wondered why my leg bothered me. I said to myself, 'What could happen if I hurt my leg and couldn't walk? This [fear] is silly.'

When I got home my [teenaged] son phoned to say that he had badly injured his leg on the glass coffee table and had to have it sutured."[18]

Another mother experienced pain at the same time her daughter sustained a severe injury. She was not aware that her own symptom had anything to do with her daughter until later. The case is on record at the American Society of Psychical Research in New York. The mother relates:

"My daughter was away at college . . . and I started to write to her as usual; when I had finished, my right hand started to burn so I couldn't hold the pen and the pain was terrific . . . Less than an hour later we received a telephone call from the college telling us our daughter's right hand had been severely burned in the laboratory with acid at the same time I felt the burn . . ."[19]

Though telesomatic reactions are frequently linked with major crises in the life of a loved one, they may also occur during less significant events. There seems to be no logical reason why some telesomatic reactions occur when they do.

Wisconsin mother Joicey Acker Hurth, who has had several dramatic psychic experiences involving her family, has experienced telesomatic reactions when her daughter has had problems such as a toothache or earache. She relates a very unusual psychic experience she had when her daughter was at school. The episode was investigated by Dr. Ian Stevenson of the University of Virginia School of Medicine.

In Mrs. Hurth's words:

"The children had left for school and the house was quiet. I was busy in the kitchen of my home at 273 East Portland Avenue, Cedarburg, Wisconsin, when suddenly I felt a sharp pain on the lower side of my right leg and buttocks. Although alone, I said aloud, 'Oh!' and rubbed the area where I had felt pain. I glanced at the clock but went on about my usual housekeeping business. When the children came home from school at lunchtime, I asked if anything unusual had happened about ten-thirty that morning. My daughter said, 'Yes, a boy ran into me with his bike. It hit me right on my backside and I hollered, "Oh!"' She rubbed the spot where she had been hit and the location was identical with the place on my own body where I had felt pain that morning."[20]

Dr. Schwarz had an experience that suggests he may have telepathically picked up his mother's anxiety about a trip to the dentist in the form of a most unpleasant physical symptom.

"Last night," he writes, "for the first time in years, I had a severe toothache. I told my wife about it at 7 A.M. and shortly afterward made an appointment with my dentist. At 10 A.M. my mother phoned to say she was having an extraction that day. Her last extraction was years ago. No one in my family knew about Mother's trouble. When I saw my dentist later that day there was neither discernible disease nor reason for my complaint. I have had no recurrence since then."[21]

Some people may be natural "telesomatic reactors." They seem to be more sensitive in terms of developing psi-caused physical symptoms than others.

One woman often has telesomatic experiences when her mother is ill. She developed a mild sore throat at the time her mother had bronchitis. One time she developed a cold with an accompanying feeling that something was wrong with her mother. Upon telephoning her, she discovered that her mother had bronchial pneumonia.

Some people may be especially prone to telesomatic reactions, perhaps as a result of some peculiarity in their energy field. Perhaps a "flaw" in the "aura," or energy field, surrounding the body, permits one person to be more open to registering the physical symptoms of another.

Psychiatrist and well-known psychical researcher Dr. Ian Stevenson points out that schizophrenic patients are particularly inclined to assume, and genuinely feel, the emotions and physical pains of persons around them.[22] But this is perhaps the result of identifying with the other person rather than a psychic phenomenon. Most persons who have a telesomatic response are perfectly normal.

The telesomatic response may be a highly modified form of what is commonly known as the "gut reaction." Though the information does not come through the known physical senses, the body seems somehow to "perceive" danger, a threat toward oneself. It may also "perceive" great stress or illness in a loved one.

Psychologist Frances Vaughn, author of *Awakening Intuition*, says that a physical response "may be experienced in a situation where there is no reason to think that anything unusual is going on. The kind of jungle awareness which enables primitive people to sense danger when there are no sensory cues to its presence is a highly developed form of intuition at a physical level."[23]

Many people seem to have this primitive extrasensory awareness on a physical level. Many seem to sense the presence of another before there are any sensory cues to the other's presence. Many have had the experience of "feeling" someone staring at them. Many have attempted with success the well-known ESP game of staring at the back of someone's head in a crowded auditorium until that person turns around. But how does this work?

That psi affects the body seems most peculiar since extrasensory perception, by its very name, is a form of perception beyond or outside of the physical senses. It is as if the human body, and perhaps all organic life for that matter, were somehow geared to pick up psi energy (if energy is an appropriate term).

Does ESP actually have a physical counterpart? This is the subject of some of the most fascinating studies in the history of psychical research. The studies began over a century ago.

In 1883 a man by the name of Malcolm Guthrie, of Liverpool, happened to read a magazine article about thought transference. Though he was quite skeptical about the phenomenon, he decided to make some trials. With remarkable results he first experimented with transferring ideas of colors, geometrical figures, and other objects, before attempting telepathic picture drawing.

He was later joined by Edmund Gurney and Frederic Myers of

the newly established Society for Psychical Research in an experiment to find out if taste—a distinct physiological reaction—could be transferred via ESP. Many parents may want to modify this experiment and try it with their children.

The experiment consisted of one person tasting a familiar substance and another trying to perceive through ESP the substance tasted. About twenty strong-tasting substances were chosen and enclosed in similar bottles kept carefully out of the subject's range of vision. The subjects were also blindfolded.

Of course, the correct taste was not transferred every time. There was much trial and error, but some of the successes were remarkable.

For example, in one trial the taster took some vinegar. The percipient responded with "a short and nasty taste."

Candied ginger was tasted. The percipient replied: "something sweet and hot."

In another trial, the taster took some alum. The percipient made this remark: "A taste of ink—or iron—or vinegar. I feel it on my lips—it is as if I had been eating alum."[24]

Nearly eighty years later, Czech neurophysiologist Stepan Figar, M.D., who had no interest in psychical research, made an amazing discovery about psi that suggests that ESP—even an ESP message of which one does not become aware—may be accompanied by a brief and subtle physiological response. He stumbled upon his discovery quite by accident. He had been working with a plethysmograph, an instrument used to measure and register variations in the size of an organ or limb and the amount of blood passing through it. He was doing research on the relationship between mental activity and vasoconstriction (the narrowing and contracting of blood vessels).

In his experiment, Dr. Figar would connect a person's hand to the plethysmograph and wait until he got a baseline reading. He would then give the person a card with instructions to complete a multiplication problem in his head. When the person did the mathematical problem, the plethysmograph registered a vasoconstriction or decreased blood volume in the hand.

On one occasion, Dr. Figar noticed an extraordinary phenomenon. He had connected a person's hand to the plethysmograph, got a baseline reading, and was thinking of getting the card with the mathematical problem, when the machine registered a vasoconstriction. The person appeared to be reacting to Dr. Figar's thoughts! This happened with several different persons.

Dr. Figar then tried a different experiment. He used two people whom he separated from one another by a curtain. Each was hooked up to a plethysmograph. Dr. Figar gave one person instructions to do a mathematical problem. In a significant number of instances, *both* persons experienced vasoconstriction. The most significant results were obtained between persons who had a mutual emotional relationship, such as mother and son.

Dr. Figar published this extraordinary phenomenon in the December 1959 edition of the British *Journal of the Society of Psychical Research.*[25] The publication of his experiment attracted the attention of electrochemist Douglas Dean, who was then doing research on the physiological dimensions of psi at the Parapsychology Foundation in New York. New research was soon underway. Dr. Dean began experiments in association with Dr. Karlis Osis, who was then with the Parapsychology Foundation and later Director of Research of the American Society for Psychical Research.

Dr. Dean repeated the plethysmograph experiments using husband and wife pairs. One person was hooked up to the machine in one room while his or her mate was wired to the machine in another. After some trial and error, Dr. Dean used names instead of mathematical problems. The subject (person receiving the message) and agent (person transmitting the message) each provided five names with which they were familiar. Added to these were five additional names from the telephone book, making a total of fifteen names. The fifteen names were written on cards handed to the agent in a random order. In a surprising number of cases, when the agent came to one of the familiar names, the subject experienced a vasoconstriction. Oddly, the physiological response was registered but the name the agent was concentrating on did not flash into the subject's mind. Nor did the subject realize ESP had occurred.

The plethysmograph experiments seem to establish two facts about psi: First, ESP can elicit a physiological response. The physiological response may be mediated by way of electrical changes in the brain. According to some Russian parapsychologists, signals traveling the psi field can produce electromagnetic changes and induce corresponding electrical changes in the percipient's brain by a process analogous to electromagnetic induction.[26] Of course, this is all quite hypothetical.

Second, ESP can affect a person without that person realizing it. One may experience a brief physiological response to a psi stimulus without being aware that extrasensory communication has occurred.

This information triggered the birth of a Psi Communications Center at Newark College of Engineering (NCE), where Dr. Dean did further research on the physiological response to psi.

The fact that ESP may have a physical counterpart may have far-reaching implications. Future research could very well lead to a communication system based on telepathy. As described in *Executive ESP*: "In the NCE telepathic communications system, psi would be coded. The sender concentrates on a name that has an emotional charge for the receiver. The receiver, hooked to the plethysmograph, registers a change in blood volume in the finger. This stands for a dot in the Morse Code. A dash is signified when nothing is sent for a specific time. In this way, a message is built up. Either a dot or a dash is sent every minute." The process is slow. A single dot or dash would be sent every minute or so. However, Dr. Dean theorizes that the method may be improved by somehow connecting directly into the sympathetic nervous system.[27]

This form of communication could span continents, work from submarines, even outer space. Moreover, as Dr. Dean pointed out when he spoke at the Canaveral Council of Technical Societies at the First Space Conference in 1964, communication based on telepathy would probably be faster than radio communication.

Oddly, the research at Newark College of Engineering has been discontinued. This, according to Dr. Dean, is the result of psi's most potent enemy: emotional prejudice.

Perhaps further research on psi-mediated responses would shed light on one of the least understood phenomena occurring in the parent-child relationship: ESP of the body. There is little doubt that the physiological response Dr. Dean recorded on the plethysmograph is kin to the parent-child telesomatic symptom. Both are physiological responses to a psi stimulus. Striking cases of psychically perceived bodily symptoms may be just one aspect of a *telesomatic response syndrome* common in the parent-child relationship.

The well-documented couvade syndrome, the expectant father's experience of prenatal symptoms, is another. The father feels dizzy, nauseous, has a backache, or experiences inexplicable weight gain, while his mate is pregnant (See examples in chapter 3). The expectant father is almost always unaware that his symptoms have anything to do with the pregnancy, as are many who experience psychic body symptoms at the time of an accident or illness in a loved one. The experiences of many expectant fathers, grandmothers, and midwives who have abdominal pains at the time a mother is giving birth fall into the same category.

The experience of many breast-feeding mothers, discussed in chapter 5, may also be a part of this telesomatic response syndrome. Some mothers report letting down their milk at the moment the baby wakes and cries for a feeding, even though they may be many miles from the child.

Sleep synchronization between mother and infant may be another form of the telesomatic response syndrome. The infant's REM (rapid eye movement) patterns may affect the mother's, or vice versa. The mother's waking just before her baby, as is often reported, may be a physical reaction to ESP.

Are we to conclude that a *telesomatic response syndrome* is part and parcel of the parent-child relationship? If sharing thoughts between parent and offspring is an enigma, an ESP-caused body response is doubly a mystery. How can we explain such ESP of the body?

The expectant father's experience of nausea and other prenatal symptoms may sometimes be anxiety-caused, and may have nothing to do with psi. Perhaps in the not-too-distant future, science may discover that whatever hormonal changes, if any, accompany expectant fatherhood predispose the father to prenatal symptoms.

But what about a mother's headache when her son is experiencing a brain hemorrhage fifteen hundred miles away? Or a mother's experience of discomfort in her own body when her daughter is injured in a car accident? A son having a toothache while his mother is at the dentist's office having an extraction? We can't blame these phenomena on hormones.

If such things happened once or twice, we could dismiss them as freaks of nature, impossible coincidences, but hundreds of people have experienced telesomatic responses. Does psi somehow influence the body directly? Does the body act as some sort of biological radio receiver picking up psi impressions even when they are transmitted from thousands of miles away, or does psi influence the body through the mind?

We know the mind can influence the body. Anxiety can cause physical discomfort. An emotional crisis can trigger a stomachache. This is known as a psychosomatic symptom (psycho referring to the mind and somatic to the body). The telesomatic response may be a *parapsychosomatic* symptom. It probably develops below the threshold of awareness. An extrasensory message somehow reaches the unconscious mind. Rather than surface as a flash of ESP or an uneasy feeling, psi triggers a symptom in the body—in many cases without the parent or child becoming aware that the other is ill or in danger. Whatever the explanation, the telesomatic response suggests that parent and child may communicate psychically when they are least aware of it.

7

Psychic Dreaming

Everyone knows that dreams are woven from the elements of our mind, our unconscious, past experiences, memories, our wishes, our fears. However, in dreams we may also pick up elements from the minds of others, and we may even glimpse scenes that have not yet occurred.

Most spontaneous psychic phenomena take place during sleep. In a vast survey of ESP cases in four countries, it was found that psychic dreams accounted for two-thirds (64.6 percent) of over 7,000 American cases, about two-thirds (63 percent) of 1,000 German cases, more than half (54.5 percent) of 900 Indian cases, and over one-third (37 percent) of 300 British cases.[1]

Sleep may open a door to extrasensory communication between parent and offspring. Dr. Joost A. M. Meerloo, psychiatrist and former associate professor of psychiatry at the New York School of Psychiatry, suggests that sleep may fortify the mutual telepathic relationship between mother and child.[2]

A sudden hunch to check on a child who is in danger, a shooting pain in a mother's arm at the moment her son falls on the ice and breaks his arm and the urge to write a daughter a letter at the very minute she is writing home, all share a common ground. They all seem to reach us via the unconscious mind. Like psi, dreaming also is an unconscious process. We may therefore be closer to our extrasensory faculties during sleep than in ordinary waking life. Dreams may create the ideal conditions for telepathy, clairvoyance, and precognition. In fact, according to many parapsychologists, dreaming is the ultimate psi-conducive state.

"Mothers and fathers are more psychically in tune with the child at night," says Dr. William Emerson, a psychotherapist with a special interest in parent-child ESP. He calls this nighttime psychic attunement "nocturnal synchronism." When nocturnal synchronism occurs, communication may take place in two directions: from the parent to the child and from the child to the parent.

Sometimes both parent and child dream similar dreams at more or less the same time. Dr. Emerson recalls a striking incident when this occurred with his twenty-two-month-old son Jamie. At the time Jamie was sleeping in another room some fifty feet away. The door to his parents' room was closed.

Dr. Emerson dreamed that Jamie was walking along the edge of a cliff and saw some bears. A baby bear fell over the cliff edge and tumbled down the ravine. Jamie wanted to save the baby bear and was close to tumbling over the edge himself. Terrified that he would hurt himself, his father yelled, "Jamie! Stop!" Then the mother bear jumped over the edge to save her baby. She was trapped on a ledge. The father bear started crawling down to help. Jamie is going to be really scared, thought Dr. Emerson.

He then woke up with the dream still fresh in his mind and thought, Jamie is going to be really frightened!

Within seconds Jamie shrieked. Dr. Emerson went into his room and picked him up. "What happened?" he asked. His child answered: "Bears fall down. Jamie scared!"

"I don't consider myself a psychic," says Dr. Emerson, "but I think every parent has psychic experiences with his child now and then."

He relates another experience that occurred when his child was having a nightmare:

"I woke up in the middle of the night and thought, Jamie is having a bad dream. I listened for a moment but couldn't hear anything. So I got out of bed, opened the door, and walked softly toward his room. As I neared his room I heard him breathing fast. Suddenly he woke up screaming."

Psychiatrist Dr. Berthold Schwarz, well-known expert on parent-child ESP, has also found that a child's fears and even nightmares are transmitted telepathically to a parent or vice versa. He was once awakened from a sound sleep at 2:30 A.M. His daughter Lisa had German measles. Early in the illness she had had a nightmare about trees with the sound of wind in them. "However, on this particular night," recalls Dr. Schwarz, "I suddenly woke up and saw a flash of a face of satanic evilness. Simultaneously with this Lisa screamed, 'I hear it again. I saw the face of a man!'"[3]

"During sleep, while falling asleep, or when awakening, the state of consciousness is attuned to telepathy," says Dr. Schwarz. He says that at these seemingly inert times, the child is quite psychically sensitive. If the parent has an anxiety-provoking experience while awake or asleep, it may be transmitted telepathically to the sleeping child. This may influence the child's dream, perhaps even cause a nightmare. Dr. Schwarz suggests that the child may also acquire values of protective significance and useful fears while sleeping or on the border between sleep and waking.[4]

He has noticed that dreams inspired by the thoughts of another are common in relationships when one person is acting in loco parentis, that is, in the place of a parent, as in the psychiatrist-patient (or psychotherapist-patient) relationship.

Many psychiatrists who have studied the subject with an open mind agree. According to Jungian psychoanalyst Dr. James A. Hall, who practices in New York City, "In clinical situations, synchronicity often appears to occur in dreams. For instance, a dream containing a dramatic motif may not be meaningful to the dreamer, but has a clear, relevant and dramatic association in the mind of the analyst. At times it seems as if the dream-making ability of the patient's unconscious has used material from the unconscious mind of the analyst."[5]

Dr. Montague Ullman, a psychiatrist and the director of the Community Mental Health Center at Maimonides Medical Center, has had patients report dreams that seem to contain elements picked right out of his mind. One case, which he refers to as the "alcoholic cat episode," is well-known in parapsychological circles. Dr. Ullman had been interested in psychical research when he was in college. This episode was the first in a series of telepathic experiences that reactivated his interest.

On the evening of February 24, 1950, he attended a meeting about animal neurosis at the New York Academy of Medicine. A film was shown about experiments conditioning cats to develop a preference for alcohol. The "alcoholic" cats preferred milk mixed with alcohol to plain milk. A few days after he attended the meeting, one of his patients reported two dreams occurring on the same night. In one, there was a bottle containing part alcohol and part cream. In the other, the patient had a small leopard. Dr. Ullman remarks, "One might speculate that after a few of those drinks the alcoholic cat might feel like a 'small leopard.'"[6] The elements in this dream are so unusual that they were very probably influenced by Dr. Ullman's experience.

This dream, along with other similar dreams, inspired Dr. Ullman to embark on a long-term ESP dream research project, which soon led to his launching the world's most famous psychic dream study—and one of the only parapsychological studies to bring the psychic dream into the laboratory.

He organized a dream laboratory at Maimonides Medical Center. There he was soon joined in his research by another of the nation's most distinguished parapsychologists, Stanley Krippner, now of Saybrook Institute in San Francisco.

In the Maimonides experiments, one person (the agent) would concentrate on something and try to influence the dreams of another person (the subject). The agent was given a sealed envelope randomly chosen from a batch of similar envelopes. Each contained a copy of a work of art selected for its emotional intensity, vividness, color, and simplicity. The agent agreed to concentrate on the picture and attempt to send a message to a sleeping subject in another room.

The agent spent the night in a room thirty-two feet away from the dreamer's room. In later studies, the agent's room was on the other side of the building ninety-eight feet away, and in still later experiments, in a different building altogether.

The subject, who slept in an isolated room, was hooked up to an electroencephalograph (EEG) throughout the night, and the EEG tracings were monitored in a room nearby. As soon as rapid eye movement (REM) activity was observed indicating dreaming, an experimenter pressed a buzzer signaling the agent, who would then concentrate on the picture. Shortly afterward, the dreamer was awakened and asked about his or her dream.

The results of this experiment are published in many journals and in the book *Dream Telepathy* by Montague Ullman, Stanley Krippner, and Alan Vaughan, and are nothing less than astounding.

In one instance the painting was Paul Cézanne's *Trees and Houses* depicting a desolate house on a hill covered by stark, barren trees. The dreamer, a clinical psychologist, reported dreaming "something about a house" in one dream. Of another dream that night he remarked: "It's been a very poor yield," meaning he didn't think he had picked up the message telepathically; then added, "It may be a great yield if there's a target picture in there that's a lonely shack sitting on a hillside."[7]

In another instance Millar Sheets's *Mystic Night* was used. This painting portrays a nighttime ritual in a wooded area surrounded by mountains. The dreamer, another clinical psychologist, reported dreaming "being with a group of people . . . participating in something." Of another dream, she recalled "driving in the country . . . looking . . . at a lot of mountains and trees. When discussing her postsleep associations she mentioned, "I can almost see it as some sort of tribal ritual in the jungle."[8]

Sol Feldstein, a doctoral student at the City University of New York, who had been working on the dream project with Dr. Ullman, suggested an innovation. He drew the picture or acted out a scene from it in an attempt to immerse himself in the theme and thereby send a more vivid telepathic message. Props were used in some of the experiments.

For example, on one occasion with Sol Feldstein acting as agent and Dr. William Erwin as subject, the picture randomly selected was *Downpour at Shono* by Hiroshige, depicting a Japanese man with an umbrella in a driving rain. The prop accompanying the picture was a toy Japanese umbrella with the instructions: TAKE A SHOWER.

The event is captured in *Dream Telepathy.* "Feldstein popped into the shower adjoining his agent's room several times that night, glad that there was no one around to see him with his toy umbrella.

"That night Erwin dreamed 'something about an Oriental man who was ill . . .' In other dreams that night he saw rain, fountains, and guessed that the picture had something to do with fountains or water."[9]

(Parents may want to try this sort of dream experiment with their children. This is discussed in chapter 10.)

Drs. Ullman and Krippner found that men were better percipients than women. They think this is perhaps because women may be more nervous than men about sleeping in a strange bed and having male experimenters.

By contrast, in most collections of spontaneous ESP dreams, women dreamers far outnumber men. Drs. Ullman and Krippner think that this may be the result of our cultural climate in which women are allowed to talk about their irrational ESP experiences and men look down on ESP. In *Dream Telepathy* they point out, "Given an open cultural attitude toward ESP, the sexes would seem to have equal potential at ESP dreaming."[10] This is probably true of all psychic phenomena.

Agent and subject made a deliberate effort to communicate telepathically in the Maimonides experiments. However, in most parent-child psychic dreams, no effort is made to receive or send a message. It just happens spontaneously. Like waking ESP experiences, nocturnal psychic phenomena often involve crisis situations: accidents, injuries, illness, and death.

Denise Hamilton reports a horrible incident in the Los Angeles Times, November 21, 1987:

"Three University of California, Santa Barbara, students were killed and a fourth was missing . . . after their car plunged off California 1 into the Pacific Ocean south of Point Mugu . . . Betty Finkel, mother of the missing young woman, said she is convinced that her daughter perished with the others because of an unsettling nightmare that awakened her early Thursday. A fisherman discovered their car at 8:40 Thursday morning.

"'I know she's gone. I'm sure it happened at 2 A.M. I woke up suddenly and I really felt like I was drowning. I sat up in bed and I couldn't breathe,' Betty Finkel recounted."

This dream was so vivid that the mother herself felt as if she were drowning. Such vivid impressions are not uncommon in psychic dreams or waking telepathic experiences. During the death of a loved one, the percipient frequently feels as if he or she were dying.

Phantasms of the Living, a vast collection of spontaneous ESP cases gathered by the Society of Psychical Research (SPR), includes one hundred and forty-nine cases of psychic dreams. Over half of these deal with death.

The following tragic dream, reported by Mrs. Morris Griffith, a mother living in North Wales, was investigated by the SPR and included in *Phantasms of the Living.*

"On the night of Saturday, the 11th of March, 1871, I awoke in much alarm, having seen my eldest son, then at St. Paul de Loanda on the southwest coast of Africa, looking dreadfully ill and emaciated, and I heard his voice distinctly calling to me. I was so disturbed I could not sleep again, but every time I closed my eyes the appearance recurred, and his voice sounded distinctly, calling me 'Momma.' I felt greatly depressed all through the next day, which was Sunday, but I did not mention it to my husband, as he was an invalid, and I feared to disturb him." Mrs. Griffith says that Mr. Griffith also suffered from intense low spirits all day and that they were both unable to eat dinner.

"The next day a letter arrived containing some photos of my son, saying he had had a fever, but it was better and hoped immediately to leave for a much more healthy station, and written in good spirits. We heard no more till the 9th of May, when a letter arrived with the news of our son's death from a fresh attack of fever, on the night of the 11th of March, and adding that just before his death he kept calling repeatedly for me." Mrs. Griffith never had another psychic dream before or after this.[11]

Most of the dramatic psychic dreams in *Phantasms of the Living* are reported by people like Mrs. Griffith, people with no special psychic talents, many of whom have never had another psychic experience in their lives.

An ESP dream may reveal information about a crisis which is not necessarily tragic. Yet the vivid nightmare may cause the dreamer to leap to erroneous conclusions. World renowned psychic Dr. Alex Tanous, who has used his psychic abilities to make psychic diagnoses and help police solve crimes, relates the story of a mother's dramatic dream about her son. The mother dreamed that her son's car was speeding toward another car. They were about to have a head-on collision. She woke in terror just as the two cars were ready to collide. She was convinced that her son had been in a terrible accident.

Later she learned that her son was driving on the highway at the time of her dream. The scene occurred as the mother dreamed it. Her son's car sped toward a head-on collision with another car, but he turned away just before colliding with the other car, perhaps at the very instant his mother woke in terror.

Whether or not they occurred at the same instant, the mother's experience coincided with her son's momentary terror. She actually perceived a precise scene from the crisis situation. She later jumped to the seemingly obvious conclusion, quite naturally, upon awakening. However, a person may overdramatize a psychically perceived crisis during the actual dream.

One seventeen-year-old girl had a chilling experience which caused her mother to have a telepathic nightmare. The daughter was living on the Lower East Side in New York City in a furnished room in a run-down building where there had been recent burglaries and other crimes. At 2 A.M. she was up studying for an anthropology final. All of a sudden the door to the room slowly started to open. She was gripped with terror. Slamming the door as quickly as she could, she cried out in a voice as tough as she could make it sound, "Get away from my door!"

Shuffling sounds came from the corridor. Someone was out there. There was no phone. She opened the window and cried for help but no one responded. The shuffling continued. In terror, she stood in the room with a knife in her hand for a full five hours. She didn't feel safe until morning came and other people were up and about and on their way to work. She went out and phoned her parents, who were living in Brooklyn, to say she was coming home.

Her mother said, "Yes, I know. I had a dream at 2:00 A.M. that you were getting murdered. I woke up screaming."

Her mother had never had a dream like this before. There is little doubt that the dream was triggered by her daughter's all-night terror which began at 2:00 A.M. However, apparently her subconscious mind overdramatized the ESP message.

Louisa Rhine reports a similar experience. While babysitting in an upper duplex apartment one night, a girl in Ohio had dozed off. She was awakened by the sound of a drunk stumbling and cursing up the stairs toward her door. She sat upright and put both hands up to her mouth. "Mother, oh Mother," she said.

Then she realized the person on the other side of the door was going to another apartment. Soon afterwards her mother called her from the lower door. She went down and let her in. Her mother said she had been dozing by the fire (where she lived three blocks away) when she was awakened to see her daughter before her, hands to her mouth, saying "Mother, oh Mother."[12]

Though telepathically perceived information is sometimes presented accurately in dreams, distortion is also common. A father reported the following dream in a letter to Sigmund Freud. If a psychic message is conveyed, it was quite distorted. The father writes: "During the night of November 16–17, I dreamt, with a vividness and clearness I have never before experienced, that my wife had given birth to twins . . ."

On November 18 the father received a telegram from his son-in-law informing him that his daughter had given birth to twins, a boy and a girl. The birth took place four weeks earlier than was expected, on the very night the father had the dream.[13]

Later he says: "My daughter is much attached to me and was most certainly thinking of me during the labor." However, in the dream the father's wife, not his daughter, gave birth to twins. Does this rule out the possibility of ESP, or did telepathy influence the dream content? If so, was the telepathic message combined with a repressed wish lurking in the dreamer's conscious, a typically Freudian wish, to substitute his daughter for his wife?

Freud leaves it up in the air "whether the dream in question is a telepathic fact or a particularly subtle achievement on the part of the dreamer's unconscious or whether it is simply to be taken as a striking coincidence."[14]

But he does say that if we assume telepathy can influence a dream, then that telepathic material is "treated as a portion of the material that goes to the formation of a dream, like any other external or internal stimulus."[15] ESP messages are subject to the same distortion and change as a sound in the street or a sensation in one's own body.

In another dream, a mother psychically perceived a crisis involving her son, yet the dream distorted the outcome. The experience was investigated by the Society of Psychical Research in London and published in *Phantasms of the Living*.

The mother was living in India as a missionary when she woke up crying bitterly from a morbid dream about her son Harry, who was living in England with her sister. "I dreamed that the sister (who acted as guardian to our boys in our absence) was reading to me a letter giving a detailed account of how our Harry died of choking while eating his dinner one day at school."

Several weeks later the mother did receive a letter from her sister, but it contained no mention of the incident in the dream. However, in another two weeks she received an additional letter in which her sister apologized for not informing her that Harry had suffered a narrow escape from death. A piece of meat had passed down his throat and he had choked. His head fell on the person supporting him and he was thought dead. However, he revived shortly afterward.[16]

Of course a dream can appear to be an extrasensory experience and actually be the result of subliminal impressions, that is, information perceived below the threshold of awareness. A mother dreams something is wrong with her child. She wakes to find that her child has fallen out of bed. More probably than not, she heard the child fall in her sleep.

Dr. Tanous tells the story of a dream that on first sight appears to be an ESP experience. Both a mother and her daughter dreamed of a fire at approximately the same time. The child woke up screaming that there was a fire. Neither of them could smell smoke, but to be safe, they made a search. Sure enough, they found a fire burning downstairs.

More likely than not, this dream is the result of a subliminal impression perceived by mother, her daughter, or both. Where there's fire, there's smoke, and where there is smoke, someone sleeping is bound to smell it even if after waking she is unaware of smelling smoke.

It is no wonder that mother and daughter would share a similar dream if they both experience the same external stimulus. It is like two or more people dreaming of a car honking outside when there really is a car honking. This doesn't rule out the possibility of ESP. It simply makes ESP impossible to verify.

It is quite another matter when one dreams accurately about a fire thousands of miles away. This is what happened to Douglas Sladen of Melbourne, Australia, whose story was investigated and confirmed by the Society for Psychical Research.

On December 22, he dreamed that the kitchen in his father's house in London was on fire and awoke from the dream to see that it was 1 A.M. Several weeks later, he received a letter from his father dated December 22, informing him that a fire had occurred.

The dream did not occur at the time of the fire but rather when the father was writing the letter. The time in Melbourne is nine and a half hours ahead of British time. The father was writing the letter at 3:30 P.M., which translated into 1 A.M. in Melbourne—the time of the dream.[17]

In another dramatic case, a woman in Wyoming not only dreamed accurately of a distant fire but actually woke up smelling smoke! Her dream may very well have been lifesaving. David Graham tells the story in his book, *Dream Your Way to Happiness and Awareness.*

For the winter, Mrs. G. D. had rented a small house in town close to her place of employment while her husband and two sons stayed at their ranch.

At 3 A.M. on a January morning, she awakened with the acrid odor of burning cloth offending her nostrils. Terrified by the thought that her house might be on fire, she got out of bed and checked the small home thoroughly. Although she found no fire in the house that she was renting, the feeling of danger persisted. She concluded that the fire must be in the home in which her husband and sons lay sleeping.

Mrs. G. D. called the ranch but no one answered. She insisted that the operator keep trying. At last she heard the click of the receiver being lifted, and nearly simultaneously with his hello, she heard her older son coughing.

"Are you all right, Billie?" she shouted into the receiver.

"Mom! Mom! The house is full of smoke!"

She told her son to wake his father and brother, to find out where the smoke was coming from, put the fire out, and then call her back.

Thirty minutes later, her husband called. The boys had put their gloves on the woodbox near the stove. Apparently a spark had ignited them. The fire was put out just as the wood in the box was beginning to burn.[18]

How could a mother smell smoke when she was nowhere near the fire? Did one of her sons or her husband smell smoke while sleeping and, though remaining asleep himself, telepathically communicate the sensation to her, or, even more remarkable, did she perceive the fire clairvoyantly? In either case, her unusual experience is apparently a form of *telesomatic response*: physiological response to psi common in the parent-child relationship (discussed in chapter 6). In this form of telesomatic response, the sleeping person has a physical sensation without any immediate cause.

Donna Ray, a midwife in Center Harbor, New Hampshire, woke in the middle of the night with a possible telesomatic response, while at the same time thinking strongly of her four-year-old daughter Jenny. "I was extremely cold," she recalls. "This didn't make any sense. It was warm in the house and I was well covered. I had an overwhelming urge to get up and check on Jenny. I don't usually get out of bed at night to check on my children, but this time I felt I had to. I didn't understand why at the time. Then, when I went into Jenny's room, I was surprised to find her lying on the floor. She had fallen out of bed, and her body felt icy cold to the point where it frightened me. I rubbed her arms and legs to warm her up, put her back to bed and covered her."

Electrochemist Douglas Dean conducted an unusual experiment focusing on a psi-mediated physiological response during dreaming. He showed that telepathy could influence the frequency of a dreamer's eye movements.

Dr. Dean has done research on the physiological correlates of psi at the Parapsychology Foundation in New York and later at the Newark College of Engineering. In a previous study (discussed in chapter 6) he showed that an ESP message transmitted by one person could affect the blood volume in the hand of another located in a separate room. He had therefore linked psi to a physical response.

In his dream experiment, he arranged for a person one hundred feet away to try to influence the frequency of a sleeping person's eye movements for one minute periods. The sleeping person was wired to an electroencephalograph (EEG) to record the frequency of eye movements. The agent (person trying to influence the dreamer) looked at a picture of horizontal movement for one minute, followed by a blank picture for one minute, continuing in random order until the dreamer's body movements indicated the end of dreaming. The EEG records were then scanned for eye movements. Four subjects out of four showed significantly more eye movements during the time when the agent looked at the horizontal pictures than when he looked at blanks.[19] This suggests that psi can cause a physiological reaction during dreaming as well as in waking life.

This means that the familiar advice about pinching yourself to see if you are dreaming may not always apply. The idea is that the sensation you dream about is all in the imagination. However, since sensory experiences such as the smell of smoke or the feeling of cold appear to be capable of psychic transmission from offspring to parent, dreams may be more real than we previously imagined. At least psychic dreams may be.

While on the one hand, psychic dreams can bring about real physical sensations, on the other, a psychic dream can trigger the most nonphysical experience of all—an out-of-body experience (OBE).

Stephen Gaskin, founder of The Farm, a world-renowned spiritual community in Summertown, Tennessee, relates a rather odd apparent OBE that occurred one night while he was sleeping. He felt something was wrong with one of his children. "I went to check on her," he recalls. "She was upset. When I bent to pick her up, I had no arms! My consciousness was there but my body wasn't. I went back down the hallway and saw my body sleeping. I couldn't wake up my body at first. I searched around my body for something to respond. I wiggled my foot and that woke me up. I went back down the hallway. My daughter was still upset. I picked her up and comforted her."

It is sometimes difficult to know whether one is having an out-of-body experience or dreaming. Popular parapsychological writer Susy Smith reports a mother's extraordinary experience that may have been a dream or an OBE:

On February 15, 1963, Polly's son became ill while on vacation in Florida. Five days later Polly lay in bed praying for her son's recovery. Suddenly she saw herself outside her body and floating, "clutching in her hand a bottle of St. Ann's oil which had been blessed . . . Soon she was standing in the doorway of her son's room, and she went over to his bed. As she caressed him and kissed his feverish face, he opened his eyes and said, 'Mom.'

"'Yes, son, I've come to help you,' answered Polly. Then she dipped her thumb into the holy oil and annointed him and made the sign of the cross. He opened his eyes again and smiled. She told him, 'You'll be all right now. The doctors will be amazed when they come tomorrow. You'll be able to leave the hospital by either Tuesday or Wednesday.'"

Waking up in her own bed, Polly told her husband that she felt their son would recover. And, in fact, he did. He left the hospital on Tuesday, recovered. Later he told her, "I got up feeling wonderful after the morning that I dreamed you were there—or were you really there?'"[20]

Sara Ani of Baltimore, Maryland, reports a remarkably moving dream which occurred a few months after a psychic premonition of her mother's death. It is uncertain whether the dream is a genuine psychic experience or a deeply emotional experience created by her own unconscious during a time of great stress:

"I was married in August 1981 in California, and moved to

Baltimore a few days after my wedding. In November 1981 my mother came to visit us. After a two week stay, I drove her to the airport. I was in a hurry as I was afraid I would be late for my college class. I left her at the waiting area for her flight, hurried down the hall, down the escalator, and out the door to the parking lot. Outside, I was suddenly struck by an intense reaction like a bolt of lightning. I was keenly aware that I would never see my mother alive again.

"With tears pouring down my face, I raced back inside the airport and up the escalator. At the top of the escalator stood my mother. Her deep blue eyes met mine in a gaze that locked all eternity into that one moment. She said, 'I knew you would come back.'

"We gazed at each other without saying anything, and yet we both knew without words each other's thoughts. I never saw my mother again. She died five months later in April 1982.

"When she died I was five months pregnant with my first baby. The pain of losing my mother was so intense it was unbearable. I couldn't face her death during a time when I was embarking on the journey of becoming a mother myself. How I longed for her to be in the labor room with me during my journey to motherhood. I was frantic. My uterus began contracting so much that the doctor prescribed muscle relaxants so I wouldn't go into premature labor. All I could think of was being with my mother.

"Then one night I had a dream, a dream so real, so vivid, I was sure it was happening in real waking life. I dreamed it was the Sabbath day and I was walking to the synagogue when I was hit by a car. I heard the screams, saw people running and crowding around me, an ambulance arrived and paramedics worked on me, my husband at my side. I saw it all because I had left my body and was up in the air looking down at the scene with a curious detached air as the paramedics worked on my body. Suddenly I felt relieved, flooded with joy. I died and could now go and be with my mother.

"I saw a blinding light and my mother in the center. I ran to her with arms outstretched crying joyfully, 'Mommy!' But she put out her hand. She would not let me touch her. She said, 'You don't belong here yet.' She told me to look down at the accident scene, to look at my husband who was then cuddling me in his arms, his face wet with tears.

"She said, 'Look again, the baby needs you too. The baby can't go on without you.' I looked and saw my pregnant belly swelling gently under my dress. I returned to my body as the paramedic revived me. My mother had come and given me a message. My life had to go on. She was healing my grief."

Whether or not the dream was a genuine psychic experience, Ms. Ani says, "It was a major turning point for me which began the process of healing."

Eileen Garrett, pioneer in the field of psychical research and founder of the Parapsychology Foundation in New York, recalls a psychic experience concerning her daughter that involved both a waking and a dreaming perception.

"In London one night I had gone to bed with a strange feeling that all was not well with my daughter, who was then away at school. It was a Sunday evening, and so I discounted the experience when I recalled that she was probably writing her usual weekly letter, believing that I had "caught" her thoughts. I awoke, however, at two o'clock in the morning with the impression that she was in the house, and had just been at my side talking to me. In the dream she had said, 'I have not written you, dear, as my chest hurt. Tonight I am coughing, and have a fever. When the principal found that I hadn't written, she was very cross, and called me neglectful and undutiful; but now she has been in my room and understands that I am not well.'

"Although I was still uncertain of the validity of this communication, I decided to write down what she had said. The next morning I again felt disturbed, since no letter had arrived. Remembering my dream, I telegraphed the headmistress to inquire if all were well. In her reply she stated that my daughter was in bed with a heavy chest cold, and then continued, half-apologetically, to blame what she termed the child's 'sullen behavior' in refusing to write to me, on the illness."[21]

Most psychic dreams involving a crisis are dramatic and highly emotional in content. They tend therefore to stick out in the dreamer's mind. However, this does not mean that all psychic dreams convey momentous information. Trivial everyday events may find their way into telepathic dreams. During her early childhood, Mary Craig Sinclair had numerous psychic experiences involving her mother. As her husband, well-known writer Upton Sinclair, describes it, "Her mother would say to a little Negro servant, 'Go and find Miss Mary Craig,' but before the boy could start, Craig would know that her mother wanted her and would be on the way."

On one occasion she had an odd dream. "Craig dreamed there was a needle in her bed," writes Upton Sinclair, "and woke up and looked for it in vain. In the morning she told her mother, who slept in another room. The mother said, 'How strange! I dreamed the same thing, and I woke up and really found one!'"[22]

Ann, a mother in Killingly, Connecticut, recalls an astounding and rather amusing experience involving her two-year-old son. She woke suddenly from a sound sleep at about the same time her son was preparing to fall out of bed! "Out of the clear blue sky, I dashed from my bed through the living room to my son's bedroom. I dove to the floor like a baseball player sliding into a home run and caught my son in midair just before he hit the floor!" She put her son, who did not wake up, back to bed. She has no recollection of a dream, or anything for that matter, that might have prompted her sudden action. "I thought it was so unreal," says Ann, "I didn't want to tell anyone about it for years!"

The only other possibly psychic experiences she can remember involved driving. One time while driving to her friend's home, she came to a sudden stop in the middle of the road. At just that instant, a car came speeding out of the side street and drove directly into the woods! She did not see the car before she stopped. Her sister, who had been in the car with her, was flabbergasted. "How did you know that car was coming?" she asked. Ann doesn't know the answer.

DREAMS OF THINGS TO COME

Sigmund Freud said that in every dream one can find a point of contact with the previous day. All dreams incorporate material from daily life—people, places, and things from the past. Elements from the previous day that find their way into a dream are referred to as day residue. The psychic dreams of parents, however, may also include future day residue—elements from days that have not yet occurred.

Dreams that accurately predict or foreshadow a future event are called precognitive. From ancient times people have studied and paid serious attention to precognitive dreams. Momentous decisions have been made, the fate of nations decided, on the strength of a dream. However, precognitive dreams are not limited to prophets and sages. Parents throughout the world have reported such dreams.

Athena Drewes, a child psychotherapist in Washingtonville, New York, who has done extensive research on ESP in children, had a dramatic precognitive dream about a car crash involving her family when she was about ten years old.

"I was the observer watching it all happen," she recalls. "I watched the crash take place. The scene then shifted to me observing myself and my brother sitting in wheelchairs, not hurt, at the hospital. I watched my mother being wheeled in on a flat stretcher. It was a type of stretcher I had never before seen or even knew existed. I knew my mother was injured, but my brother and I were not."

A week after this dream, the scene occurred in real life precisely as Ms. Drewes had dreamt it.

This had a profound effect on her. She wondered how dreams

could tell us about the future. She began to think that her anger at the time may have caused the accident and she felt guilty about this. Unanswered questions led her on a quest to learn more. She first got involved in psychology. Then when she was about nineteen, she became a research assistant at the Maimonides Dream Laboratory, where three of the top parapsychologists in the country—Stanley Krippner, Montague Ullman, and Charles Honorton—were doing their history-making research on dream telepathy. There, at Maimonides, she learned that psychic dreams were normal.

Since that dramatic precognitive dream, she has had many other psychic experiences involving her family. When she was pregnant with her first child, she dreamed of pink presents that kept getting covered over with blue wrapping paper. "I knew I was going to have a boy, as much as I wanted to have a girl," she says.

Many people who readily accept the reality of telepathy and clairvoyance balk at the idea of precognition, and for good reason. It upsets our notion of the reality of time. How can one perceive what is going to happen before it happens? Not all parapsychologists believe that true precognition exists. Another interpretation of precognitive dreams has been offered. The dreamer supposedly uses ESP to scan the possibilities and chooses the most likely. However, it is difficult to imagine how "scanning the possibilities" could give a little girl a dream of a type of stretcher she had never before seen.

Whatever the explanation, precognitive dreams, like other dramatic psychic experiences, often involve crises. Psychiatrist Dr. Jan Ehrenwald records a tragic event that occurred while Charlotte, the daughter of a friend and classmate of his, was vacationing in Puerto Rico. Charlotte recalls: "I woke up in the middle of the night in a sweat, full of anxiety. I dreamed that Daddy was stricken with a brain hemorrhage."

The following day, while opening the refrigerator to help himself to a drink, her father collapsed on the floor. It is not certain whether he died of a brain hemorrhage or an acute coronary attack.[23]

Maria Cotty, a registered nurse practicing in Whitestone, New York, recalls the following crushingly tragic dream: "I awoke from the nightmare gasping, sweating, paralyzed with fear and grief. I knew that it was more than just a bad dream; it was a scene from the future.

"The dream occurred on a January night in 1973. After a normal day with the kids, April, six years old, and Georgie, almost two years old, I tucked them in and went to bed. I fell asleep peacefully and at some point during the night the horror began. I was walking in a very dimly lit room holding one of my children by the hand. We walked past rows of chairs occupied by people I knew, family and friends. As we reached the front of the room, there was a small coffin and when I looked into it I realized that I was at the wake of one of my children. Because the room was too dark, I couldn't tell which one it was. I was still holding the hand of one of them and the other was in the coffin.

"I fought and screamed my way out of the dream, running into my children's room to make sure they were safe. They were. This awful dream stayed with me, making me shudder at its thought. I discussed it with some friends who made light of it, saying 'It was just a bad dream.' I'd had similar experiences with dreams twice before in my life, and I knew this was more than just a dream.

"In February 1973 during a routine pediatric exam, my son Georgie was suspected of having mononucleosis or hepatitis because of swelling discovered in his abdomen. Laboratory tests were performed and the diagnosis of neuroblastoma, a childhood cancer, was made. I was shocked, devastated, and because of my dream completely unnerved.

"On September 20, 1973, my precious son died of the disease. During the six and one half months of his illness we shared many intuitive connections and grew and learned from one another in ways in which only human beings so close in mind and spirit can."

One could go about looking for elements from future days in every dream and probably always make a connection by looking hard and waiting long enough. Sometimes the connection may exist only in the imagination. However, other times the connection is obvious and undeniable, particularly in dreams that contain scenes from a crisis.

Jeriann Fairman, a midwife in Sugarloaf, California, has had numerous precognitive experiences involving her clients. She will often have an intuition to go to bed early and get extra rest, to turn down a wine cooler at a party, and so on, the evening before a client goes into labor. One evening she had a dramatic precognitive dream about an expectant mother. "The night after I met her," Jeriann recalls, "I dreamed she hemorrhaged and was taken away on a stretcher to an ambulance. This was peculiar because the expectant mother appeared to be in excellent health with no apparent risk factors. Besides, I had never used an ambulance to transport a client to the hospital.

"Later, when the mother went into labor, I remembered my dream and asked my apprentice to prepare Pitocin, a hormonal solution to keep the uterus contracted and to prevent hemorrhage (I don't ordinarily use Pitocin) and to have emergency oxygen handy.

"The mother had a short labor but a difficult birth. As soon as the baby was born, there was a gush of blood and a massive hemorrhage. After I administered the shot of Pitocin, the hemorrhage seemed to be under control for a while. However, the mother began bleeding again and I had to call an ambulance to transfer her to the hospital."

The realization that what one has dreamed has become a reality can be quite striking. A person who recognizes that a scene has already been glimpsed in a dream is frequently seized with a feeling of the uncanny.

David Graham records a rather macabre precognitive dream. A fourth-grade boy was involved in a playground accident during recess. Later as an adult he recalls: "I ran home from school, my upper lip slit quite badly. As I opened the screen door to our kitchen, my mother caught sight of me. She screamed, 'My God, Steve, oh my God! I dreamed this morning just before I woke up that you came home from school with all your teeth knocked out, and all you said was, "You shoulda seen the teeth fly!"'"[24]

Precognitive dreams may help to explain the peculiar feeling of déjà vu—the sense of having been in a particular place or having done something before. Most people have had this experience at one time or another. A place seems strangely familiar yet one knows one has never been there before. Sometimes a déjà vu experience can have a haunting quality.

Some parapsychologists suggest that déjà vu can often be explained in terms of precognitive dreams. We may feel that we have lived through a particular scene before or have been to a particular place because we have glimpsed it in a dream. Perhaps some precognitive dreams are completely or partially forgotten by the conscious mind yet, retained in the unconscious, still contribute to the feeling of déjà vu.

Most memorable precognitive dreams are realistic. However, the dream mechanisms that distort familiar people, places, and things of the past may also distort glimpses of the future.

Nancy Sondow reports a dream in the *Journal of the American Society for Psychical Research* that she believes has precognitive elements involving her son. She writes:

"I took some bubble gum out of my mouth . . . I threw it in the garden . . . It became large, and first one, then many chickens jumped into the garden and started pecking and eating the gum . . . I continued walking past the garden in the backyard and felt a sharp sting on my leg. There was an insect with sharp spikes like a thistle embedded in the skin. I pulled some of it out . . . My mother was there. She told me those insects were around. I felt there might be others on me, on my clothes, my hair. I wanted my mother to help me take off the jacket I was wearing, which was Jimmy's . . . I had an impulse to sing so we wouldn't be so scared."

In the days following this dream, Dr. Sondow noticed many correspondences. "After I woke up," she writes, "Jimmy, my oldest son, told me he had a splinter in his foot he couldn't remove. I tried to get it out, but only managed to remove part of it. I noticed the correspondence to the dream, in which I was wearing Jimmy's jacket and asked my mother for help. Three days later, I went to a school show that included Jimmy's class. I knew nothing about it, except that as a parent I had received an invitation. In the middle of the performance, the teacher stopped the show and asked one child to give her the gum he was chewing. She added it to a large pile of chewed gum on the stage floor. Then the show resumed. When Jimmy came out, he played the part of a chicken and sang a song. I hadn't known about the show or his role as a chicken."

She believes that Jimmy was the connecting link through time. "It is his splinter, his chicken suit, his song, his class's pile of gum, and in the dream I am wearing Jimmy's jacket."[25]

In this example, rather than capturing a complete scene precisely as it later occurs, the mind's dream-making mechanism apparently wove elements from several future scenes into the dream. It is unlikely most people would even notice such a precognitive dream.

For that matter, the vast majority of psychic dreams—precognitive or otherwise—may elude our notice. Those that are remembered and capture attention may be a mere fraction of those that occur. There are several possible reasons for this.

One may forget a large portion of psychic dreams. Most people recall only a small percentage of their dreams. There is no telling how many of those that were forgotten contain psychic elements.

Even if the psychic dream is remembered, there is another reason it may go unnoticed. Not all psychic dreams tell a straightforward story. ESP-triggered scenes may be woven into a dream in a distorted way and be barely recognizable.

Scenes that are accurate pictures of what a parent or child is experiencing in another location may still fail to capture attention. One may think the correspondence between the dream and real life is a coincidence and therefore dismiss the dream.

It is also quite possible to have an ESP dream without knowing it. The daughter who dreamed she found a pin in her bed at the time her mother actually found one will be aware that she has had a psychic dream only if she or her mother happens to mention it. And this is not the sort of incident one is sure to talk about. How often do such psychic dreams escape our attention?

As parapsychologist Dr. Sally Ann Drucker, who has done extensive research on ESP in children, points out: "Without feedback you may never realize you've had a psychic dream." She suggests attempting to verify any dream that you think may be psychic. If something seems to announce itself as an ESP message—words in a foreign language, a sentence written on a blackboard, and so forth—she suggests checking it out. If the message is about someone you know, ask if it is relevant.

Finally, psychic dreaming may frequently go unnoticed because the elements communicated paranormally are often trivial. The common pins of the parent-child relationship hardly capture the same attention as do more dramatic psychic phenomena. Hearing a child's voice calling for help when he is miles away facing disaster, feeling a sharp pain on the very spot a mother is injured, dreaming a daughter is being murdered at the same time a robber is stalking her apartment; these are the sorts of phenomena that grip our interest. They are remembered, recorded, repeated.

But when it comes to learning about the parent-offspring ESP connection and to experiencing it in our own lives, the common pins may actually be of far greater value. In themselves the details are unimportant. It is what they signify, namely, that psi need not encompass a once-in-a-lifetime drama to be an intimate part of the parent-child relationship, but may affect us in the more familiar realm where parents and children continually interract:

Everyday life.

8

The Parapsychology of Everyday Parenting

A father thinks of his daughter whom he hasn't heard from in months. Seconds later, she telephones. On sudden impulse, a mother sits down to write a letter to her son at college. At the same moment, he is writing a letter to her. Their letters cross in the mail. Most parents can recall such incidents. This is the ESP of everyday life.

Unlike the more dramatic crisis telepathy, everyday ESP encompasses trivial details and ordinary events. It is the most common form of psychic phenomenon in the parent-child relationship, and it is the most overlooked. Most people associate psychic phenomena with the extraordinary. The very expression conjures visions of ghostly visits and other uncanny encounters with the world beyond the senses.

While never to be forgotten encounters with the paranormal do occur in the parent-child relationship from time to time, they are quite rare. Parent-child ESP is usually much less exciting. It is easy to overlook or shrug off as coincidence. After all, intuiting who is on the phone the instant it rings hardly captivates the same attention as a mother's sudden anguish when her son is killed in a war thousands of miles away. Yet everyday ESP may be the most important psychic phenomenon parent and child share. A closer look at this often overlooked facet of psi may shed the most light on the parent-offspring ESP connection.

EVERYDAY ESP

Probably no one has collected more everyday ESP experiences with his own family than psychiatrist Berthold Eric Schwarz. Of the 1,521 episodes he has recorded in meticulous detail, 505 are published in his book, *Parent-Child Telepathy: A Study of the Telepathy of Everyday Life.* This book remains one of the very few studies of everyday ESP in all parapsychological literature. Dr. Schwarz gives us a vivid picture of the personality of psi as it appears in day-to-day life.

For example, one day while sitting under the Christmas tree, his daughter Lisa held up a Santa Claus doll to her mother, Ardis, and asked: "What do you want for Christmas?" Caught by surprise, Ardis thought of the word "car," but before she had a chance to voice her thought, Lisa loudly interjected, "You want a car for Christmas?"

According to Dr. Schwarz, "Ardis had not given a second thought to a car since we had bought one last September."[1]

Another day Ardis was in her bedroom speaking on the telephone to her mother-in-law who, unknown to the rest of the family, was sick in bed at the time. Dr. Schwarz recalls: "Lisa was in her crib in her room and the two heavy doors which separate it from Ardis's room were closed. When Ardis finished her conversation she went into Lisa's room and Lisa said, "You were talking to Grandma; she's sick in bed."[2]

Writing in the well-respected journal, *Psychoanalytic Quarterly*, in 1935, Dr. D. T. Burlingham remarked that there are "striking parallelisms between the thought or behavior of the mother and that of the children, which do not seem to be understandable in terms of familiar forms of communication between mother and child."[3]

Dr. Jan Ehrenwald, who theorizes that all psychic phenomena are rooted in the maternal-child bond, gives the following example of just such a parallelism between a mother and her two-year-and-nine-month-old daughter. In the mother's words:

"I was standing folding Lisbeth's diapers on the counter in the bathroom when I thought idly that it would be fun for us to go away somewhere over Labor Day and wondered if this would be practical, and if so, where we should go. At this precise instant, Lisbeth ran in from her bedroom, where she had been playing quietly for some time, and asked, 'Pat, we going on a trip?' Absolutely nothing had been mentioned on this subject; the thought had just struck me at that moment." And it apparently had also struck her daughter by means of that inexplicable form of communication we call ESP.

A mother who is thinking about taking a vacation might think it perfectly reasonable that her child would be thinking the same thing and overlook the ESP episode. It could simply be coincidence.

Much of what appears to be ESP really is coincidence triggered by external causes. A father and son drive by a dairy bar and simultaneously think about ice cream a minute or so later. But it is difficult to write off as coincidence the following incident involving Dr. Ehrenwald's wife and four-year-old daughter. Dr. Ehrenwald writes:

"My wife had just received a letter from her cousin Clarence in the United States. She had spent a happy time with his family a few years before we got married, and Clarence, too, had married in the meantime. There was a photograph of Clarence's wife, Matilda, attached to his letter, showing her in the company of two more ladies. My wife, engaged in housework, was pondering the letter and photograph, while Barbara was absorbed in play by her side. At that very moment, the child, for no apparent reason, uttered the name 'Matilda.' I may add that this name in its English version had been quite unfamiliar to the child."[4]

Everyday ESP is most common between mother and child, who traditionally have the most intimate parent-offspring relationship, but fathers too share extrasensory communication with their offspring. Approximately two-thirds of the 505 parent-child ESP episodes Dr. Schwarz published are father-child experiences, that is, they took place between himself and his children.

Former school psychologist and well-known psychic Alex Tanous and author Katherine Fair Donnelly relate the following incident about a doctor and his son in their book, *Understanding and Developing Your Child's Natural Psychic Abilities:* "When he was five years old, the boy would always 'know' five minutes before his father arrived home, whether late or on time. The child would run to his mother and announce, 'I see Daddy. He is coming home now.' And Daddy always showed up five minutes later."[5]

ESP communication passes from father to child as well as from child to father. Stephen Gaskin, the founder of The Farm, a world-famous spiritual community in Summertown, Tennessee, recalls a fleeting ESP experience. "I was in bed in a meditative doze when I heard in the kitchen my wife Ina May offer one of the children something to eat. The thought flashed through my mind: Too hot! A second later I heard a loud 'Ow!' from the kitchen."

Occasionally a thought transmitted psychically from a mother or father to a child triggers a physical response without child or parent even realizing that ESP has occurred. "I walked into the kitchen feeling quite exuberant," writes Dr. Schwarz, "and thought I would clown by showing Lisa a Nijinsky-like kick. However, before I could demonstrate, she started to kick and do a little dance. She had never done this before. In this way, perhaps, she acted out, in motor fashion, my happy behavior that was about to emerge from its silent incubation."[6] This is an example of what Dr. Schwarz refers to as "motor compliance." A child acts on a parent's feelings or thoughts perceived telepathically.

Dr. Schwarz recalls a time when Ardis and Lisa were in the kitchen. "Lisa was frying four pieces of bacon for herself. Lisa is very fond of bacon and takes care of her own needs. Ardis thought, 'Lisa shouldn't have so much bacon; it isn't good for her.' Just then Lisa turned completely around and offered her mother two pieces of bacon."[7]

Another example of motor compliance Dr. Schwarz records is equally subtle. His son's actions neatly dovetailed with his mother's wishes. "Ardis was standing at the hallway door to Lisa's room watching the painters put the finishing touches. Eric was inside the room following them around. Ardis had a good dress on and didn't want to get near the wet paint. Eric was standing approximately fifteen feet away from the radiator cover and his face was out of his mother's view. Ardis noticed something that looked like dirt on the radiator cover. . . . She wondered, Where did that come from? Eric immediately went over to the radiator and carefully brushed the dirt off with his hand. His action was perfectly timed and in harmony with his mother's wishes."[8]

Most people associate ESP with the crystal-clear examples. You think of your daughter while she is dialing your telephone number. A child perceives precisely what its mother is thinking. The message is clear. However, ESP appears to come to us through the unconscious mind, and despite the name extra*sensory* perception, cannot be compared to information perceived directly through the sensory organs. According to Dr. Charles Tart, professor of psychology at the University of California at Davis and a renowned parapsychologist, ESP is a complex phenomenon. The information we perceive psychically is subject to all sorts of changes and distortion as a result of our beliefs, psychological makeup, and unconscious process.

A single ESP impression may combine several ideas with the poetic economy of a dream image. Dr. Schwarz gives a good example of this: On the afternoon of January 13th, "while washing the dishes, Ardis was looking outside at the trees and wondering how long they would last with all the ice on them." Shortly before she had been thinking, "The children need so much to get outside and get rid of some of their energy!" Lisa came up to her and said: "The trees are crying for the children to come out." Here, Lisa picked up her mother's thoughts and feelings telepathically and condensed two separate thoughts into a single poetic metaphor.

Young children seem to have a natural gift for ESP. Parapsychologist Ernesto Spinelli tested one thousand subjects in ten age groups each with fifty males and fifty females. He discovered that children aged three to four scored highest on ESP tests. There was a gradual lowering of scores in the older child, young adult, and adult groups.[9] Several other studies have confirmed that ESP is most common in children.

One reason may be that children are dependent on their parents. They have a need to share intimate communication with mother and father. They may therefore be more attuned to the parent-offspring ESP connection. This may influence a child's general psychic ability whether or not ESP communication involves a parent.

In addition, children seem to take ESP more in stride rather than suppressing telepathic messages. As Dr. Schwarz puts it, "Children haven't learned that ESP can't happen. Society hasn't gotten to them with the acculturation. They haven't yet discovered that ESP is all superstition, that it's a whole lot of garbage, that it can't possibly be, and isn't there at all. They *know* it's there because they experience it."

Who is more likely to have more extrasensory experiences, a girl or a boy? Several studies with schoolchildren have addressed this question and found that girls scored highest on ESP tests. However, there are exceptions. In the Spinelli study, boys and girls did equally well.

In our culture women seem to have more psychic experiences than men. Mothers report more parent-offspring ESP episodes than fathers. The majority of examples in this book involve mothers and children. This does not mean that females are naturally more psychic than males. However, in this culture women pay more attention to their inner feelings and intuition and are therefore more open to extrasensory experiences.

In some situations men may appear more psychically attuned.

For example, in the Maimonides dream research experiment discussed in chapter 7, Drs. Ullman and Krippner found that men were better percipients than women. They think this is perhaps because women may be more nervous than men about sleeping in a strange bed and having male experimenters.

By contrast, in most collections of spontaneous ESP dreams, women dreamers far outnumber men. Drs. Ullman and Krippner think that this may be the result of our cultural climate in which women are allowed to talk about their irrational ESP experiences and men look down on ESP. In *Dream Telepathy* they point out: "Given an open cultural attitude toward ESP, the sexes would seem to have equal potential at ESP dreaming."[10] This is probably true of all psychic phenomena.

In India, a country where paranormal phenomena are much more widely accepted than they are in the U.S. or Europe, a survey by a prominent psychologist and educator, Dr. Jamuna Prasad, showed that boys and girls reported almost the same percentage of ESP experiences.[11]

Do personality characteristics have any bearing on extrasensory ability? Is a child with one type of personality more likely to have a psychic experience than another? To answer this question, Eloise Shields, former school psychologist in the Los Angeles County district, divided schoolchildren into a withdrawn group and a nonwithdrawn group and tested them. Using picture cards for testing, she found a significant difference in scoring between the two groups. The withdrawn group scored below chance. They seemed to have a tendency toward "psi-missing"—they got more incorrect answers than the laws of chance indicate. According to Ms. Shields, "This only seems possible providing that they in some way knew the correct guesses at times and were occasionally or preponderately missing the known targets in a meaningful manner."[12]

She says that her research in this area is only exploratory. No hard conclusions can be drawn. Meanwhile, even if withdrawn children are less prone to do well on an ESP test, this does not necessarily mean there is less chance of psychic experiences in the parent-child relationship.

In the past, some parapsychologists have associated ESP with neurotic characteristics. High ESP ability, it was thought, could be a compensation for character maladjustment. However, this impression probably stems largely from considering the number of odd personalities in the psychic field. The majority of studies seem to show that the highest ESP scores are obtained by extraverted, expansive, and well-adjusted persons.

In biological parenthood, the parent-offspring ESP connection is apparently forged while the child is still in the womb. However, when it comes to extrasensory phenomena, the emotional relationship, not the biological connection, seems to be paramount. Next to ESP in the parent-child relationship, extrasensory phenomena are most common between lovers. As mentioned before, adoptive as well as biological parents develop a psychic bond with their children.

On the other hand, it is not uncommon for an adopted child to question the authenticity of his parents. He may sense the truth as a result of subliminal impressions received from his adoptive parents, ESP, or both. Dr. Ehrenwald cites an example of a four-year-old boy, Dick, who was the offspring of his mother and a man with whom she had had an affair. The boy repeatedly asked, "Is Daddy my real daddy? Yes, he is Daddy, but is he my real daddy?"

Dr. Tanous and Ms. Donnelly cite another example. "Vera R. Webster, science editor for a major publishing firm, tells of a younger sister who was adopted at a very early age after her mother had died. When the little sister was two years old, she was sitting on the front porch one day and was overheard talking to someone. Queried about whom she was speaking to, the child replied, 'To my mother.' When told that her mother was inside the house in the kitchen, the girl replied, 'No, I mean to my mother up in heaven.'" The girl did not know she had been adopted, or, more accurately, she hadn't been told she was.[13]

One of the most important factors in parent-child ESP is a

home atmosphere conducive to extrasensory experiences. ESP is more likely to occur if it is valued and if people in the family pay attention to their intuition.

In the Schwarz family, Lisa and Eric had an unusually high number of spontaneous ESP experiences. This may be partly the result of their own psychic talents and partly the result of a home atmosphere conducive to spontaneous ESP.

Dr. Schwarz noted that telepathy occurred most frequently when he was oriented toward the possibility of ESP and when he went to the trouble of writing down the episodes.[14]

Being on the lookout for parent-child ESP experiences may bring to light many more episodes than one might expect. Few parents would want to go to the trouble that Dr. Schwarz did. This requires scrupulous attention to detail and the willingness to take the time to write down an episode immediately after it occurs, which is not always convenient. However, a nod to psi may be all that is needed to encourage it to perform. Many gifted psychics refer to "tuning in" when having an ESP experience. As mentioned before, thinking of ESP may help the mind attune to ESP's "frequency" and make more open to psychic experiences.

Dr. Schwarz also found that ESP occurred frequently when he felt "in rapport" with his children. Everyday ESP also occurred most often in the Schwarz family during both periods of mental tranquillity and during periods of emotional upswings such as those following the children's victories or awards in athletic contests.

Of course, parent-child ESP experiences are bound to be more common if one or more persons in the family is physically talented. Some children are more psychically gifted than others for reasons we don't understand. Unfortunately, the child who is remarkably intuitive is often dismissed as being overimaginative. Sometimes a child who accurately reports an ESP experience is actually threatened with punishment for telling "tall tales."

Dr. Tanous believes that a child's psychic abilities should be cultivated, not repressed. This doesn't mean that parents should encourage their children to aspire to be fortune tellers. However, being open to their psychic ability may enhance children's creativity. Dr. Tanous suggests that children recognize psychic ability as a natural aptitude. Some parents react to the psychically gifted child with fear, fear of the unknown and fear stemming from religious prejudice against psi. Perhaps fear that the child will bring out some of the forbidden material in the parents' unconscious, or reveal a secret that the parents would like to keep.

A few are afraid the psychic child will pick up all their thoughts, hidden desires, and the sort of stuff most want to keep tucked in the very back room of the mind. However, this is not likely. If anything, telepathy picks up an element here and there, but rarely a meaningful idea that would embarrass a parent. Even if the child did pick up a secret desire, it would most likely be without understanding.

The following example illustrates this:

On Saturday afternoon, November 13, 1965, Dr. Schwarz was out shopping with his daughter Lisa. "While in the store," he writes, "I noticed a very attractive, sexy teenager and mused on how nice it would be if I were young again. Lisa was in another part of the store at this time, and it was impossible for her to see the object of my admiration. As we were driving home, I fantasized on this well-endowed teenager, when Lisa broke into my daydreams by saying, 'Teenagers cheat.' She then proceded to berate them in a way that was not appropriate for her train of thought but which seemed to complement my thought."

In this example, a girl telepathically reacts to a thought her father would have preferred to keep hidden. However, the content of the ESP episode is still unknown to the child. Lisa has no idea of her father's thoughts, or even of the fact that telepathy has occurred.

Why does ESP occur when it does? Of the many unanswered questions about everyday ESP, this is near the top of the list. It remains a mystery why a father thinks of his daughter the instant before she telephones on one occasion, and not on another. If ESP is going to occur at all, why doesn't it happen all the time?

When everyday spontaneous telepathy occurs, a parent or child does not consciously attempt to send a message. The communication just seems to occur. For no apparent reason, we suddenly seem to have contact with the mind of another, or as the writer Upton Sinclair expresses it, "Is it some contact with a deeper level of mind, as bubbles on a stream have contact with the water of the stream?"[15]

This is one of the most frustrating facets of psi, its utter unpredictability. Psi just pops into our head out of the blue and flits away. Thanks to this behavior, many scientists refuse to take it seriously. Though they may know ESP is a reality, may even have personal experience of ESP, it is unsatisfying to investigate a phenomenon that seems to follow no rules. However, some suggest that there is a sort of internal logic to spontaneous ESP episodes.

According to Dr. Schwarz: "Telepathy occurs when there is, underneath if not evident at the surface, a very meaningful communication."[16] Though the vast majority of everyday ESP episodes encompass trivial details, ESP flashes may be similar to dream images in that they may actually overlie an emotionally charged thought or feeling. The important ideas associated with the telepathic message never reach the surface of our consciousness.

PSYCHIC PARENTING

For that matter, it is possible that most extrasensory communication between parent and child never reaches the surface of consciousness. The everyday ESP of which we become aware may be the mere crest of the wave.

Some parents have psychic experiences frequently. ESP is second nature to them. They use their ESP to tune into one another consciously, or they have extrasensory experiences spontaneously. Another group, perhaps the majority, experiences ESP only rarely. A third group of parents and children never have ESP experiences. But all may share extrasensory communication on an unconscious level. The existence of telesomatic reactions suggests that we can be affected by ESP without being aware of it. Those parent-child ESP experiences that do reach consciousness may be linked to a deeper psychic relationship like waves to the sea.

Some sort of psi energy may function as a silent vital current linking parent and offspring in the deepest part of the mind. In some part of us, we may share what Dr. Taub-Bynum calls a "family unconscious." And the psychic experiences that are never brought to light, that we never realize have occurred, may be the most important of all. For it has been suggested that ESP plays an important role in parental "hunches," in the child's emotional, social, and moral development, in the development of conscience, and in learning.

ESP may influence our decisions without us being aware of it. ESP is probably behind a large number of sudden hunches. Dr. Tanous recalls an incident involving a mother and daughter driving along the highway. The mother was about to pass a car. Reacting to a sudden hunch, the daughter suddenly said, "Slow down, don't pass." Consequently the mother didn't pass. Almost immediately another car that apparently had just come onto the road, came speeding behind them. If the mother had passed at that time, they would have collided.

Similarly, ESP may trigger sudden compulsions. Out of the blue, a mother has an urge to check on her infant. At the moment she walks into the room, the baby is choking on something it picked up from the floor. The urge to check on the baby was apparently triggered by crisis telepathy.

It is a familiar scene. A parent or child acts on an unconscious flash of ESP. When this happens, the person is usually unaware of the ESP and does not know why the sudden urge arose. He may not even stop to think about it.

An incident recorded by Dr. Schwarz appears to be an ESP-triggered compulsion. While on a business trip, a man decided to photograph his birthplace. He had been in the area many times before but this was the first time he looked up his place of birth. Later a telegram informed him that his mother, who had been in apparent good health, had died at the time he was photographing his birthplace. An extrasensory flash, of which the man remained unaware, had apparently motivated his action.

ESP may also play a role in child development and contribute to molding the child's character. Our concepts of right and wrong, good and evil, may in part stem from psi communication. Dr. Schwarz suggests, "Conscience involves more than identification with and introjection of parental values. It might have a telepathic core."

Parent-offspring psi may have a darker side when it comes to influencing child development. For most, the darker side of psi connotes strange phenomena they only read about, and hope they will never experience—ghosts, hauntings, things that go bump in the night. However, there is a far more subtle side to psi, an aspect of ESP of which most people are unaware. The messages we unconsciously transmit to our children.

If parents can sometimes sense a child is in danger during a moment of crisis, or can share everyday ESP experiences, it stands to reason that on occasion negative thoughts and feelings, things that we might even wish to repress, might also travel from parent to child.

Science has only recently revealed that what the pregnant mother thinks and feels can and often does affect her unborn child. The parents' thoughts and feelings may continue to affect the child throughout its development. The parents' feelings may influence their behavior in subtle ways, which in turn will affect the children, though this may take place beneath the surface of consciousness. In addition, strong emotions or emotionally charged thoughts may be transmitted to the child telepathically, or in another way of looking at it, they may become part of the "family unconscious" of which the child's own unconscious is a part.

"When carried to excess," states Dr. Schwarz, "confused or pathological parental thoughts, affects, and complexes could contribute to their children's behavioral disturbances, bizarre ideations, speech problems, and so forth. In such cases, the child could telepathically detect the parent's warped thoughts, which the parent would pathologically dissociate from or deny. . . . In everyday life, when the parents are disturbed the children are upset. This is particularly noticeable in the relationship between the mother and her infant."[18]

On the other hand, tuning into the ESP connection may broaden the parent-child relationship and allow parents to consciously send positive thoughts and healing messages to their children. It can, from time to time, give us a glimpse beneath the surface of appearances and allow deep communication to flow from mind to mind. Robbie E. Davis-Floyd, Ph.D., an anthropologist at Trinity University in San Antonio, Texas, relates the following healing exchange between herself and her son, Jason:

"Jason's leg started hurting one Monday night. He screamed every time anybody tried to turn it a certain way. On Tuesday I took him to the chiropractor, and then when the adjustment didn't ease the pain, to the pediatrician. He told me that it could be very serious, and to take him to a pediatric orthopedist. I made the appointment for Thursday morning. On Wednesday his leg was still hurting. I kept him with me all day. We went all over the campus where I teach with him in a stroller.

"We went to the auditorium to buy some tickets. We ordered them and were told that it would be a few minutes. I sat down with Jason on a soft bench and took him on my lap and held him close, trying to get a sense of what was bothering him. I just held him, and sensed him, and silently asked myself/himself why he would be needing his leg to hurt. And then I said, 'Jason, are you making your leg hurt so that I will stay home with you all the time?' He looked up at me so gratefully and sobbed, 'Yes!'

"I was suddenly swept with a wave of fear. I realized that, if he chose to get very sick, he could force me to give up teaching, which I love. I began to understand that he was in part mirroring my own guilt over not seeing him from eight to six every day.

"I said, 'Jason, I love you and I always will. You and your sister and your Daddy are the three most important people in the world to me, but I can't spend all my time with you. My work is very important to me too, and I am just not happy if I am not doing my work.' I started to cry, and I continued speaking from my heart to his. 'I love to teach and I love to write. I am writing a book right now, and doing that makes me very happy. I would feel so bad if I couldn't finish my book or teach my classes. You are a very powerful person. If you decide to make your leg sick, then I will have to stay home with you, and I will do my best to be a good Mommy, but I will not be happy staying at home and not doing my work. I know that you need to be with me more, so I have an idea: On Fridays I could pick you up at three o'clock right after nap, and we could spend some special time together. How does that sound?'

"He was crying too, and he said, 'I don't know, Mommy, I really want to be with you more.' And I said, 'You really want to be with me all the time. That would be so wonderful for you.' He said, 'Yes, all the time, but then you couldn't do your book and you would be unhappy. I don't know what to do.' I said, 'Why don't you just think about it, and you can tell me what you have decided at suppertime. You can choose where we go to eat.'

"For supper he chose his favorite cafeteria. In the middle of dinner he put his fork down and proudly informed his sister that he had had a long talk with Mommy, and now he had decided that he was going to let her write her book and teach her classes, and that she would pick him up early on Fridays, and so he wasn't going to need his leg to hurt any more.

"The next day when the pediatrician's office called to find out what had happened at our appointment with the pediatric orthopedist, I started to explain our talk, but couldn't figure out how to convey what had occurred between Jason and me. So I simply said, 'He's fine now, so we didn't go. But thank you for calling!' "

Just as parapsychology could unite in fruitful marriage with the fields of obstetrics and of prenatal and perinatal psychology, it could join hands with childhood education. Research into the psychic life of children could very well revolutionize the field of child education and broaden our perspective on how children learn.

When parent and child or teacher and child are in a state of telepathic rapport, says Dr. Schwarz, "a parent's or teacher's approval or disapproval of a child's act can have a great emotional effect."[19] If this is so, psi could have a tremendous impact on a child's ability to learn, an impact that educators have not even begun to measure.

When there is a positive telepathic rapport between parent or educator and child, knowledge may be exchanged more easily. Learning, therefore, may be enhanced. One evening Dr. Schwarz was reading a fable to his daughter Lisa. "A child has made something with clay," he read. While discussing this, his eye went to the next fable which began, "A boy went to the park." Lisa, who could not yet read and was out of view, said, "The child put it [the clay] back in the park."[20] Lisa was not merely hearing the words her father read. She was apparently picking up some of his thoughts as well. Such a transference of information may occur unconsciously without either educator or child being aware of it, and it may occur with greater frequency than most educators realize.

In 1951, J. G. Van Busschbach, state inspector of Amsterdam primary schools, undertook a massive investigation of telepathy in schoolchildren. This was prompted by several teachers who claimed that they were in telepathic contact with some of the children in their classes.

Using an exceedingly boring but by no means untypical ESP test, Mr. Van Busschbach tested 673 fifth and sixth graders in twenty-one different classes. The teacher sat at the rear of the class hidden from view behind an arrangement of maps. He was given five cards face down, each with one of the five following symbols, arranged in a random order: + O − : x.

These symbols were also placed on a blackboard for the

children to see. They were told that the teacher would look at one of the symbols and they were to guess which one it was. The teacher would then turn one card over at a time and concentrate on it. The children were asked to indicate on a form which card they thought the teacher had turned over. A similar procedure was followed using five colors and five words. When the results were evaluated, Mr. Van Busschbach discovered that the "guesses" were significantly higher than chance.[21]

In 1953, a similar experiment was done with twenty-six classes in Utrecht. The results were comparable to the Amsterdam experiment—significantly above chance.

Were young children particularly open to telepathy with their teachers, or would they have just as many correct hits if another person, unknown to them, broadcast the message? To find out, a similar test was administered with some of the same children. This time, however, a man the children didn't know acted as the "sender". The result was a noticeably smaller number of correct hits. This left little doubt that the teacher was a significant factor in telepathy in children."[22]

When the results of these experiments appeared in the *Journal of Parapsychology*, published in The Netherlands, it attracted the attention of J. B. Rhine at the Parapsychological Laboratory at Duke University in North Carolina. He invited Mr. Van Busschbach to Durham to help parapsychologists there repeat the tests. The results of telepathy tests among American schoolchildren matched those of the Netherlands.[23]

Later, when Mr. Van Busschbach made similar tests with older children, the result fell within the range of chance. This is not surprising if, as the research of several parapsychologists has shown, ESP is more common in younger children.

Actually, it is amazing that the experiments provided above-chance results with any age group of children considering the symbols chosen. It is a wonder that a child, or teacher, for that matter, could keep his mind on such a boring enterprise. One would think that parapsychologists would devise more interesting material, and particularly, subjects suitable to hold the interest of children. Though the material transmitted via spontaneous ESP between parent and child is sometimes trivial, it is hardly of the order of +, O, and so on.

In 1955, Miss N. G. Louwerens of the Parapsychological Institute of the State University of Utrecht, did devise a more interesting test. Her experiment involved 1,188 kindergarten children and twenty-nine teachers from twenty-nine classes in fifteen different schools. Rather than abstract symbols, she used colored pictures of five objects—a blue car, a red doll, a green ball, a stack of yellow cubes, and a Bambi deer with orange and brown spots. The pictures were arranged in a looseleaf notebook (for the teacher) and envelopes with one hundred and fifty prints (for the children).

Instructions were presented to the children in the form of a fairy tale: A little princess had a picture book that was mixed up by the wind. A good fairy (the teacher who had the notebook) had to rearrange the pictures. The brownies (the children) had to guess how she arranged it.

Behind a blind, the teacher then looked at the book. The children were asked to guess which print the teacher was looking at and to put their cards in the same order. When the children finished, the cards were collected and the tests evaluated. The kindergarten children produced such a high number of correct hits that the chances of their doing this by accident were one in ten million, or just about nil.[24]

Miss Louwerens repeated the experiment with ten classes, but this time she acted as "sender" rather than a teacher with whom the children were familiar. The results were strikingly different. They were within the range of chance.[25]

It seems to be well established that children do better on ESP tests when a teacher with whom they are familiar, rather than a stranger, acts as sender. But does the personality of the teacher have any effect on the child's telepathy? Will a particular personality type elicit a greater telepathic response in the child?

This was the subject of Miss Louwerens's further investigation. She had all the teachers involved in the experiment take an extensive psychodiagnostic examination. She found that, as a general rule, pupils did best on telepathy tests with teachers who could be described as "motherly types."[26]

We can hypothesize that the teacher is a parent substitute, especially for younger children. Teacher-child ESP may therefore be an extension of parent-child psi. With this in mind, it is easy to imagine why the teacher whose role comes closest to that of mother may be most likely to have the greatest telepathic rapport with her pupils.

Psychic experiences seem to be especially common among children with learning disabilities. In 1935, Ferdinand von Neureiter, a German professor of forensic medicine, published an extraordinary account of a mentally retarded nine-year-old Latvian girl by the name of Ilga K. She could "read" any text if and when her mother was reading it at the same time. The mother's lip movements could not have cued the daughter since Ilga could read the text even when her mother was behind a curtain or in another room.

German parapsychologist Dr. Hans Bender investigated and verified the case in 1937. He published it in the *Journal of Parapsychology* under the title, "Report of a phenomenon of unusual perception."[27]

Unusual it is. But it is not an isolated case. In 1938, R. M. Drake of Wesleyan College in Macon, Georgia, published a similar case in the *Journal of Parapsychology.* It involved an eleven-year-old retarded boy named Bo who was once thought to be a "lightning calculator" because he was able to do complicated sums or multiplication despite his very low IQ. However, it was soon found that he could do these calculations only when his mother was doing them at the same time.[28]

Another somewhat similar case of unusual perception was published in the *Journal of the American Society for Physical Research* in 1968. A boy known as the "Cambridge Boy" suffered from spastic diplegia and congenital cataracts in both eyes. His ophthalmologist couldn't figure out how the boy could clearly "read" the visual acuity charts when his mother was nearby. The boy was unable to read the charts in her absence.[29]

Retarded children or those with other handicaps may be more dependent on the parent-offspring psychic relationship than are those who can function normally in other ways. As former school psychologist Eloise Shields puts it, "If they have a good rapport with an adult, they may lean on that person telepathically because they don't have sophisticated thinking of their own."

As a result, learning-disabled children may display unusual psychic sensitivity. For example, Ms. Shields relates an incident about a six-year-old boy named Carl who had difficulty learning. One day, out of the clear blue, Carl came out with a mind-stopping request of his mother. "Tell me about that accident I had the day I was sitting in the front seat with you." It was an innocent question, except that the mother had never experienced such an accident with her son, at least not yet. Two hours after Carl asked the question, she was on the way to the store with him. They were in a car accident, but fortunately it wasn't serious.

One fourteen-year-old retarded boy in the Torrance school district of Los Angeles County told his teacher: "I saw you last night. You were sitting in a rocking chair watching TV."

The teacher was astonished. For what the boy had said was true. He consulted school psychologist Eloise Shields, who had a special interest in parapsychology. Ms. Shields explained that retarded children often have a high degree of telepathy and clairvoyance. "The child probably didn't have anything to do and wanted to be with his teacher." She hastened to add, "Don't worry. The telepathic or clairvoyant child doesn't see everything you do!" Most people would find this last fact very reassuring.

Ms. Shields noticed that ESP appeared to occur more frequently among retarded children than among other children with whom she worked. This led her to embark on a formal study of psi in retarded children in the spring of 1975. Two others on the school staff, the speech therapist and the school nurse, joined her and made up the research team.

They made up a deck of twenty-five cards. In place of the abstract symbols of the Zener cards traditionally used in ESP testing, they chose pictures of five animals—horses, dogs, cats, sheep, and roosters.

The school nurses arranged the cards in a random sequence. The speech therapist then showed a sample card of each of the five animals. The five cards were then left in front of the child during the tests.

For the telepathy test, the speech therapist sat opposite the child being tested. A cardboard blind was placed between her and the deck. She said, "I have some more cards like this behind my paper. I'm going to look at one of them and I want you to read my mind, and tell me which picture I'm looking at." She then proceeded to take the top card in the deck, turn it over, and look at it. "Which picture do you think I'm looking at now?"[30] She continued this way until she finished the deck. Then the school nurse scored the results.

For the clairvoyance test, the process was similar except that the speech therapist took the top card off the stack and held it face down behind the cardboard blind as she said, "Now let's see if you can guess what picture is on the card I'm holding. I don't know what it is either, but you guess. What do you think this one is?"[31]

Was Eloise Shields correct in her hypothesis? Were mentally retarded children really psychically gifted? Says Ms. Shields, "The children scored at a phenomenally high level in the telepathy test." One girl made twenty-three hits out of twenty-five. She sensed when the speech therapist began to become bored, as experimenters often do in such repetitive testing. When the therapist's mind began to wander instead of sticking to "sending" the impression on the card, "the girl piped up and said, 'Think *close*,' which brought the therapist back to the job immediately!"[32] The children did less well on the clairvoyance test but still above chance.

We must bear in mind that the children were not doing the psi tests with strangers but with persons with whom they were in close contact and had a rapport. Ms. Shields points out that the superiority of the telepathy scores may reflect the high degree of rapport between the children and the speech therapist.[33]

Ms. Shields regards telepathic ability in those with learning disabilities as a fact of life. She does not, however, feel that it is particularly useful in enhancing the learning process. This is because telepathy is "too unpredictable," too hit or miss.

On the other hand, Dr. Tanous, another former school psychologist, strongly believes that ESP has a very definite impact on educating the learning-disabled child.

Dr. Tanous has worked with many children with severe learning disabilities and other handicaps. "Primarily their intuition and their insight into a subject are often much stronger than their logical ability," he says. "They are therefore sometimes able to grasp the totality of a subject instead of coming to it through step by step logic." He believes that such children can be helped to supplement their learning by using the high degree of telepathic ability they frequently have. For this reason, part of the training he has given disabled children involves ESP testing.

He is the first to point out that working with learning-disabled children is no easy road. It takes a great deal of effort. As he puts it, "It takes a lot of patience, and a lot of courage, but even a lot more love."[34]

Though his methods certainly seem unconventional in comparison to most contemporary American education, his results are eye-opening. In *Understanding and Developing Your Child's Natural Psychic Abilities,* Dr. Tanous records one remarkable case among many of his success stories working with retarded children:

"One of my earliest cases dealt with a sixth-grader who was considered retarded. He had an IQ of 80. The boy came from a family of well-known musicians. His teacher told the parents that the child would never make it, and recommended a school for retarded children. The parents then sent him to a private school, where the staff had little success trying to teach him, although he was able to learn to a certain degree. After years of frustration the parents brought him to me. I found out that he was very interested in music. He always listened to music; he would play records and go to concerts. I also discovered that he had many psychic experiences, but had been afraid to tell them to anyone. After I worked with him and put his psychic abilities to use, his flair for music flourished and he was able to return to school later majoring in music. Today he is attending a well-known music school. His marks are superior. Soon he will graduate and embark on a series of concerts throughout the country."[35]

This wonderful success story is not an isolated case. Dr. Tanous himself was considered retarded as a child.[36] He did very poorly in school and received D's and F's through high school. However, as he writes, "I was able to use my perceptivity and psychic ability to overcome my 'retardation.'"[37] And he did indeed overcome whatever learning disabilities stood in his way. Today he holds a doctorate in divinity and advanced degrees in philosophy, history, government, and student counseling; not bad for a so-called retarded child!

Scoring high on an ESP test is by no means a sign that a child has a learning disability. In fact, a study conducted by Sally Ann Drucker, Ph.D., and Athena Drewes suggests the very opposite. Dr. Drucker and Ms. Drewes are both psychical researchers and members of the Parapsychological Association in Durham, North Carolina. They have conducted and published several controlled studies on ESP in schoolchildren. In addition, Athena Drewes has written an exhaustive annotated bibliography of every research study on children and ESP in the English language.

In their study involving ESP and IQ, they used M&M candies. A child was to "guess" the color of an M&M a teacher drew from a bag which contained one hundred candies, twenty each of the five colors. The children with higher IQ's did significantly better on the second trial. This implies that some kind of learning process may have occurred. The high IQ child's ESP improved with practice.[38]

Judging by this study we are led to believe that high IQ children seem to be able to learn to improve their psychic abilities. Judging from Eloise Shields's studies, we find that children with low IQ's are more psychic. Yet other studies suggest that intelligence level has little or no bearing on extrasensory ability. What are we to conclude? Is this another of psi's elusive tricks, a manifestation of its difficulty in being categorized that frustrates parapsychologists and laymen alike? At best we can conclude that children from a wide range of intelligence levels have ESP.

While the role that intelligence level plays on the transmission of extrasensory information is uncertain, the importance of emotional rapport with the sender is clear. Agreeing with the results of the previous Dutch studies, Ms. Drewes says, "If there is an emotional link between subject and agent, the ESP scores are much higher. The strong emotional bond facilitates the psychic transmission."

This brings us back to the strongest emotional bond of all—the parent-child relationship. As already mentioned, in a study involving intuiting the color of M&M's, Elaine Shrager, Ph.D., found that children scored highest when their own mother rather than another mother acted as sender. This links up with Czech neurophysiologist Stepan Figar's observation about psi-mediated physiological responses measured by a plethysmograph (discussed in chapter 6): best results were obtained when sender and recipient had a mutual emotional relationship such as mother and son.

Quite a bit of research has been done on ESP in children—most of it between teacher and child and very little between parent and offspring. But we can speculate that ESP uncovered in the teacher-child relationship is but a shadow of parent-child psi at home, where ESP flows most freely.

And in so doing, we are left with many unanswered questions. What undiscovered role does ESP play in the learning process?

How does parent-offspring ESP influence our decisions? What role does it play in our everyday lives at home? How does psi affect the child's character development, his or her sense of values, emotions? To what degree does psi affect the lives of parents and children or our destiny? What role does it play in the deepest and most lasting of our inner experiences and the parent-child love bond?

It may be decades, perhaps even centuries, before these questions are fully answered. Today, the psychic life of parents and children is at much the same point that the science of chemistry was centuries ago when it was just beginning to emerge from medieval alchemy. Psi is just beginning to emerge from occult trappings and pseudoscience. But unlike chemistry, the world of parent-child ESP is more than a science of hard facts and neat formulas. It is part of a deeper reality—our interconnectedness with the universe, the living connection we share with those who gave us life and with those whom we are privileged to nurture.

Psi invites us to embark on a vast inner exploration of an entirely new world. To appreciate it, we must approach it as we would approach a developing child waiting to be born, with hard science, yes, but also with the heart.

Psi offers a compelling invitation. It is an open door. It is for us to discover what is on the other side.

9

Tuning into the ESP Connection

The parent-child relationship offers the ideal opportunity to explore the world of psi on the other side of the door. All parents and children share an ESP connection. From time to time all parents and children can probably communicate in the realm beyond the senses.

A few gifted psychics assume that everyone can develop ESP to the same degree, but there is no evidence for this. Not everyone can learn to perform remarkable psychic feats; neither can everyone learn to become a Mozart or a Rembrandt. ESP does not come equally easily to all people. Some are able to tune in to their psychic abilities immediately. Others must practice weeks or months before getting results. Still others never seem to be able to develop extrasensory abilities.

But everyone probably does have latent psychic ability. Everyone can probably learn to heighten his or her intuition to a greater or lesser degree.

GUIDELINES FOR MAKING THE ESP CONNECTION

Though there is probably nothing you can do to guarantee a psychic experience, you can create the conditions most conducive to ESP.

The exercises in the following chapters are designed to heighten your intuition and to create the optimal conditions for ESP. They are not meant to test you or your child for ESP ability. Therefore there are no right or wrong answers.

The exercises in the following two chapters are entirely different from tests designed by parapsychologists to detect ESP in the laboratory setting. Experiments to test for ESP can be inconceivably boring. They often consist of such things as "guessing" the patterns on cards—hundreds of cards—over and over, ad nauseam. Even the tests designed for young children often transcend dullness. Actually, when you come to think of it, it's amazing that laboratory tests produce the dramatic results they do, and that they have yielded such staggering statistics in favor of telepathy, clairvoyance, and precognition. Indeed, it's a wonder that ESP works at all under tedious laboratory conditions.

Quantitative testing can contribute much to our knowledge of parapsychology. The ESP tests designed by such pioneers as J. B. Rhine and others in the field have led to amazing breakthroughs in our knowledge of psi, but ESP in "real life" is a world removed from ESP in the laboratory. At best, ESP in the lab is a thin slice of psychic phenomena. What we glimpse in the lab is psi hemmed in, divested of its spontaneity, its liveliness, its sense of sudden drama, and above all, its peculiar unruly quirks. In the words of psychiatrist Berthold Eric Schwarz, who has probably collected and published more accounts of ESP between parent and child than any other living writer, "Psi is the essence of spontaneity, the unexpected, and unprecedented. . . . It can catch one off guard, knows no boundaries, and cannot be controlled. The wild animal in his habitat is a different beast from the forlorn creature caged in a zoo."[1]

One purpose of the exercises in the chapters ahead is to catch a glimpse of the wild animal in its habitat. All of the exercises are designed for the relaxed atmosphere of your own home. Home is the ideal place to experiment with parent-child ESP and to work on developing your intuitive skills. A study conducted by Athena Drewes and Sally Ann Drucker showed that children tested at home scored higher than those tested in a nursery or day-care situation.[2]

Parapsychologists sometimes go to great lengths to rule out the possibility of fraud, subliminal impressions, or anything other than ESP that could conceivably explain a correct "hit." Percipients and agents are carefully separated, isolated in soundproof rooms. Random sampling is frequently assured by the most elaborate means. Cards are shuffled by machines. If, after taking all of these precautions, there is the least possibility that a test has not been executed under the most severely controlled conditions, the parapsychologist responsible is likely to see his work torn to shreds by other parapsychologists who, if anything, can be a critical bunch.

However, unless you plan to publish your results in a parapsychological journal, you can safely forget about rigid controls. In fact, you can even make many ESP exercises into a game with your child.

As stated earlier, a positive mental attitude toward ESP is a key factor in success with psychic experiments. ESP is far more likely to work for those who believe in it.

ESP is also likely to be more common in persons who pay attention to and value their intuition. Just paying attention to your intuition may be a way of opening the mind to ESP. In the words of transpersonal psychologist Frances Vaughan, Ph.D., of Marin County, California, "Attention is the psychic energy which can activate your intuitive ability."[3] It may both heighten your extrasensory ability and make you more aware of everyday ESP experiences that might otherwise be overlooked. It is like paying attention to dreams. Many are not aware of having a rich dream life until they begin to recall their dreams on a regular basis. They then find they are dreaming more frequently and more vividly. This is largely because the dreamer's ability to recall dreams has improved.

Dr. Schwarz advises writing telepathic experiences down, the obviously genuine as well as the "gray" ones. "Before you know it," he says, "the spark jumps the gap and you may find yourself getting some spectacular accounts." Recording bonafide ESP experiences may also give you confidence in your psychic ability and lead to more episodes. "Success breeds success," says Dr. Schwarz. And if anyone should know, he should. He has recorded 1,521 ESP episodes in his own family.

Acting on your intuition, your "gut" feelings and hunches when it seems reasonable to do so can also increase your intuitive abilities. By so doing, you learn to trust your intuition and perhaps to tune into your psychic ability more easily. "The more you act on your feelings and take the risk of checking out the validity of your intuition," says Dr. Vaughan, "the more reliable it can become."[4]

When you have a hunch or intuition, it is wise to examine it in the light of common sense. As Dr. Vaughan points out in her book *Awakening Intuition*, "Rational, discriminating judgment is essential to checking the validity of intuitive perceptions and evaluating the process."[5]

Most psychically talented persons agree that a relaxed state of body and mind is essential to success with ESP. Some will find it helpful to do the following simple relaxation exercise before attempting the psychic exercises in the next chapters. It will give you the feeling of total body relaxation and help you get in the right state of mind for ESP. It is based on Autogenic Therapy, a method of relaxation and healing developed in the 1920s by Dr. J. H. Schultz, a German physician.

• ● •

Get into a comfortable position. Some people find relaxation exercises most effective when they are lying down flat on the back, hands at the sides. Others, while doing psychic work, prefer to sit with the spine straight in a meditative posture.

Close your eyes.

Inhale deeply and slowly through the nose. Exhale through slightly parted lips.

Continue to breathe this way for a minute or so.

Now let your breathing become a little deeper, a little slower, without forcing the breath in any way.

Continue to breathe in this slow, relaxing way through the exercise.

Now, with each breath in and each breath out, mentally repeat the following words: My right arm is heavy and warm.

Do this for a couple of deep breaths.

Now, with each breath in and each breath out, mentally say: My left arm is heavy and warm.

Now, with each breath in and each breath out, say: My right leg is heavy and warm.

Now, with each breath in and each breath out, say: My left leg is heavy and warm.

Now say: My abdomen and pelvic organs are warm, comfortable, and relaxed.

Observe your breathing, calm and regular.

With the next breath out say: It breathes me . . . it breathes me.

Now say: The muscles of my back and neck are warm and relaxed.

After a half minute or so, with the next breath out say: My jaw muscles are loose and relaxed.

Now with the next breath out say: My forehead is cool.

With the next breath out say: My eyelids are heavy and relaxed.

Enjoy the sensation of complete relaxation for a minute or so.

While in a state of deep relaxation, go ahead with one of the exercises in this book.

When you have finished, take a deep breath, stretch gently, and open your eyes.

In addition to relaxation, a passive yet alert state of mind seems to be most conducive to ESP. The trick is to relax completely, yet keep the mind open and alert. For many, this is difficult at first. Improvement comes with practice.

A nonjudgmental attitude is also essential to success. You must temporarily suspend the critical faculty. Allow yourself to perceive an ESP impression without trying to analyze it at first. Just let the thoughts or impressions come. You can always analyze them later.

Concentration is also important. If you are trying to send a message telepathically, blank out all other thoughts to the best of your ability and fix your attention on the message you are trying to send. If you want to receive a telepathic message, let go of all other thoughts and keep your mind as blank as possible.

Don't "try" too hard to get a psychic impression. This can inhibit intuition. Put yourself in the right state of mind, tell your inner mind what you want, and "let it happen."

Gifted psychic Ingo Swann says that the developed psychic has learned to switch gears, to shift focus from everyday consciousness to a communion with the deeper self. In his book, *Natural ESP*, he writes: "The developed psychic creates an unimpeded pathway from the deeper self to conscious awareness in which the incoming psychic information can be perceived with relative clarity. In psychic parlance, this is often referred to as 'focusing.'"[6]

Quieting the mind increases the ability to think in images, the language of most ESP experiences. Psychic perceptions most often come in the form of images. When trying to communicate telepathically or pick up an impression about someone, you are more likely to see a picture before the inner mind than to think of an idea.

Sometimes one glimpses a trivial rather than an important detail. For example, in attempting to connect telepathically with someone at a distance, you may glimpse the bright-green jacket the person is wearing rather than the person himself, or you may catch a glimpse of a seemingly unimportant object in the person's field of vision—a passing train, a wall poster, and so forth.

ESP often seems to work in such patches of information. Sometimes the details glimpsed before the mind's eye are so trivial, or flit by so quickly, that one does not recognize them for ESP.

Czech parapsychologist Dr. Milan Ryzl of San Diego State University gives an example of a woman getting a psychic impression of a pair of scissors. The impressions came to mind gradually:

"First a series of quickly changing pictures appeared to me; such details were dancing before my eyes as if a quickened film were being projected. A metallic color with a dim luster appeared to me, an acute angle, an obtuse angle, but I was unable to locate either the color or the angles more closely in space. Then the acute angle became more distinct to my vision. I noticed that there were two acute angles with their tips pointing toward each other. The metallic gray color became localized to the obtuse angles on the sides. . . . It reminded me of two crossed pencils. . . . When I said it looked like two crossed pencils, I now had the impression that it actually was something across each other, but it was definitely not pencils . . . the ends away from me were pointed . . . but those near me did not appear to me. I had not gotten it sharp enough yet . . . It struck me as if two circles were projecting out of a thick fog . . . it was a pair of scissors."[7]

Often instead of getting the complete picture one will get only a fragment. For example, the woman quoted above first saw only a metallic color with a dim luster, then angles, then something like two crossed pencils. Many would get only these impressions without later receiving the distinct impression that the object was a pair of scissors.

One obstacle to success with telepathy is the tendency to write off an image as unimportant. Pay careful attention even to seemingly irrelevant details. Write down your images or fix them in your mind and try to verify them for accuracy later.

If you glimpse a detail that you don't recognize or which has no meaning for you, ask your inner mind for clarification or more information. You may get more details or an insight.

An ESP impression frequently comes through like a radio station with a faint signal or with much static, especially when you first begin. The extrasensory message may include what parapsychologists refer to as "noise"—our own contribution and distortion. It may take considerable practice to get a clear message.

ESP often conveys information in the form of symbols. Interestingly, one may perceive an ESP-inspired symbol yet misinterpret the meaning. World-renowned parapsychologist Dr. W. H. C. Tenhaeff gives an example:

While with a woman he did not know, a psychic "saw" an image of a case of Smyrna raisins. Quite naturally, he asked her if she liked to eat raisins. She did not. The psychic then asked her if Smyrna raisins played a role in her life. The woman said she was born in Smyrna.

Why did the psychic think of a case of raisins? Perhaps the contents of his own mind influenced the telepathic message that he had received. The psychic had formerly worked in a grocery store and continued to be interested in things connected with the business. Had he been a postage stamp dealer, Dr. Tenhaeff suggests, he might have seen an image of a postage stamp with the word "Smyrna" on it.[8]

Symbolism such as this is very common in psychic impressions. In one case Dr. Tenhaeff describes, the psychic saw six glasses of beer over a person's head. The psychic first thought the person had something to do with a café or restaurant. But it turned out that the person was born in a village named Sexbierum![9]

In another striking example, a psychic was given a portrait of a man. He asked, "Does this man often come to Belgium?"

He was told no.

He then asked, "Did this man recently join a procession?"

Again no.

The psychic commented: "I cannot understand this. It makes me think of a Belgian market town, Hoogstraten, where I once saw a procession as a young boy. Now I am seeing the procession distinctly."

The name of the man in the portrait was Hoogstraten.[10]

It is easy to see how one can get an accurate psychic impression and come to an incorrect conclusion. With experience psychics are often able to interpret their impressions.

People respond to a wide variety of methods to tap intuition. You may find some exercises more effective than others. Some parents and children are prone to a particular type of psychic experience. One may have a tendency to clairvoyant dreams, a second person to hunches, a third to feeling another's symptoms in his own body, and so on.

Some psychics do best when holding an object, often metal, that belongs to the person with whom they are working. This is known as *psychometry*. Gifted psychic Peter Hurkos says he does best when holding someone's shoe!

Odd as it may seem, some people are good at picking up information only about certain subjects. George Tyrrell, a past president of the Society for Psychical Research, had an adopted daughter with a talent for finding lost objects. This led him to devise an automatic ESP testing device. The apparatus consisted of five closed boxes with a tiny electric lamp in each. He lit up one bulb at a time by means of mechanism that insured a random selection. His daughter, and later other persons, had to "guess" in which of the boxes the bulb was lit.[11]

The individual personality may have a tendency to determine the kind of information one best attunes to psychically. In a study conducted by Dr. K. Ramakrishna Rao, past president of the Parapsychological Association in Durham, North Carolina, and B. Kanthamani, subjects produced better results with symbols they chose than they did when using standard ESP cards. This is called the *differential* or *preferential effect*. One usually (but not always) obtains better results under conditions that are agreeable to the subject and with symbols the subject *prefers.*[12]

For example, Dr. Tenhaeff refers to a case of a psychic who could tune in on details of other people's sex lives—people entirely unknown to her! She was a very temperamental and sensual woman, says Dr. Tenhaeff, and this was where her interest lay.[13]

Speaking of sex, two researchers, G. W. Fisk and D. J. West, discovered a person who did particularly well with crosses and circles because they represented for him male and female genital organs. Following the subject's lead, they devised a test to see whether he would score higher with just erotic symbols. They made up a special deck of ESP cards with male and female symbols. The man was highly successful with the erotic symbols but obtained only chance scores with other symbols![14]

If you find you get best results with one particular subject or one type of ESP exercise, by all means work with this. Don't force yourself to do exercises that produce no results or that you don't like.

Don't expect to get consistent results every time you practice the exercises in this book. One thing that most psychics agree about is that ESP is difficult if not impossible to control. Even the most psychically talented do not always obtain accurate results. They frequently lose their ability from time to time. This is probably the main reason why fraud is so common among those who have genuine psychic talents (as well as those who don't). Many gifted psychics have been caught "cheating" despite the fact that their psychic ability has proven accurate on other occasions. Some who use their paranormal talent to entertain others perhaps feel they sometimes have to resort to trickery to produce consistent results.

Pay attention to your inner experience when you feel you have been successful with ESP. Psychic Ingo Swann, justly criticizes parapsychologists for ignoring the subject's inner experiences during ESP episodes. Indeed, inner experiences may be the key to unlocking untapped extrasensory potential.

You may find that you have a "psychic feeling" when receiving a telepathic impression. This is sometimes described as a tingle or a sense, difficult to describe, of having entered an altered state of mind. On the other hand, you may not notice any feeling or change in consciousness, yet still get results with ESP.

Some find that a particular symbol comes spontaneously to mind just before a telepathic or clairvoyant impression. The symbol seems to indicate a shift in consciousness to the psi-conducive state of mind.

Eileen Garrett, a talented psychic, the publisher of many books in the field of parapsychology, and the founder of the Parapsychology Foundation of New York, associated a symbol with ESP in her own life. In her book, *Telepathy*, she writes:

"Through all my supernormal life one particular symbol has recurred with regularity, and I find that this symbology serves for me as a key to unlock that condition of superreceptivity in which I can best accomplish significant telepathic communication."[15] Her symbol is an English yew tree.

A symbol like this may vary from time to time. Of her inner yew tree, Ms. Garrett writes:

"It grew as high as a church steeple. It split and became two trees; it bent over and became a tuning fork; and sometimes it buried itself in a stumpy cabbage. At times, it slipped off its heavy greenness and danced into a double-V shape; and at other times, it uprooted itself and curled, root in mouth, as a serpent. In turn, it became a wren's nest as it spread and widened itself or bent or danced or rocked.

"Sometimes the yew tree changed into a beautiful woman, though more often it became a giant. But more often still, the tree whirled and danced in a spinning circle, and then repeated itself many times and became a wood full of singing birds. It slipped away from itself and its own dark green foliage and hid in the trunk of the slender larch or likened itself to an oak. Sometimes it was a cavern in which I had hidden, and again it became an exotic plant that bore strange and lovely flowers."[16]

If you have a symbol that you associate with ESP, recalling it to mind may trigger the psi-conducive state, or what Ms. Garrett calls the "alertness necessary for supernormal functioning."[17]

"In working telepathically," she writes, "I have often to play games with my mind in order to escape from my surroundings." To do this she thinks of the yew tree symbol.

Though the ESP connection is a natural part of the parent-child relationship, it may take time to tune into your intuition. Don't expect immediate results. A few people have psychic experiences the first time they try, but most find that it takes time and energy to develop psychically. Just as other skills must be learned and exercised before they are fully developed, extrasensory skills must be practiced before they fully flower. With practice you will probably find yourself becoming gradually more intuitive.

Feel free to adapt any of the exercises in this book in any way you want. Let your intuition be your guide. Change the details in any way that is comfortable for you and that seems to yield results. Be creative. Explore new worlds.

10

ESP Exercises for Pregnancy

Both parents may be more open to ESP during the life-creating months than at any other time. Of course, not all expectant mothers and fathers have extrasensory experiences. But pregnancy is an ideal time to tune into the inner self and awaken latent ESP abilities.

Pregnant women and frequently their mates often have a sense of heightened intuition. Sometimes this is the result of listening to the body's subtle signals and increased self-reflection; sometimes, ESP.

Appreciating pregnancy and the body's amazing changes will provide a strong foundation toward heightening prenatal intuition. You are more likely to be intuitive if you have a positive attitude about pregnancy and birth. A positive attitude will also increase your chances of a more fulfilling childbearing experience.

The pregnant mother has a beauty and a vitality no one else shares. When you reflect on her ability to create, nurture, and give birth a new life, she is nothing short of awe-inspiring. It is perhaps for this reason that in many ancient cultures goddess figures were fashioned to look like expectant mothers with expanded bellies and pendulous breasts. Such images call to mind the power of nature, whom we still call "Mother Nature," as well as that aspect of nature which is woman's ability to create a new being.

Things have changed since our ancestors of 30,000 B.C. sculpted goddess figures in the shape of expectant mothers. Today volumes of scientific literature are written on conception, fetal development, and birth. We know much about the process of childbearing. However, pregnancy and birth still inspire awe; pregnancy is still a magical state of being.

Take a few minutes to consider the awesome changes your body is experiencing:

Get into a comfortable position and relax. Take a mental journey within.

Imagine the baby in his or her own private world surrounded by a sea of crystal clear water.

Imagine the curly white and blue umbilical cord connecting the baby to the placenta attached to the side of the uterus.

Through this amazing organ, the baby receives everything he or she needs to grow and develop.

Explore in your mind's eye the strong walls of the powerful uterus that keeps the baby snug and secure.

Thank your body for the miracle it is now working and will continue to work.

Then go ahead with one of the exercises following:

THE RADIANT LIGHT

During pregnancy you are the center of incredible energy. This exercise can make you more aware of the prenatal energy field and may increase your intuition. You and your partner have created a new being. Your womb is the source of all the changes taking place in your body, in your emotions, in your partner, and in your home. One of the first things to do to heighten your intuition is to center on your pregnancy, on the miracle that is taking place right now within your body. From this center, you can allow yourself to open. Let your awareness expand.

Sit or lie in a comfortable position.

Relax your body and mind.

Forget your responsibilities for a little while. You can always return to them later.

Focus your mind on your breathing. Allow it to become just a little slower and a little deeper without forcing the breath in any way.

Now, as you breathe in, imagine that your in-breath is a soft golden light.

Imagine that you are breathing this light directly into the womb. Sense the light entering your womb and surrounding your baby while he or she floats in a private sea of crystal clear water.

Imagine that the soft golden light you take in with each in-breath fills the womb until it begins to expand outward from the womb in all directions. Imagine it expanding further and further until your entire body is surrounded by a beautiful aura or halo of soft golden light.

If you wish, you can let the aura keep expanding until it surrounds your partner, even your entire home, with a soft golden glow.

Now imagine that your awareness is also expanding with the golden light.

Dwell on this image for a few minutes or as long as you like. Enjoy it.

Then, when you are ready to return to your everyday life, count slowly to five, stretch gently, and open your eyes.

Or, if you prefer, go ahead with either the *inner voice* or the *mind to mind* exercise ahead.

THE INNER VOICE

Your deeper mind knows what you and your baby most need for a healthier, happier pregnancy and a safe, fulfilling birth. This exercise can help you tap this knowledge and perhaps receive guidance from your inner self.

Do the *radiant light.*

Now, while dwelling on the image of the soft golden light radiating from your womb and surrounding your body, ask yourself any of the following questions:

What do I most need to do right now to enjoy a healthy pregnancy?

What do I most need to do to prepare for a safe, fulfilling birth?

What do I most need to do to prepare for a joyful beginning to parenthood?

Or any other question you want.

If thoughts or feelings come into your mind, let them drift freely. Don't attempt to analyze them just yet.

Then, when you are ready to return to your everyday life, count slowly to five, stretch gently, and open your eyes.

You may get a practical answer to one of your questions, such as more effective support to help you through labor, a different birthing environment, and so forth. By analyzing this with your rational mind, you can make a decision and act on it.

Always examine information received intuitively in the light of common sense.

You may get no impression at all when you do this exercise. If this is the case, don't be concerned. Even if you receive no direct answer to your question, this exercise can still make you more aware of your own and your baby's needs.

MIND TO MIND

If you would like to attempt sending and receiving thoughts with your partner, try this exercise.

Arrange a time when you and your partner can do this exercise at the same time. Take turns sending and receiving.

•●•

Do *The Radiant Light* on pages 208-209.

Now imagine that the soft golden light is surrounding your partner as well as yourself. It doesn't matter where he is—in the same room, across town, or on the other side of the world.

Tell yourself you are open to receiving thoughts or impressions from your partner during this meditation.

Or, imagine yourself sending a thought or impression to your partner along a current of soft golden light.

If thoughts or impressions come into your mind, let them drift freely. For the moment, just observe rather than react to whatever images arise.

Then, when you are ready to return to your everyday life, count slowly to five, stretch gently, and open your eyes.

If thoughts or impressions come to your mind, make a mental or written note of them after doing the exercise and discuss your impressions with your partner.

To further experiment with prenatal telepathy with your mate, you can also try the telepathy exercises designed for parents and children in chapter 11.

COMMUNICATING WITH YOUR UNBORN CHILD

Psychic experiences involving the unborn child, from flashes of intuition to prenatal dreams, are common. Many mothers and fathers feel they are able to communicate with their child in a language beyond the senses.

Of course, impressions about the unborn baby do not always imply ESP. Some are explicable in terms of subtle body signals; others are the result of the parents' imagination.

The exercises in this section will help you connect with and experience ESP with your baby in the womb. They also have other benefits whether or not you have a psychic experience.

Parent-unborn communication on whatever level can enrich the prenatal experience for both mother and father. Psychologist Leni Schwartz, Ph.D., who has taught hundreds of parents to communicate with the unborn child (though not necessarily in the context of ESP), believes that including your unborn child in meditation enhances the family relationship before birth. You accept the baby and see the unborn child as already part of your unfolding family. This may assist you to more fully develop the love bond with your child. As you "get in touch with your unborn child," you may also begin to confront your feelings about becoming a parent. Nothing can prepare you for what it will be like to be a mother or father twenty-four hours a day, seven days a week. But confronting your feelings now can help you make emotional adjustments to new parenthood. In addition, as you pay more attention to your child within, you may begin to think of your baby's experience of birth. This can inspire you to evaluate your choice of caregiver and birthing environment with the baby's experience in mind.

The first step in communicating with your unborn child is turning inward and paying more attention to the baby and to your feelings for your baby.

Sylvia Klein Olkin, author of *Positive Pregnancy Fitness,* suggests that parents meditate on sending their love to their child and opening up to receive love from the baby. She calls this process "inner bonding."

The following "inner bonding" exercise for both parents is based on an exercise designed by Ms. Olkin and Frederick Leboyer, French obstetrician and author of *Birth Without Violence.* While its purpose is to promote prenatal bonding and not necessarily to increase parapsychological communication, it can heighten your awareness of the parent-offspring ESP connection.

• ● •

Relax completely, body and mind.

Quiet your mind by concentrating on your breath flowing in and out.

Allow your breath to settle down and become a little slower, without forcing the breath in any way.

Imagine your whole being opening up to your unborn child.

Let the love you feel for your child well up within you. Imagine it pouring into your baby.

Now also imagine the bliss, the contentment, the security and happiness your baby feels and lives with in the womb pouring into you.

Imagine that these wonderful feelings can pass to you through a secret doorway. Open the door a bit wider so you can be flooded with these good feelings.

Dwell with your child and with these feelings for a few minutes.

• ● •

Franz Veldman, quoted by European psychiatrist W. Ernest Freud, recommends that the mother, after midpregnancy, put her hands gently on her abdomen, one on each side. "By leaving them there in the same position and without exerting pressure, she can cause the child in the womb to move from one side to the other. Thus she can gently 'rock' the child from left to right and from right to left. If she wishes to touch and caress her child she can do so by letting her feeling of love flow into one of her hands."[1]

Getting In Touch With Your Unborn Child

This exercise provides a peaceful inner journey that can leave you feeling refreshed and more centered on your baby. That alone can heighten your awareness of the ESP connection even if you don't get immediate results.

One father who used this exercise when expecting his first child remarked: "When I do this imagery, I have a peaceful sense of staring into my child's eyes, just sharing love between the two of us."

An expectant mother who tried it remarked: "It gives me a wonderful reassuring feeling—a sense of inner strength and power—and of knowing that my baby and I are making this passage together."

While doing this exercise, imagine the baby in any way that feels natural and comfortable for you. Don't be concerned about how the baby actually looks at this particular stage of development. Whether or not you imagine the baby as he or she actually appears is unimportant.

•●•

Mother's Version

Relax completely, body and mind.

Focus your mind on your breathing for a minute or so.

Allow your breathing to become a little deeper, a little slower, without forcing the breath in any way.

Imagine that you are breathing directly into the womb, where your baby is surrounded by crystal-clear water in his or her own private universe.

Now imagine that the in-breath is a soft, radiant, golden light.

Continue to breathe in the light until it fills your womb and surrounds your baby with a warm, vibrant glow.

Dwell for a minute or so on the soft, glowing, golden light filling your womb.

Now imagine that your mind is able to travel and you are able to enter the womb—face to face with your baby.

Allow the love you feel for your child to well up within you.

Speak to your baby—tell your baby anything you wish—how you are feeling right now, how you are looking forward to the day when you will hold him or her in your arms.

If you find your attention wandering, mentally repeat the words "baby, baby, baby" and let yourself drift into a peaceful, relaxed state, dwelling on your baby.

Enjoy this imagery for a few minutes.

When you are ready, count slowly to five, stretch gently, and open your eyes.

Or, if you wish, remain in your relaxed state and continue with Talking With Your Baby, the next exercise ahead.

• ● •

Father's Version

Relax completely, body and mind.

Focus your mind on your breathing for a minute or so.

Allow your breathing to become a little deeper, a little slower, without forcing the breath in any way.

Now imagine that the in-breath is a soft, radiant, golden light.

Continue to breathe in the light until it fills your entire body and radiates from your body in all directions.

Imagine that the golden light also surrounds your baby with its soft, vibrant glow and links you with your unborn child. It doesn't matter whether you are in the same room with your mate and developing baby or a thousand miles away. Right now, the soft golden light that you breathe in connects you with your unborn child.

Now imagine that you are cradling the baby in your arms.

Allow the love you feel for your child to well up within you.

Speak to your baby, tell your baby anything you wish—how you are feeling right now, how you are looking forward to greeting him or her on the day of birth.

If you find your attention wandering, mentally repeat the words "baby, baby, baby" and let yourself drift into a peaceful, relaxed state, dwelling on your child.

Enjoy this imagery for a few minutes.

When you are ready, count slowly to five, stretch gently, and open your eyes.

Or, if you wish, remain in your relaxed state and continue with Talking With Your Baby, the next exercise ahead.

• ● •

Talking With Your Baby

In this exercise, you ask the baby a specific question and remain open to receive an answer.

This is a form of *receptive visualization*—a method of tuning in to your intuition, in which you put yourself in a receptive mood to receive the answer to a general or specific question.

According to Mike Samuels, M.D., and Nancy Samuels in *The Well Baby Book,* "Through receptive visualization a parent may catch a glimpse of the unborn baby and come to know the baby's personality. Even answers to direct questions about the baby may come in the form of visual impressions or thoughts."[2]

To get results, it is not necessary to believe that you are actually communicating with the baby. Some parents think of this exercise as a means of tapping their own inner minds. Answers they receive, including information acquired extrasensorily, may spring from their own unconscious. Others feel that the answer they receive is from the baby. As one father put it: "I feel that I'm receiving guidance from the baby in some way I can't quite understand."

• ● •

Relax completely, body and mind.

Do the previous exercise, Getting In Touch With Your Unborn Child.

Then, while dwelling on your unborn child, ask a question.

You can ask a specific question, such as "Where would you like to be born?" or a more general question like "What do you need most right now?"

Imagine that your baby can answer you, not necessarily in

words, but in images, impressions, or by painting a picture in your mind's eye.

When you are ready, count slowly to five, stretch gently, and open your eyes.

• ● •

The Chevraux Pendulum

In *The Well Baby Book* Dr. Mike Samuels and Nancy Samuels suggest the Chevraux pendulum to tap one's intuition.

For some this simple method works effectively. One study which the Samuels cite claims that the method was greater than 90 percent accurate regarding the unborn baby's gender for those who got a definite yes or no answer in the third trimester. Not all parents do get a definite yes or no, however.

• ● •

Tie a small weight such as a ring with a one-foot piece of string or thread. Sitting comfortably, hold the cord lightly between your thumb and forefinger while asking yourself a simple question to which the answer is "yes," such as, "Am I pregnant?" See which way the pendulum swings.

Now ask another question to which the answer is "no." The pendulum may begin to move in another direction. You can also ask yourself another question with an "I don't know" answer. The pendulum may make a third and different motion.

Once you are familiar with the pendulum's motions corresponding to "yes," "no," and "I don't know," ask: "Is my unborn child a boy?" According to the Samuels, "the pendulum will begin to swing in one of its characteristic motions."[3]

• ● •

Many parents who have done exercises like those in this section have a heightened feeling of intuition and a sense of communicating with the baby in a preverbal language. Ria, one mother whom Dr. Leni Schwartz quotes, remarked, "I began to picture the development of the baby. I was acutely aware that my baby isn't ready to be born yet. I can't explain how I know that, I just know it in a lot of ways. The baby and I seemed to understand about that."[4]

However, it is often difficult to tell if you are actually communicating with your baby in a language beyond words. When your baby kicks in response to your thoughts, moves in the uterus when you are excited, seems to share your emotions, are you really communicating psychically? Or is the communication just the result of biological processes? Or both? Perhaps no one will ever know. And perhaps it doesn't make any difference. If, in your attempts to turn inward, you are sharing love with your child, you are communicating in the most important way of all. And one doesn't have to be psychic to do that.

11

ESP Exercises for Parents and Children

The exercises in this chapter are designed to help you explore ESP in the parent-child relationship and to develop your intuition. You can do them with your children whether they are preschoolers or adults and whether they are living with you or in a distant area.

You may find the exercises work best with young children. This is because children are frequently more open to ESP and find it easier to be in turn with their intuition. In her book *Awakening Intuition*, Frances E. Vaughan, Ph.D., a psychologist in Marin County, California, who has taught intuition workshops, says: "Many adults in my groups have said they felt they were more intuitive as children, and that they learned to keep their intuitive perceptions to themselves after encountering skepticism or ridicule from adults."[1]

It is never too late, however, to learn to tune into your intuition. The exercises in this chapter may awaken skills you perhaps experienced as a child. Or they may help you develop intuitive ability even if you have never had an ESP experience.

Not everyone responds equally well to the same exercise. Do those you feel most comfortable with and which you find most effective. You may do well in telepathic picture drawing, which many find a very effective way to develop psychically. Or you may be more interested in exploring psychic dreams. Some methods of psychic development may work better for you than others. Many gifted psychics excel in one area. Some specialize in psychic diagnosis and healing. Some are good at giving readings (picking up and interpreting psychic impressions) about a wide range of subjects, while others are able to tune into psychic information only about specific areas—crime detection, for instance.

If you get no results with one exercise, wait for another day. Or try another exercise. It may take many attempts before you find what works best for you. Keep at it.

Do the exercises as often or as seldom as you want. You may want to do them just once or twice to experiment with parent-child ESP. Or you may want to do them on a regular basis to develop your intuition and strengthen the family bond.

Don't let ESP exercises develop into a competitive affair. If you are doing extrasensory exercises with two or more children, one may excel and do better than the others. This is to be expected. Though everyone probably has latent ESP ability, some are more psychically gifted.

If one child does exceptionally well, don't let the others feel bad by overpraising that child. Treat ESP as a natural and normal part of parent-child relationship, which in fact it is. Don't allow one child to feel inferior because he doesn't do as well on an ESP experiment as another. Siblings have enough of a struggle without feeling less competent as a brother or sister at ESP.

Two of the exercises ahead are "serious" meditations—The Psychic Umbilical Cord and The Aura of Light. They focus on love, healing, and strengthening the family bond. Others such as The Taste Test and The Colored Candies Test can be used as family games.

However, *all* of the exercises open the door to what is for many parents and children a new and uncharted world of self-exploration. All of them can help you awaken and develop your intuition and make you more aware of the parent-offspring ESP connection.

THE PSYCHIC UMBILICAL CORD

The parent-offspring ESP connection may be compared to a psychic umbilical cord which unites parent and child regardless of how far geographically they may be from one another.

This simple but very effective meditation can make you more aware of the parent-offspring ESP connection. You can use this meditation whether your child is a newborn or an adult, whether he or she is living with you or on the other side of the world. You may also find it a particularly effective way to connect psychically with an infant.

• ● •

Relax completely, body and mind.

Imagine that you and your child are connected by a psychic umbilical cord.

Visualize the cord as an endless stream of light extending from you to your offspring.

Mentally tell yourself that only positive, constructive thoughts and energy can flow along this cord and that negative thoughts or energy cannot enter it.

Dwell with this image in your mind's eye for a few minutes.

If you wish, send a message along this stream of light—a thought, a feeling, or simply your love.

Then, when you have enjoyed this exercise for as long as you want, tell yourself that you are returning to the world of everyday life, that you will feel relaxed, refreshed, and in greater touch with your child.

Stretch gently, count slowly to five, and open your eyes.

•●•

If thoughts, images, or impressions enter your mind while you are doing this exercise, let them drift freely before the screen of you inner mind. Don't attempt to analyze them while you are meditating. Just let them be there. Make a mental note of whatever has come to you. If you think you may have perceived a telepathic impression about your child, you can later verify it.

You can use this exercise to "set the stage" for sending a telepathic message, or for sending thoughts of healing or love. To do this, imagine that the thoughts or feelings that you direct to your child, or parent, are reaching him by way of the psychic umbilical cord.

In his book, *Wisdom of the Mystic Masters*, Joseph Weed, a Rosicrucian, suggests visualizing the recipient's name or face and sending a telepathic idea out on a stream of love.[2] You can imagine the telepathic impression traveling to the recipient with a stream of love along this psychic umbilical cord.

When you attempt to receive a telepathic impression, you can imagine it traveling to you with a stream of love along this umbilical cord.

AURA OF LIGHT

You can use this exercise to send healing energy or simply your love to your child.

•●•

Relax completely, body and mind.

Imagine that your child is surrounded by an aura of white light.

Picture the entire body surrounded by glowing, radiant light.

Imagine your child's whole being becoming filled with healing energy.

With each breath you take in, imagine that the energy is getting stronger and the light glowing more brightly.

Tell yourself: Only positive energy can enter this aura. Negative energy cannot enter.

Dwell with this image for a few minutes, directing your love, your energy, to your child.

Then when you are ready, open your eyes.

• ● •

If, while using this exercise for healing, you perceive one part of the aura as murky, make it bright. If you sense that a particular area of the body is most in need of healing, send light to that area.

Dr. Mike Samuels and Nancy Samuels, authors of *The Well Baby Book* and *The Well Child Book*, recommend using a similar exercise for healing.

Here are their suggestions:

Imagine the person you wish to heal surrounded by white light.

Imagine yourself at one with the person in an atmosphere of love.

Imagine energy flowing from or through your body to the body of the person you wish to help.

Visualize yourself, helpers, or tools going into the body of the person you wish to heal and changing a sick area to a healthy one.

Mental imagery can be an effective way to help bring about healing. Your child can do imagery himself when ill while you reinforce his imagery (or do the imagery for him) by sending a psychic impression. The following images are adapted from *The Well Child Book:*[3]

• ● •

Relax completely, body and mind.

Imagine that you are sending one of the following images to your child:

FOR PAIN: Imagine the pain coming out of the body and blowing away like smoke.

FOR FEVER: Imagine a cool wind blowing over the body, or imagine that the body is covered with snow.

FOR CUTS: Imagine that the sides of the cut get sticky, then join together, and the bleeding stops. Imagine that the line of the cut gets smooth and disappears.

FOR BRUISES: Imagine the black and blue mark turning into tiny dots and gradually fading away.

FOR BROKEN BONES: Imagine the bones being stuck together with glue and being stronger than ever.

FOR BURNS: Imagine the burned area feeling as if it were in ice water.

FOR NOSEBLEEDS: Imagine the blood is coming from a tiny faucet which you can slowly shut off.

FOR A RUNNY NOSE: Imagine the lining of the nose shrinking and becoming dry. Imagine a faucet at the top of the nose being shut off.

FOR RASHES: Imagine the skin feeling smooth as silk. Imagine the redness disappearing as if it were being erased.

FOR ITCHES: Imagine the skin feeling as if a cool breeze were blowing over it. Imagine floating in cool water.

FOR A SORE THROAT: Imagine cold ice cream sliding down the throat.

FOR EARACHE AND STUFFED-UP EARS: Imagine that the tubes that go from the ear to the back of the throat are opening.

FOR COUGHS: Imagine the chest becoming warm.

FOR STOMACHACHE: Imagine the stomach calm like a smooth lake.

THE TASTE TEST

This is a very simple exercise to elicit a telesomatic response (physical reaction to ESP). One person tastes a substance while another attempts to receive an impression of the object tasted. Some find this quite effective. You can turn it into a game with your child.

TASTER:
Go into a separate room with the door closed.

Choose a familiar substance with a distinct flavor to taste. Examples are vinegar, salty snacks, mustard, ketchup, Worcestershire sauce, pickles, lemon, orange, lime, licorice, or spices such as cayenne, cinnamon, cloves, and nutmeg.

Tasting a small quantity is sufficient.

If the substance tasted has a strong odor, be sure you and the receiver are sufficiently far apart to rule out the possibility of smelling it.

Signal the subject when you are ready. You can use a bell or other sound-producing device, or simply say you are ready.

RECEIVER:
Relax and remain open for impressions. Try to sense the substance being tasted.

TASTER AND RECEIVER:
Compare impressions with the actual substance tasted.

Allow a few minutes to elapse between each two substances tasted to be sure the taste or impression of one substance is not still lingering when trying another.

You can try to intensify the telepathic message by getting involved in what you taste, as fully as possible. Suppose you have chosen a lemon. Hold the lemon in your hand, feeling the texture of the skin. Bring the lemon close to your nose and smell the fragrance. Peel it, appreciating its texture and fragrance. Finally, eat a small portion.

More than two people can try the taste test at the same time. For example, a parent can do the tasting while two or more children in the other room try to identify the substance. Or two or more tasters can taste the same substance and send a message to one person.

THE COLORED CANDIES TEST

This exercise, especially good for young children, is adapted from an ESP test several parapsychologists have used to test ESP in children. The object is for your child (the recipient) to perceive the color of a candy chosen by you (the sender).

Choose candies with several colors such as colored lollipops or M&M's. Place these in a bowl.

You can check results after each choice of candy or you can do a run of several trials before checking the results. If you do several trials, the sender should write down the color chosen and the recipient should make a note of the response. Limit the number of trials to twelve to avoid boredom. Parapsychologists have found that as the recipient grows bored, ESP scores decline and the recipient sometimes even produces reverse results.

During this exercise sender and recipient should be in separate rooms with a door closed between them.

SENDER:
When you are ready to begin, signal the recipient with a bell or simply say, "ready."

Now, with eyes closed, choose one of the colored candies from the bowl. Look at the color. Write the color down. Then concentrate on it.

RECIPIENT:
Relax. With eyes closed, try to "see" what color candy was chosen in the other room. When you think you have an answer, note it down.

SENDER AND RECIPIENT:
Compare results.

Reverse roles if you want and have the child send you the message.

If your child is too young to write down his response, try using different colored crayons to correspond to the colors of the candies. Your child can note his impression of the color by making a mark or even drawing a picture of the candy on a sheet of paper.

The sender can try to intensify the telepathic message by using crayons also. Instead of merely concentrating on the color of the candy, draw a picture of the candy with a colored crayon.

THE TELEPATHIC PICTURE EXERCISE

This exercise can be a fascinating and enjoyable way to explore parent-child telepathy. It uses pictures, which are far more interesting and easy to concentrate on than ESP cards or abstract symbols. The object is to transmit a detail or, if possible, an entire picture via ESP. Use simple scenes to begin with. Then if the results are good, gradually work up to more complex pictures.

During this exercise, sender and recipient should go into separate rooms with a door closed between them.

SENDER:
Select a picture from a book or magazine or use an art work, whichever you prefer. Try choosing pictures that elicit an emotional response.

In a quiet room, concentrate on the picture, blocking out all other thoughts to the best of your ability, and attempt to transmit the picture telepathically to the receiver.

There are several ways to intensify the telepathic image:

Try drawing the picture as you concentrate on it.

Get involved in the picture using as many senses as possible. For example, if the picture depicts a bowl of oranges, you may want to eat an orange or imagine yourself eating or squeezing an orange.

If the picture shows action, imagine yourself somehow participating in the action. You may even want to act out a scene. For example, if the picture shows a backpacker hiking through the woods, you may want to put on a backpack and hike around the room with a walking stick.

Have fun with this exercise!

RECIPIENT:

Relax completely body and mind.

Write down your impressions of the picture.

Or sketch your impressions. This often conveys a telepathic image more accurately than words.

Also note down your reactions—moods, thoughts, images, and feelings that the picture evokes.

SENDER AND RECIPIENT:

Compare impressions with the actual picture.

If you want, select another picture and switch roles.

Results are likely to improve with practice, Transpersonal psychologists Gay Hendricks, Ph.D., and Thomas Roberts, Ph.D., who have designed a wide variety of exercises to be used with children to heighten awareness (included in their *Second Centering Book*), find this a particularly good one for testing and developing extrasensory abilities.

TELEPATHIC PICTURE DRAWING

Many people find telepathic picture drawing the most effective way to get results with ESP. Some who have difficulty with other psychic exercises excel at this. Gifted psychic Ingo Swann believes that picture drawing is the ideal way to develop psychic ability and has devoted much of his illuminating book, *Natural ESP,* to mastering this method. Picture drawing works with an elemental, nonverbal language bypassing verbalization. For this reason it may be closest to most parent-child ESP taking place below the threshold of awareness.

Telepathic picture drawing can be a fascinating "ESP game" for children who often love to draw what is on their minds. And the results can be startling.

In 1971 Ingo Swann participated in an experiment with the American Society for Psychical Research in New York, which involved attempting to clairvoyantly perceive objects at a distance. Experimenters selected a wide variety of objects, from a notebook to a 7-Up can. Mr. Swann was to try to "see" the objects and describe what he perceived. When he verbalized his impressions, the results, though impressive, were not what he wanted. Suddenly he got the idea of drawing his impressions as they came to mind. He says that the shift from verbalizing to picture drawing was the key ingredient responsible for his achieving significant results. In one experiment he drew a rectangular shaped object surrounded by what he thought looked like Arabic letters. Upon turning his picture upside down, he found that it was the exact replica of an object hidden in another room—a 7-Up can. Upside down, the letters and numeral appeared to be in a foreign language.

He then did extensive research and experimentation with telepathic picture drawing before coming to the conclusion that it was the best way to convey information psychically.

One does not have to be artistic to succeed with this method of telepathic communication and psychic development. Successful psychic drawings are almost always mere sketches—attempts to translate on paper what the inner mind perceives. Picture drawing, Ingo Swann says, "translates the incoming psychic information into basic forms and shapes which are recognized by the individual's psychic system and consciousness. The picture drawing mechanism seldom goes beyond this specific task, and it is unusual to find picture drawings fleshed out into highly artistic renderings. When the drawing *is* fleshed out, we are most likely to discover that it has been done so by consciousness trying to fill in the holes and that what has been filled in is erroneous."[4]

The Sinclair experiments in telepathic picture drawing, involving well-known novelist Upton Sinclair and his wife, Mary Craig (discussed in chapter 2) remain one of the most fascinating and often quoted studies in parapsychological literature, more than fifty years after being published in the book *Mental Radio* in 1930. Mrs. Sinclair points out: "This technique takes time, and patience, and training in the art of concentration."[5]

Though concentration may be essential to achieve consistently striking results, anyone can try telepathic picture drawing. You can try this ESP exercise with a young child so long as he is old enough to draw.

First read through the directions and, if the child with whom you are doing this exercise is very young, explain the directions to him in simple language.

Sender (the person doing the original drawing) and recipient (the person attempting to reproduce the drawing telepathically) should go into separate rooms.

SENDER:

Sketch a drawing on a plain, unlined sheet of white paper—a geometrical shape, a figure, a design, a scene—whatever you wish as long as it is distinct and clear. Choose subjects that are easily recognized at first. As you gain proficiency you can try more complicated subjects.

When you are finished with the drawing, tell the recipient you are ready. Then concentrate on what you have drawn.

RECIPIENT:
Relax. Tell your inner self that you want to see what has been drawn in the other room. Don't try to create an image. Just wait expectantly and allow an image to form in your mind's eye. Observe whatever forms appear on the screen of your inner mind.

If you receive an image, draw it immediately even if the image seems foolish to you. Don't omit fragments that seem to be out of place. Just draw what you see in your mind's eye.

Also make a note of any thoughts or impressions that may have come to mind in connection with the drawing.

SENDER AND RECIPIENT:
Compare the drawings.

VARIATION:
You may want to try this variation of telepathic picture drawing. It is based on instructions given by Mary Craig Sinclair in *Mental Radio:*

SENDER:
Sketch a design, figure, scene, or geometric shape on a piece of paper. Fold the paper in two so the drawing cannot be seen, or place the paper in an envelope.

RECEIVER:
Relax completely body and mind, with the sheet of paper or envelope nearby. When you are completely relaxed, take the drawing in your hand and hold it over your solar plexus.

Give your inner mind the suggestion: "I want to see the drawing on this paper."

Remain relaxed and in a passive but alert state of mind.

Try gently and without straining to see whatever forms appear on the screen of your inner mind.

Don't try to create an image. Just wait expectantly and allow an image to form in your mind's eye. Observe whatever forms appear on the screen of your inner mind.

If you receive an image, try to fix it clearly in your mind.

If you wish, repeat this process two or three times to see if the same image persists in coming back.

As soon as you feel you have the correct image, sketch the details you have perceived. Don't omit fragments which seem to be to be out of place.

Record also your thoughts or impressions about the image.

Now compare what you have drawn and recorded with the actual original drawing.

You may have to try this exercise several times before getting results. The process of receiving images can be subtle. Mrs. Sinclair's experience may give others a better understanding of how psychic images sometimes form in the mind. She writes:

"Fragments of forms appear first. For example, a curve line, or a straight one, or two lines of a triangle. But sometimes the complete object appears; swiftly, lightly, dimly drawn, as on a moving-picture film. These mental visions appear and disappear with lightning rapidity, never standing still unless quickly fixed by a deliberate effort of consciousness. They are never in heavy lines, but as if sketched delicately, in a slightly deeper shade of gray than that of the mental canvas. A person not used to such experiments may at first fail to observe them on the gray background of the mind, on which they appear and disappear so swiftly. Sometimes they are so vague that one gets only a notion of how they look before they vanish."[6]

You may find that you get some elements correct but that your imagination has contributed others. Or you may actually sketch the drawing with a fair amount of accuracy yet misinterpret it. In one of the Sinclair examples mentioned in chapter 2, Upton Sinclair sketched a volcano with black smoke pouring out. Mary Craig sketched a practically identical drawing yet called it a black beetle.

You may get the message or part of the drawing but associate it with something in your mind and, as a result, create an entirely different drawing. As Ingo Swann points out: "Associations take place when the incoming ESP information gets far enough into the system to trigger some sympathetic image, feeling, taste, smell, etc., but not far enough to objectively emerge as a totally correct drawing.[7] Perhaps this is analogous to what happens during many experiences of parent-child crisis telepathy when a parent (or child) is inexplicably depressed yet does not perceive the actual crisis.

Telepathic images often come in bits and pieces. Sometimes the individual elements of the original drawing are reproduced in the telepathic drawing yet don't fit together in a coherent whole. For example, in one of the Sinclair experiments, the original was a diamond and the reproduction was two triangles without bases at a distance from one another. Had the triangles been put closer together, they would have matched the original. Ingo Swann calls this phenomenon "lack of fusion."[8] He says that it is a "hopeful and positive signal" that ESP is definitely working but is perhaps still learning to perceive a complete image.

Study how your telepathic drawings correspond to the originals, paying special attention to errors. According to Ingo Swann, the ESP process seems to "learn" from this type of comparison. He says, "if you do an intellectual analysis of your attempt, you will find that your picture drawings will gradually improve, sometimes considerably so."[9]

TRAVELING ESP

In this exercise you imagine that your consciousness is able to be present with the person with whom you want to communicate telepathically. It makes no difference whether the person is in the next room or 3,000 miles away.

Most people think of ESP ability as something deep within them. Some parapsychologists, however, have suggested that the mind—or a portion of the mind—is external to the body (or perhaps in a spaceless dimension of its own). You can think of this idea as a metaphor and imagine that your extrasensory faculty is outside of yourself and able to extend externally to a distant point.

Traveling ESP is not the same as an out of body experience during which the mind, or soul, actually appears to leave the body. During traveling ESP you simply imagine that your are in a distant location.

To experiment with traveling ESP you can try to perceive an object in a distant room. Have someone place an object on a table or elsewhere in a distant room.

• ● •

Relax body and mind.

Imagine that you are in the room and able to see the object.

Describe or sketch your impressions.

Compare your impressions with the actual object.

• ● •

If you are successful with this exercise, it is difficult to tell whether you are actually perceiving the object clairvoyantly or are picking up an impression telepathically from the other person.

You can try traveling ESP to pick up a telepathic impression from your offspring:

• ● •

Relax completely, body and mind.

Tell yourself that you are able to be present with your child wherever he or she is.

Mentally travel to the place where your child is. Look around as if you were there.

Visualize the place in as much detail as you can. When you do this, observe whether the sun is out or whether it is cloudy— and any other details you can.

See yourself walking into the house where your child is— actually being there.

Allow thoughts, impressions, or images to come into your mind. Let them drift freely. Don't try to analyze them. Just let them be there.

If you feel you have had a psychic impression but it doesn't make sense to you, ask your inner mind for more information.

When you are ready, open your eyes.

• ● •

If possible, verify your impressions for accuracy.

TUNING INTO PSYCHIC DREAMING

The world of psychic dreams is one of the most fascinating dimensions of parent-child ESP to explore. Many parapsychologists believe that during dreaming we are closest to our unconscious ESP processes. This is probably the reason that some people find psychic experiences occurring more frequently during dreams than during waking life.

Paying greater attention to psychic dreams can teach us about ourselves and shed light on the often unnoticed extrasensory relationship we share with our children. Dreams provide a wealth of possibilities for exploring parent-offspring ESP. You can heighten your awareness of spontaneous ESP dreams, discover whether or not you and your child share similar dreams on occasion, and try to influence a dream telepathically. You can also experiment with ESP during the imagery-rich "twilight state" just before falling asleep.

Becoming Aware of Spontaneous ESP Dreams

Some people seem to have a natural propensity for psychic dreaming and have more psychically meaningful dreams than others.

Psychic dreams in the parent-child relationship either encompass a telepathic message from a parent or offspring or include precognitive elements. In telepathic dreams one glimpses a scene from an event that is occurring to a parent or child at the same time the dream is unfolding. This is most common during a crisis or other situation likely to involve strong emotions. In precognitive dreams one glimpses a scene from a future event.

In either case, the process of becoming more aware of spontaneous psychic dreaming is similar.

The first step is to remember what you have dreamed. Most people forget most of their dreams by morning. However, virtually everyone can learn to remember his or her dreams accurately with conscious effort.

Before going to bed, give yourself the suggestion that you will remember your dreams upon waking. Then, as soon as you wake up, think about what you have dreamed. Try to recall the dream in as much detail as possible. After practicing this for a short while, you will no doubt find that your dreams become more vivid and that you are able to remember more details.

The second step is to focus on just that small percentage of dreams which contain extrasensory elements. To do this, enlist the help of your inner mind. Before going to sleep, give your inner mind a suggestion such as, "I will wake when I have had a psychically meaningful dream."

Most people find it helpful to make a note of their dreams. To do this, keep a pencil and pad of paper by your bed so you can write down a dream immediately after waking while it is still fresh in your mind.

Write down as many details as you can remember, even if they seem unimportant. This is a key step in detecting a psychic dream. It is the unusual, often trivial, details rather than the dominant themes or major characters that frequently represent psychic impressions.

You may find that psychic impressions in dreams stand out in some unique way from the rest of the dream. For example, you may dream of a word or phrase written on a blackboard or spoken in a foreign language. Perhaps telepathy may be symbolized by a telephone call. There are any number of possibilities.

If you think that a dream or an element in a dream is psychically meaningful, try to verify it as soon as you can. For example, if you have dreamed that a son at college is having a difficult time preparing for an exam, call him and ask if this is so. Otherwise you may never know that your dream scene corresponds to a real life event.

Keep a record—mental or written—of actual psychic dreams. This will give you encouragement as your inner mind "learns" to make you more aware of psychic dreaming.

Becoming Aware of Shared Dreamscapes

Parents and offspring occasionally have synchronous dreams. Their dreams may share similar elements, identical images, and even the same scenes. This is sometimes the result of coincidence. For example, both dreams may be triggered by the same external stimulus—an odor, a sound outside, and so on. Other shared dreams result from parent-child psychic empathy.

Shared dreams can be quite striking as, for example, when father and son wake the same instant from the same or a similar nightmare. However many, if not most, shared dreams may be entirely unnoticed.

With practice you can become aware of spontaneous, shared ESP dreams. To increase your recognition of such dreams, Dr. Edward Taub-Bynum, a clinical psychologist at the University of Massachusetts who has done extensive research on shared dreams within the family, suggests setting aside a specific time each day—in the morning or evening—to discuss the dreams you had the night before. He has found that breakfast is the ideal time to discuss dreams. He suggests making dream discussion a family ritual. He says, "This is not only a way for the family to increase their sense of intimacy and empathy with each other, but it may also reveal—from time to time—a shared dream landscape either in terms of symbols or actual dream imagery."

If you are really interested in exploring shared dreams on a regular basis, Dr. Taub-Bynum suggests keeping a written dream log. Enter all of the dreams that seem to include a shared inner landscape within the family. Note as many details and similarities as possible and date each dream.

You may be surprised with your results.

TELEPATHIC DREAMING

An exciting way to explore the world of psychic dreaming, this exercise is based on the world-famous Maimonides Medical Center dream research experiment conducted by parapsychologists Dr. Montague Ullman and Dr. Stanley Krippner (discussed in chapter 7). One person (the sender) concentrates on an image and tries to influence telepathically the dream of another person (the recipient).

Famous artworks were chosen for the Maimonides experiment. However, you needn't use a famous painting unless you want to. Find any picture, preferably of a pleasant scene. Use a photo of a friend or relative, a page from a child's picture book, a nature scene from a magazine such as *National Wildlife.* Choose a scene from a faraway place that you would really like to visit, or something as familiar as your own backyard.

According to Ullman, Krippner, and Vaughan writing about the Maimonides project in *Dream Telepathy,* "The targets which are incorporated most easily into dreams generally depict people and are often archetypal (emotional) in character (which is why we have relied so heavily on art-prints rather than magazine pictures, for instance). If there is a person in the target picture with whom the dreamer can identify, a telepathic incorporation is more apt to occur."[10]

Choose something that elicits emotion so you will better able to concentrate on it and to increase your likelihood of sending an intense telepathic message.

Be sure to avoid giving hints about the picture you choose. Otherwise you will never know whether it was your suggestion or telepathy that influenced the dream.

• ● •

RECIPIENT:
Before going to sleep, give your inner mind a suggestion to increase your chances of telepathic dreaming. Tell yourself that you are open to include in your dream the image that the sender chooses.

SENDER:
Concentrate on the picture when you are least likely to be disturbed and when you know the recipient is asleep. Make a deliberate attempt to send the message.

RECIPIENT:
Report your dreams in as much detail as possible as soon as you wake up. Describe whatever feelings and associations the dream evoked. Your associations with the dream may be a more accurate impression of the image than the main body of the dream itself.

• ● •

If you want, you can try to send the image to two or more persons at the same time. For example, if you have three children, you may want to try this exercise with all of them at the same time. Then in the morning you can compare their dreams.

To intensify the telepathic message, try sketching the picture. This will aid your own concentration and make the exercise more interesting.

You may also want to act out a scene from the picture. For example, if the picture depicts bathers at a beach, put on a bathing suit.

Try a multisensory approach using as many senses as possible. For example, if your target picture depicts oranges, draw an orange with an orange crayon, eat an orange, and so on.

TWILIGHT ESP

Many parapsychologists believe that the borderland between waking and sleeping is especially conducive to ESP. The imagery-rich state between waking and sleeping is called "hypnagogic" and that between sleeping and waking is called "hypnapompic." Images often flow freely, dreamlike, during these "twilight" states.

You can try either sending or receiving telepathic images while in the twilight state. This is a fascinating state of mind to explore. It is almost like a waking dream. You may find that the thought you wish to send takes the form of a vivid image with a life of its own—a bird in flight traveling to the person you wish to impress, a ray of light, perhaps the psychic umbilical cord, or any number of images.

Before experimenting with ESP in this unique state of mind, you should bear in mind that the twilight state and sleep is by no means clear. It is often difficult to remain alert in the twilight state, particularly when first attempting it. You may find yourself drifting off to sleep and popping awake repeatedly. This is perfectly normal and to be expected. It takes considerable practice to maintain a passive, alert, relaxed frame of mind.

To remain awake, try the following: Keep one arm upright balanced on your elbow, so that your arm stays up without your expending much energy and growing tired. If you fall asleep, the muscle tone in your arm diminishes, your arm falls, and you awaken.

To send a telepathic message during the twilight state, fix your mind on the thought or impression that you wish to send. Picture the person with whom you wish to communicate telepathically in your mind's eye.

Now concentrate on the thought you wish to send. Let it take on a life of its own and perhaps become an image.

Imagine that the image is reaching the person with whom you are trying to communicate.

To receive a telepathic impression during the twilight state, first picture in your mind's eye the person from whom you want to receive the telepathic impression.

Give your inner mind the suggestion that you are in contact with that person.

If thoughts, images, impressions, come to mind, let them drift freely. Don't try to analyze them. Just let them be there.

If an impression comes to mind which you think may be psychically meaningful, yet you don't understand it, ask your inner mind for more information.

When you are ready, open your eyes and make a note—mental or written—of your impressions.

Verify your impressions for accuracy later.

EPILOGUE

A NEW LOOK AT THE PARENT-CHILD RELATIONSHIP

We can't avoid the conclusion that extrasensory phenomena, sometimes trivial, sometimes momentous, are a real and living part of the parent-child relationship. The experience of thousands makes this point. And we can verify the reality of parent-child psi in our own lives by taking the time to turn inward. For that matter, ESP may play a role in the parent-child relationship even if we are wholly unaware of it.

We have barely scratched the surface of this fascinating subject. The little we know about parent-child ESP is a mere prelude to what may turn out to be one of the most fascinating tales about parents and their offspring.

Many people, scientists and laypersons alike, tend to overlook this facet of reality. In our society rational knowledge is favored over intuitive knowledge. Intuition is devalued, ridiculed, and all but ignored in our daily lives. But this is changing as more and more people become aware of the awesome potential of the mind and the reality of the world beyond the senses.

Parapsychology has opened the door to the still virtually unexplored world of psi. Psi has emerged from occult trappings as a reality in its own right. But up to the present time, most parapsychologists have concerned themselves with statistical studies and with exploring psi in the laboratory. This has improved our knowledge of ESP immeasurably. However, it can no more give us a complete picture of the world of psi than can studying the behavior of a caged animal in the zoo give us the complete story of the animal in its natural habitat.

It is time that we went deeper.

Exploring parent-child ESP enables us to see that psi is a silent actor in the greatest and most lasting of all human bonds. From the moment of conception (and perhaps even before), psi functions in the parent-offspring relationship like barely audible background music. From birth on, it unites parent and child as if by a psychic umbilical cord, a cord that remains intact throughout our lives and—who knows—perhaps even beyond.

It is impossible to make sense of this side of reality in terms of modern family psychology or any other science for that matter.

Indeed, to come to terms with parent-child psi, we must rewrite the script. We must rethink our views. Not just about the way we look at parents and their children. But our view of the universe. Everything.

Eastern religious thought and mysticism teaches that on some level nature is fundamentally one. "The most important characteristic of the Eastern world view—one could almost say the essence of it," writes Fritjof Capra in *The Tao of Physics*, "is the awareness of the unity and mutual interrelation of all things and events, the experience of all phenomena in the world as manifestations of a basic oneness. All things are seen as interdependent and inseparable parts of this cosmic whole; as different manifestations of the same ultimate reality."[1]

In its search for the ultimate reality, modern theoretical physics has embraced a strikingly similar world view: that nature, on some level, is fundamentally interconnected. Or, in the language of mysticism: everything is part of the one.

Perhaps parapsychology too is headed toward this same view. Psychical researcher and psychic Ingo Swann puts it this way: "What if extrasensory perception is but a vast, not particularly individual, gigantic plane that interconnects all humanity with itself and with all existence, that the developed psychics are special only in that they are better integrated into this plane, whereas all others have individuated from it for one reason or another. . . . At a basic level, we are all interconnected."[2]

Perhaps psi is the connecting link. As marine biologist Sir Alister Hardy has suggested, psi may be a silent link that unites life with life through the never ending stream of creation and may somehow direct the course of evolution.

And perhaps the branches of science that touch on parents and their children—from psychology to education—could benefit from considering such views.

For through psi we may be vitally linked with all other human beings, with all forms of life everywhere, with the universe.

And especially with our children.

NOTES

CHAPTER ONE

1 J. Rhine, "A Review of the Pearce-Pratt Distance Series of ESP Tests" (*Journal of Parapsychology*, 18: 165–177, 1954).

2 S. Soal, K. Goldney, "Experiments in Precognitive Telepathy" (*Proceedings of the Society for Psychical Research*, 47: 21–150, 1943).

3 J. Eisenbud, "Psi in Psychotherapy" (ASPR Newsletter, October 1987, vol. XIII, no. 4).

4 B. Schwarz, *Parent-Child Telepathy* (New York: Garrett Publications, 1971), p. 88.

5 J. Meerloo, *Hidden Communion* (New York: Garrett Publications, Helix Press, 1964), p. 66.

6 S. Ostrander, L. Schroeder, *Psychic Discoveries Behind the Iron Curtain* (New York: Bantam Books, 1971).

7 M. Ryzl, *Parapsychology: A Scientific Approach* (New York: Hawthorn Books, Inc., 1970), p. 152.

8 J. Rhine, "A Brief Introduction to Parapsychology" (Durham, N.C., Institute for Parapsychology).

9 M. Ryzl, op. cit., p. 141.

10 A. Hardy, "Biology and Psychical Research" (SPR Proceedings, 1953).

11 J. Palmer, "A Community Mail Survey of Psychic Experiences" (*Journal of the American Society for Psychical Research*, 73: 221–251, 1979).

12 B. Schwarz, op. cit., p. 65.

13 B. Schwarz, op. cit., p. 228.

CHAPTER TWO

1 J. Rhine, "Evidence of precognition in the Covariation of Salience ratios" (*Journal of Parapsychology* 6: 111–143, 1942).

2 D. S. Rogo, *Parapsychology* (New York: Taplinger Publishing Company, 1975), p. 111.

3 B. Schwarz, "Psi and the Life Cycle" (*Journal of the American Society of Psychosomatic Dentistry and Medicine*, 1974).

4 U. Sinclair, *Mental Radio* (Springfield, Ill: Charles C. Thomas, 1930), p. 106–107.

5 Ibid., p. 62.

6 Ibid., p. 73.

7 C. Jung, *Psychological Types* (New York: Harcourt, Brace, 1933).

8 C. Young, "Intuition and Nursing Process" ("Holistic Nursing Practice" 1987, I(3), p. 56.

9 H. Berger, "Psyche" Jena, Verlag Gustav Fischer, 1940.

10 G. Schaut, M. Persinger, "Subjective Telepathic Experiences, Geomagnetic Activity and the ELF Hypothesis: Part I," *PSI Research*, March 1985, pages 4–20.

11 C. Tart, *Journal of the American Society for Psychical Research*, April 1988, 82:2, p. 129–146.

12 M. Ryzl, *Parapsychology* (New York: Hawthorn Books, 1979), p. 157.

13 L. Vasiliev, "Experiments in Mental Suggestion" (Church Crookham, Institute for the Study of Mental Images, 1963, p. 178).

14 L. Vasiliev, "Long-Distance Suggestion" (Moscow, Gospolitizdat, 1962), p. 160. (In Russian. English translation in manuscript available at Parapsychology Laboratory at Duke University).

15 A. Luria, *The Working Brain* (New York; Basic Books, 1973).

16 J. Ehrenwald, *The ESP Experience* (New York: Basic Books, 1978), p. 217.

17 G. Murphy, R. Ballou (eds.). "William James and Psychical Research" (1961) p. 324, cited in J. Wheatley, H. Edge, eds., *Philosophical Dimensions of Parapsychology* (Springfield, Ill: Charles C. Thomas, 1976), p. 88.

18 H. Price, "Psychical Research and Human Personality" (Hibbert J., 47: 105–113, 1949) cited in K. Ramakrishna Rao, *Experimental Parapsychology* (Springfield, Ill: Charles C. Thomas, 1966), p. 222.

19 R. Haynes, *The Society for Psychical Research 1882–1982* (London: Macdonald & Co., 1982), p. viii.

20 D. S. Rogo, op. cit., p. 26.

21 G. Schmeidler, "Separating the Sheep from the Goats" (*Journal of the American Society for Psychical Research* 39: 47–49, 1945).

22 B. Schwarz, *Psychic Nexus* (New York: Van Nostrand Reinhold Company, 1980), p. xvii.

23 G. Murphy, "Field Theory and Survival" (*Journal of the American Society for Psychical Research* 39: 181–209, 1945).

24 R. Haynes, op. cit, p. ix.

CHAPTER THREE

1 L. Rhine, *ESP in Life and Lab* (New York: Cillier Books, 1967).

2 R. Hunter and I. Macalpine, editors, *Three Hundred Years of Psychiatry* (London: Oxford University Press, 1963), p. 207.

2A L. Rhine, "The Invisible Picture: A Study of Psychic Experiences" (Jefferson, N.C.: McFarland & Company, Inc., 1981), p. 190.

3 R. Heywood, "Case of Rapport between Mother and Daughter" (*Journal of the American Society of Psychical Research* vol. 42, 1963), p. 187–189.

4 L. Rhine, "Psychological Processes in ESP Experiences, Part I: Waking Experiences" (*Journal of Parapsychology*, vol. 29: 96–108, 1965), p. 106–107.

5 L. Schwartz, *The World of the Unborn* (New York: Richard Marek Publishers, 1980), p. 78.

6 C. Jones, *Mind Over Labor* (New York: Viking/Penguin, Inc., 1987), p. 23.

7 L. Schwartz, op. cit., p. 73.

8 L. Schwartz, op. cit., p. 86–87.

CHAPTER FOUR

1 D. Chamberlain, *Consciousness at Birth: A Review of the Empirical Evidence* (San Diego: California, Chamberlain Communications 1983), p. 35.

2 Ibid., p. 41.

3 Ibid., p. 46.

4 C. Riley, "Transuterine Communication in Problem Pregnancies" (*Pre- and Perinatal Psychology*, 1 [3], spring 1987), p. 183.

5 D. Cheek, "Prenatal and Perinatal Imprints: Apparent Prenatal Consciousness as Revealed by Hypnosis" (*Pre- and Perinatal Psychology*, 1 [2], winter 1986), p. 106–107.

6 A. Buchheimer, "Memory—Preverbal and Verbal," chapter in *Pre- and Perinatal Psychology*, T. Verny, editor (New York: Human Sciences Press, Inc., 1987), p. 53.

7 D. Cheek, op. cit., p. 99.

8 E. Parsons, "Pregnancy Taboos," chapter in *Birth: An Anthology*, D. Meltzer, editor (San Francisco: North Point Press, 1981), p. 97–99.

9 D. Stott, "Follow-up Study from Birth of the Effects of Prenatal Stresses" (*Develop. Med. Child Neurol.* 1973, 15), p. 781.

10 Ibid., p. 787.

11 M. Huttunen, P. Niskanen, "Prenatal Loss of Father and Psychiatric Disorders" (*Archives of General Psychiatry*, April 1978), p. 429–431.

12 L. Sontag, "Prenatal Determinants of Postnatal Behavior," chapter in *Fetal Growth and Development*, Waisman & Kerr, editors (New York: McGraw-Hill, 1970).

13 G. Rottmann, cited in W. Freud, "Prenatal Attachment and Bonding," chapter in *Pre- and Perinatal Psychology*, T. Verny, editor (New York: Human Sciences Press, 1987), p. 100.

14 T. Verny, *The Secret Life of the Unborn Child* (New York: Dell Publishing Co., 1981), p. 7.

15 Ibid., p. 29.

16 Ibid., p. 89.

17 Ibid., p. 23.

18 A. Liley, "The Foetus as a Personality" (*Australia and New Zealand Journal of Psychiatry*, 6, 1972), p. 100.

19 E. Sidenbladh, *Water Babies* (New York: St. Martin's Press, 1982), p. 63.

20 T. Verny, op. cit., p. 87–88.

21 I. Stevenson, "Characteristics of Cases of the Reincarnation Type in Turkey and Their Comparison with Cases in Two Other Cultures" (*International Journal of Comparative Sociology*, vol. 11, no. 1, March 1970).

22 Ibid., p. 10.

CHAPTER FIVE

1 D. Cheek, "Maladjustment Patterns Apparently Related to Imprinting at Birth" (*American Journal of Clinical Hypnosis* 1975, 18: 75–82).

2 D. Chamberlain, "Reliability of Birth Memory: Preliminary Observations from Mother and Child Pairs in Hypnosis" (initial report presented to the American Society of Clinical Hypnosis, Minneapolis, November 1980), p. 6.

3 D. Chamberlain, *Babies Remember Birth* (to be published by J. P. Tarcher, Los Angeles, CA, 1989), chapter 19.

4 Ibid.

5 Ibid.

6 Ibid.

7 Ibid.

8 J. Meerloo, *Hidden Communion* (New York: Garrett Publications, 1964), p. 65.

9 C. Little, "The Journal of Soil and Water Conservation."

10 J. Ehrenwald, *The ESP Experience* (New York: Basic Books, Inc., 1978), p. 23.

11 Ibid., p. 22.

12 Ibid., p. 22.

13 Ibid., p. 6.

14 Ibid., p. 23.

15 L. West, "Forward to Dream Psychology and the New Biology of Dreaming" M. Kramer, ed. (Springfield, Ill: Charles C. Thomas, 1969).

16 W. Sears, *Nighttime Parenting* (La Leche League International, 1985) p. 162–163.

17 Ibid., p. 162.

CHAPTER SIX

1 I. Stevenson, *Telepathic Impressions* (Charlottesville, VA: University of Virginia, 1970), p. 42–43.

2 Ibid., p. 185.

3 F. Saldana, *San Diego Tribune* November 26, 1987. p. B-1.

4 B. Schwarz, *Psychic Nexus* (New York: Van Nostrand Reinhold Co., 1980), p. 123.

5 I. Stevenson, op. cit., p. 56–58.

6 Ibid., p. 61–62.

7 L. Dale, "Spontaneous Cases" (*Journal of The American Society for Psychical Research* 46: 31–35, 1952).

8 E. Gurney, F. Myers, F. Podmore, *Phantasms of the Living* (New York: Arno Press, reprint edition 1975), p. 173.

9 L. Dale, op. cit., p. 31–35.

10 S. Freud, *Studies in Parapsychology* (New York: Collier Books, 1963), p. 78.

11 L. Rhine, "The Invisible Picture: A Study of Psychic Experiences" (Jefferson, N.C.: McFarland & Company, 1981), p. 46

12 E. Gurney et al., op. cit., p. 438.

13 Ibid., p. 498.

14 Ibid., p. 394.

15 L. Rhine, op. cit., p. 77–78.

16 E. Gurney et al, op. cit., p. 418.

17 Ibid., p. 502.

18 B. Schwarz, op. cit., p. 124.

19 I. Stevenson, op. cit., p. 111.

20 Ibid., p. 115.

21 B. Schwarz, op. cit., p. 114.

22 I. Stevenson, op. cit., p. 108.

23 F. Vaughan, *Awakening Intuition* (Garden City, N.Y.: Anchor Books, 1979), p. 66.

24 E. Gurney et al., op. cit., p. 44–45.

25 S. Figar, *J. Soc. Psych. Res.*, 40, 702: 162–172, 1959.

26 M. Ryzl, *Parapsychology: A Scientific Approach* (New York: Hawthorn Books, 1970), p. 157.

27 E. D. Dean, "Plethysmograph Recordings as ESP Responses" (*International Journal of Neuropsychiatry*, September/October 1966), p. 446.

CHAPTER SEVEN

1 I. Stevenson, *Telepathic Impressions* (Charlottesville, VA: University of Virginia Press, 1970), p. 2.

2 J. Meerloo, *Hidden Communion* (New York: Garrett Publications, Helix Press, 1964), p. 65.

3 B. Schwarz, *Parent-Child Telepathy* (New York: Garrett Publications, 1971), p. 101.

4 Ibid., p. 83.

5 J. Hall, "Jungian Analytic Meaning of Clinical Parapsychological Phenomena" ("ASPR Newsletter," April 1988, vol. XIV, no. 2).

6 M. Ullman, S. Krippner, A. Vaughan, *Dream Telepathy* (New York: Macmillan Publishing Co., Inc., 1973), p. 47.

7 S. Krippner, "An Experimental Approach to the Anomalous Dream" (to be published by Plenum Press, New York): *Cognitive Approaches to Dream Research,* 1989), p. 5–6.

8 Ibid., p. 8–9.

9 M. Ullman, S. Krippner, op. cit., p. 119–120.

10 Ibid., p. 214.

11 E. Gurney, F. Myers, F. Podmore, *Phantasms of the Living* (London: Trübner, 1886) (2 vols.) (page unavailable).

12 L. Rhine, *The Invisible Picture: A Study of Psychic Experiences* (Jefferson, N.C.: McFarland & Company, 1981), p. 88.

13 S. Freud, *Studies in Parapsychology* (New York: Collier Books, 1963), p. 66–67.

14 Ibid., p. 72.

15 Ibid., p. 74.

16 E. Gurney, F. Myers, F. Podmore, *Phantasms of the Living* (New York, Arno Press, reprint edition 1975), p. 227–228.

17 Ibid., p. 224.

18 D. Graham, *Dream Your Way to Happiness and Awareness* (New York: Warner Books, 1975), p. 40–41.

19 D. Dean, "Plethysmograph Recordings as ESP Responses" (*International Journal of Neuropsychiatry* September–October 1966), p. 440–441.

20 S. Smith, *Out of Body Experiences for the Millions* (New York: Dell Publishing Company, 1969), p. 51–52.

21 E. Garrett, *Telepathy* (New York: Helix Press, Garrett Publications, 1968), p. 70–71.

22 U. Sinclair, *Mental Radio* (Springfield, Ill: Charles C. Thomas, 1930), p. 16.

23 J. Ehrenwald, *The ESP Experience* (New York: Basic Books, Inc., 1978), p. 89.

24 D. Graham, op. cit., p. 44.

25 N. Sandow, "The Decline of Precognized Events with the Passage of Time: Evidence from Spontaneous Dreams" (*Journal of the American Society for Psychical Research,* January 1988, vol. 82 no. 1), p. 37.

CHAPTER EIGHT

1 B. Schwarz, *Parent-Child Telepathy* (New York: Garrett Publications, 1971), p. 40.

2 Ibid., p. 24–25.

3 D. Burlingham, "Child Analysis and the Mother" (*Psychoanalytic Quarterly* 5: 69–92, 1935).

4 J. Ehrenwald, *The ESP Experience* (New York: Basic Books, Inc., 1978), p. 14–15.

5 A. Tanous, K. Donnelly, *Understanding and Developing Your Child's Natural Psychic Abilities* (New York: Simon & Schuster, 1979), p. 5.

6 B. Schwarz, op. cit., p. 24.

7 Ibid., p. 173.

8 Ibid., p. 187.

9 E. Spinelli, "The Effects of Chronological Age on GESP Ability," J. Morris, W. Roll, R. Morris, eds., *Research in Parapsychology 1976* (Metuchen, N.J.: Scarecrow Press, 1977), p. 124.

10 M. Ullman, S. Krippner, A. Vaughan, *Dream Telepathy* (New York: Macmillan Publishing Co., Inc., 1973), p. 214.

11 J. Prasad and I. Stevenson, "A Survey of Spontaneous Psychical Experiences in School Children of Uttar Pradesh, India" (*International Journal of Parapsychology*, 10, 1968, p. 241–261).

12 E. Shields, "Comparison of Children's Guessing Ability (ESP) with Personality Characteristics" (*Journal of Parapsychology* 1962, vol. 26).

13 A. Tanous, K. Donnelly, op. cit., p. 32–33.

14 B. Schwarz, op. cit., p. 209–210.

15 U. Sinclair, *Mental Radio* (Springfield, Ill: Charles C. Thomas, 1930), p. 5.

16 B. Schwarz, op. cit., p. 189.

17 Ibid., p. 193.

18 Ibid., p. 85.

19 Ibid., p. 188.

20 Ibid., p. 53.

21 J. Van Busschbach, "An Investigation of ESP between Teacher and Pupils in American Schools" (*Journal of Parapsychology*, 1956, 20: 71–80).

22 W. Tenhaeff, *Telepathy and Clairvoyance* (Springfield, Ill: Charles C. Thomas, 1972), p. 117.

23 J. Van Busschbach, "An Investigation of ESP between Teacher and Pupils in American Schools" (*Journal of Parapsychology* 1956 20: 71–80).

24 N. Louwerens, "ESP Experiments with Nursery School Children in the Netherlands" (*Journal of Parapsychology*, 1960, 24: 75–93).

25 Ibid., p. 75–93.

26 W. Tenhaeff, op. cit., p. 130.

27 H. Bender, "The Case of Ilga K.: Report of a Phenomenon of Unusual Perception" (*Journal of Parapsychology*, 2: 5–22, 1938).

28 R. Drake, "An Unusual Case of Extrasensory Perception" (*Journal of Parapsychology*, 2: 184–198, 1938).

29 E. Recordon, L. Stratton, J. Peters, "Some Trials in a Case of Alleged Telepathy" (*Journal of the American Society for Psychical Research*, 44: 390–99, 1977).

30 E. Shields, "Mental Retardation: Subliminal Stimulation" (*Research in Parapsychology* 1975), p. 137.

31 Ibid., p. 137.

32 Ibid., p. 138.

33 Ibid., p. 183.

34 A. Tanous, K. Donnelly, op. cit., p. 34.

35 Ibid., p. 76–77.

36 Ibid., p. 36.

37 Ibid., p. 71.

38 S. Drucker, A. Drewes, L. Rubin, "ESP in Relation to Cognitive Development and IQ in Young Children" (*Journal of the American Society for Psychical Research*, 71: 289–298, 1977).

CHAPTER NINE

1 M. Ullman, S. Krippner, A. Vaughan, *Dream Telepathy* (New York: Macmillan Publishing Co., Inc., 1973), p. 252.

2 S. Drucker, A. Drewes, L. Rubin, "ESP in Relation to Cognitive Development and IQ in Young Children" (*Journal of the American Society for Psychical Research*, vol. 71, July, 1977).

3 G. Hendricks, T. Roberts, *The Second Centering Book* (Englewood Cliffs, N.J.: Prentice-Hall, Inc., 1977), p. 77.

4 F. Vaughan, *Awakening Intuition* (Garden City, N.Y.: Anchor Books, 1979), p. 71.

5 Ibid., p. 4.

6 I. Swann, *Natural ESP* (New York: Bantam Books, 1987), p. 122.

7 M. Ryzl, *Parapsychology: A Scientific Approach* (New York: Hawthorne Books, Inc., 1970), p. 110.

8 W. Tenhaeff, *Telepathy and Clairvoyance* (Springfield, Ill: Charles C. Thomas, 1972), p. 40.

9 M. Ryzl, op. cit., p. 111.

10 Ibid., p. 111–112.

11 R. Haynes, *The Society for Psychical Research 1882–1982: A History* (London: Macdonald & Co., 1982), p. 213–214.

12 M. Ryzl, op. cit., p. 136.

13 W. Tenhaeff, op. cit., p. 35–36.

14 G. Fisk, D. West, "ESP Tests with Erotic Symbols" (*Journal of the Society for Psychical Research* 38: 1–7, 1955–56).

15 E. Garrett, *Telepathy* (New York: Helix Press, Garrett Publications, 1968), p. 35.

16 Ibid., p. 37–38.

17 Ibid., p. 39.

CHAPTER TEN

1 T. Verny, editor, *Pre- and Perinatal Psychology* (New York: Human Sciences Press, Inc., 1987), p. 103.

2 M. Samuels and N. Samuels, *The Well Baby Book* (New York: Summit Books, 1979), p. 64.

3 Ibid., p. 65.

4 L. Schwartz, *The World of the Unborn* (New York: Richard Marek Publishers, 1980), p. 117.

CHAPTER ELEVEN

1 F. Vaughan, *Awakening Intuition* (Garden City, N.Y.: Anchor Books/Doubleday, 1979), p. 62.

2 J. Weed, *Wisdom of the Mystic Masters* (West Nyack, N.Y.: Parker Publishing Company, Inc., 1968), p. 134.

3 M. Samuels and N. Samuels, *The Well Child Book* (New York: Summit Books, 1982), p. 268–269.

4 I. Swann, *Natural ESP* (New York: Bantam Books, 1987), p. 187.

5 U. Sinclair, *Mental Radio* (Springfield, Ill: Charles C. Thomas, 1930), p. 125.

6 Ibid., p. 121.

7 I. Swann, op. cit., p. 149.

8 Ibid., p. 157.

9 I. Swann, op. cit., p. 128.

10 M. Ullman, S. Krippner, A. Vaughan, *Dream Telepathy* (New York: Macmillan Publishing Co., Inc., 1973), p. 211.

EPILOGUE

1 F. Capra, *The Tao of Physics* (Berkeley, CA: Shambhala, 1975), p. 130.

2 I. Swann, op. cit., p. 192.

INDEX